Shame, Gender Violence, and Ethics

Feminist Strategies: Flexible Theories and Resilient Practices

Series Editors: Sharon Labrot Crasnow and Joanne Beil Waugh

Advisory Board: Samantha Brennan, Sandra Harding, Jose Medina, Kelly Oliver, Georgia Warnke, Shelley Wilcox, and Naomi Zack.

Feminist Strategies encourages original work in contemporary philosophical feminism that recognizes that while women have achieved a significant measure of equality, discrimination nonetheless persists through the intersection of gender with other systems and practices of oppression. Such work includes the formulation of theories that are sufficiently flexible, and the promotion of practices sufficiently resilient, to address these changing contexts and forms of oppression. The volumes that comprise this series thus examine current practices, actual cases, and historical episodes of discrimination in which gender has intersected with systems of oppression including those involving feminism and disability; women, animals, and emotion; extended cognition and feminism; women and depression; motherhood, and the new materialist feminism.

Titles in the series

Shame, Gender Violence, and Ethics

Terrors of Injustice

Edited by Lenart Škof and Shé M. Hawke

LEXINGTON BOOKS
Lanham • Boulder • New York • London

"To Believe in the Words of Justice" chapter To Believe in the Words of Justice Reprint
First published as Introduction in *International Conference Terrors of Injustice: Gender
Violence and Ethics of Shame/Programme and Abstracts,* Koper, Science and Research
Centre, Publishing House Annales, 2018, pp. 7-8.

Published by Lexington Books
An imprint of The Rowman & Littlefield Publishing Group, Inc.
4501 Forbes Boulevard, Suite 200, Lanham, Maryland 20706
www.rowman.com

6 Tinworth Street, London SE11 5AL, United Kingdom

British Library Cataloguing in Publication Information Available

Library of Congress Control Number: 2020050829
ISBN 978-1-7936-0467-5 (cloth : alk. paper)
ISBN 978-1-7936-0469-9 (pbk : alk. paper)
ISBN 978-1-7936-0468-2 (electronic)

Contents

To Believe in the Words of Justice

Farida Khalaf (Farida Global Organization)

We live in a world about which the least you can say is that it is unsafe and unjust.[1] The general sense we had after World War II—that the world was a safer place and a more civilized place—is just untrue. Today, humanity is not better than seventy years ago, and not better than 300 years ago. We live in constant fear, and violence has become a global phenomenon. I know it is an unjust world, because I, as a person, my family, and we as a community, have suffered injustice for the past four years. We were villagers of a region in northern Iraq called Sinjar—a region where people lived in harmony. There was simplicity in our lives, there was happiness, and there was a struggle to face the hardships of everyday life, just as in every corner of the world. ISIS attacked our peaceful Yazidi community on August 3, 2014, and committed genocide. They took our women and children as slaves, and they killed thousands of men, women, and children. I was lucky—and so were my mother and brother—because I was able to escape captivity. My other brother survived a mass shooting. My father was among those killed. Many innocent people were unlucky too; thousands remain missing and most of them probably will never come back. Among them are many of my relatives and friends. ISIS left behind tens of mass graves, a homeland filled with landmines and explosives; they wanted to make sure that my people will never have a homeland to return to.

The genocide was not only in Iraq; today our Yazidi community and the Christians in Syria, and in particular in the Afrin region, are facing another genocide due to the domination of extremist groups. There will be no Yazidi community in Syria in the next few years. What is most striking to me is that until today none of the ISIS criminals have been held accountable for genocide, war crimes, and crimes against humanity whose victims have been the Iraqi and Syrian communities. They have been free in Iraq and Syria, with many returning to their countries in Europe and to other countries without any prosecution. We have been fighting for justice, and the Yazidi women in particular have showed so much courage. Many have spoken up against ISIS, and we have tried to shake up the world system in hope that it will work. You would think that basic human rights and the preservation of basic human dignity would be at the top of interests in the United Nations (UN), EU, and governments around the world. But the truth is, it is not. In face of all this insensitivity, we must act. I believe in the power of people, normal people like us, who will make real, lasting change. I believe in the voices of women, girls, youth, and students—because the power we have is genuine. It is not centered around self-interest or geopolitical interests. We have to act because what makes us human is how we treat each other. When justice is absent, violence becomes cyclical. This is very obvious in Iraq. In the absence of justice every day dozens of crimes are committed against innocents. Everyone in our country has suffered because we live in a cycle of violence.

NOTE

1. First published as Introduction in *International Conference Terrors of Injustice: Gender Violence and Ethics of Shame/Programme and Abstracts*, Koper, Science and Research Centre, Publishing House Annales, 2018, pp. 7–8.

Introduction

Shé M. Hawke and Lenart Škof

In her text addressing injustice, gender, shame, and terror at the opening of this book, Yazidi survivor Farida Khalaf brings us a formidable account of genocide and enslavement that she and her family from northern Iraq could not have imagined prior to their capture and attempted cultural mutilation. Now free, Farida is part of the Yazda global advocacy campaign to bring ISIS militants to justice, raise awareness, and bring international attention to this particular genocide, transposing her experience of terror and violence into education, reparative action, and a sustained call for justice. In the first instance, we dedicate this book to the Yazidi women and their families. We also dedicate this book to all innocent victims and survivors of war, terror, and violence.

> In no dialogue can everything be said, and it is recognizing the necessity of something unspeakable and its preservation that allows an exchange of words between two different subjects.[1]

Testimonies of terror and gendered violence convey an incredible courage and resilience in the face of what are arguably the worst horrors a human being can face: rape, torture, and the threat of death, along with witnessing the murder of friends and relatives, and the environment. This book is not intended only as a series of memorial but it also recognizes the critical need for "memory in place" to be acknowledged, respected, and responded to. We also value "witnessing" as a valid discourse represented in this collection through diverse and meaningful modes of expression. Moreover, this volume is intended as a critical survey and analysis of some of the terrors of injustice in the world today and asks questions about the genealogy of gendered violence, complicity, and resistance. While differently positioned, we are all implicated in the atrocious acts that subsist in all parts of the world and have done for millennia. But what is the circuit breaker for this cycle of violence that has become second nature?

Overwhelmingly, the chapters in this book report on current acts of gendered violence, in which shame is variously embedded and understood, and where justice is sought and ethics are reimagined. By interrogating the systemic violence and practices of our own political creation, we hope to offer here a reparative opportunity for justice through "textual witnessing" that may provoke further action and nonviolent outrage, scholarly and legislative debate, along with critical and tactical response to existing regimes of violence, recklessness, and incivility, particularly against women. As Irigaray suggests, no dialogue is ever complete, but without a beginning there is only silence, as several chapters testify. We offer this book as a beginning among other beginnings.

This volume traverses an array of perspectives on issues intersecting between gender, shame and violence, and ethics, as examples of the operationality of terror, fear, and the assemblage of power relations that sustains them. Part of our intention is to hear voices less often heard in Western academia, and to include both junior and senior scholars to gain both older and fresher perspectives on the concerns of the book. Some authors take up Agamben's[2] notion of "bare life" to help us understand how power relations determine what constitutes a human life, while others critique notions of inclusivity and exclusivity specifically.

To fulfill our aim to hear voices from across the world—on both its genocides and everyday inhumanity—we invited a diverse range of scholarship from fields such as philosophy, sociology, media and cultural studies, law and theology, masculinities and gender studies, disabilities studies, queer theory, and GLBTQI communities. What follows are the contributions we received from fields including sociopolitical, legal and human rights responses to femicide (Barter; Marrero; McKay), philosophy and theoretical reflections on shame (Sashinungla; Strahovnik; Looney), media and cultural studies (Anderson and Duerr; El Helou-Sensenig), and ecofeminist, sociocultural, and theological contexts of shame and gender (Emery; Herles; Sanderson), in whose chapters the diverse intentions of the book are embedded. Some of these contributions are challenging in what they disclose. This book is not a quiet read—it is unsettling in the territory it navigates and the examples it exposes, and acts as a springboard for further analysis.

As several authors convey, the immorality and injustice of violence produces shameful effects among the subjects that experience violence and terror. On one hand, shame appears as an affect that is culturally, ethically, and morally suppressed, burdening victims, instead of being a possible vehicle for the (re)constitution of ethical relations and/or moral order. But there is more to shame than that as several chapters suggest. One of the intentions of this book is to reconceptualize shame beyond its relation to subordination, humiliation, and disgrace (although those things are never far away), and constituent parts of broader stories, philosophies, and histories. Building on previous works, from primarily feminist scholarship, that mobilizes shame as a tool of transformation (Tomkins, Nussbaum, Probyn, Bartky, Mann, Lewis, and Fricker),[3] and the terrors of injustice that bring the ethical tragedy of violence against the "Other" into clear view, we offer an intentionally diverse and disruptive collection of chapters. We remind ourselves that we are ethically implicated subjects, and that gender violence is a symptom of both cultural habitus (Bourdieu) and unruly power relations predicated on the subordination of certain subjects in our uncanny webs of relation in life.

In part 1, our book opens with "Responses to Gender Violence," which details, with at times shocking acuity, injustices toward women, and the gender violence they have endured. Jane Barter's comment that "Biopolitics leaves no stone unturned in the power it extends over life" (7) is judiciously reasoned in her chapter dedicated to the families of murdered and missing Indigenous women of Canada. This chapter achingly narrates the horrors of racist sexual violence against women by predominantly white male perpetrators. The two cases of Cindy Gladue and Tina Fontaine are skillfully but sensitively exposed in such a way that there is no doubt that these women were considered "disposable" due to the intersection of their gender and race. The redemptive memory enacted in this chapter as part of a "witnessing" is richly woven against a backdrop of scholarship and The Final Report of the National Inquiry into Missing and Murdered Women and Girls (2019) in which the terror and violence against Indigenous Canadian women is finally heard. Barter engages the Final Report against the backdrop of Canada's efforts toward reconciliation after the Truth and Reconciliation Commission's exposure of its national shame and the ensuing apology by Prime Minister Stephen Harper in 2008. She warns against a reading of reparative justice predicated on an outsideness of being, as if marginalization was all that belonged to the identity of Indigenous Canadian women and girls, deemed by successive governments as being in need of managing. She notes the lack of accountability on the part of settler descended society, despite the well-intentioned Report and "its trauma-informed affective modalities" (9). Her comparison with Agamben's *Remnants of Auschwitz*[4] is adroit in terms of what witnessing, surviving, and testifying really mean, and how biopolitics manages agency, and what is forgettable, what is unforgettable, and what is unimaginable in a politics of disclosure. A critically important essay, appropriately titled: "'Speaking About her Just Might Heal': Witnessing to Canada's Missing and Murdered Indigenous Women."

As with Barter's chapter, Danny Marrero's work on femicide in Colombia is challenging and disturbing in what it reveals about the abject vulnerability of women. Drawing on the Nobel Prize author Garcia Márquez's *Chronicle of Death Foretold*,[5] Marrero equates the violence against women in that story to historical and current incidences of femicide that he argues could have been avoided. Using Russell's definition of femicide as "the killing of females because they are female,"[6] Marrero explores the shame associated with inaction on the part of these "deaths foretold," that is, the stated intentions of the perpetrators known among the community. Judith Butler's work on precarity and what it means to be a "life . . . produced according to norms that qualify it as a life"[7] is strategically embedded in his narrative that interrogates historical developments leading to the creation of femicide as a specific offense in the Colombian Penal Code.

Melissa McKay, a barrister and lawyer from Canada interrogates positions of power and patriarchy in criminal law. Reading patriarchy as a framework for social regulation, she questions the capacity of law to uphold or subvert the power relations of the privileged, in tension with the victim/survivors present in courtrooms. Her focus is shame and gendered violence, specifically within the legal processes of accountability for sexual violence at the international criminal level and in Canadian domestic law. She considers normatively produced behavior through both a legal optic, and everyday lives of women, and critiques neoliberal understandings of autonomy and equality of power. McKay also excavates underlying power structures and language and explores how they act covertly to disempower women in the courtroom, women who seek justice in the very environment that often appears to contain their subjectivity and minimize their experience of sexual violence and rape. She cites several cases in Canadian law and surveys the Canadian Criminal Code in terms of what is understood as consent. She calls for a revision of the Code toward a more humanist criminal law in which legislative reform is the first step. Her reformative vision includes "broadening considerations of social conditioning (including inherited notions of gendered shame) . . . that can push the boundaries of what it means to be truly equal" (45).

Part 2 brings us to "Theoretical Reflections on Shame" and explores philosophical examinations of justice, injustice, and epistemic and agential understandings of shame and its associated power relations, through theoretical reflections. Aaron Looney opens this section and sketches an anthropological frame of shame as it evolved through the history of Western thought, by offering a philosophical reconceptualization of subjectivity that accounts for shame as arising from exposure. He progresses his thesis through three conceptions of shame for femininity: protective shame, moral or rational shame, and traumatic shame. Looney provides a very informative survey of shame from Plato to Hannah Arendt, and more latterly Martha Nussbaum[8] who suggests "shame is necessary and inevitable," and the converse position from Michael Lewis. Lewis poses a question rather than a *fait accompli*, "What is an exposed self and to who is it exposed?" He concludes that "the self is exposed to itself, that is, we are capable of viewing ourselves,"[9] thereby characterizing shame as a feeling of negative self-assessment, taking into account the emotive force of shame and the *uniquely* human capacity for self-reflection. Looney produces an exceptionally interesting account of shame with both concision and breadth of engagement, which brings us finally to Judith Butler's[10] comments about advocacy for embracing our common exposure without disavowal and exploitation.

Sashinungla's chapter first brings to us a theoretical history of shame and segues into an innovative account of shame as both a tool of change and an agent of oppression. Rather than binarize attitudes toward shame, Sashinungla dismantles its hinges offering a different optic that also subverts the power relations of shame, and considers the "epistemic injustice" and "epistemic ignorance" put forward by Miranda Fricker that empowers and feeds shame. She says, "Shame as I conceive of it mirrors the complexity of its latent potency."[11] Sashinungla also draws deftly on the work of Jill Locke, who critiques the notion that "Shame is a negative self-assessment,"[12] and Elspeth Probyn, who problematizes shame through a Bourdieurian lens of the dispositional, and who suggests that shame can be "positive in its self-evaluative role."[13] While Sashinungla doesn't tie herself to any of these positions, she draws them into clear exegetical view, by effectively retheorizing some theories to dislodge others. Her discussion on Bonnie Mann's analysis of masculinities of shame and shaming that secure men's power is perceptive. The very original contribution that Sashinungla makes, aside from her philosophical and sociological interventions, is her important account of shame and women of color and class, in particular the Dalit, tribal and poor women in India, who are shamed generationally because of their place in the Caste System. Consolidating the lead of Audre Lorde and Sara Ahmed on the various axes of oppression (and speaking self-reflexively) she argues that women's identity is not universal. Her discussion on casteism, sexism, and racism invites readers to consistently reexamine privilege, as the anger of others is given voice, and to value the "righting of wrongs" that should never eclipse *being-alongsideness*.

Following on from Sashinungla's chapter on a feminist ethics of shame, Vojko Strahovnik focuses on epistemic or intellectual (in)justice and situates it in the framework of a discussion on epistemic agency. Strahovnik argues for epistemic justice as an ancillary epistemic virtue, being hybrid in its character, for example, by bringing in itself both epistemic and moral aspects. Epistemic injustice as a lack of epistemic justice appears when an individual or group is given either less credibility or cannot participate equally in the practices through social meanings that are generated. Strahovnik links epistemic justice to epistemic humility, which is also related to moral shame. As such, shame and humility are closely connected and thus directly related to the epistemic justice as a virtue. According to Strahovnik, finally, it is the recognition of suffering, and recognition of epistemic injustices, that should guide our quest for justice and position ourselves in relation to others—beyond preexisting biases, prejudices, or stereotypes.

In part 3, "Gender Violence in the Media," we hear from both Western and Middle Eastern journalists and advocates of law, ethics, and human rights, whose accounts are also somewhat ethnographic, informed by the embodied nature of the work they do. Janet H. Anderson, who is a UK-based journalist, human rights lobbyist, and media trainer, teams up with international law expert and human rights advocate Benjamin Duerr, to deliver up-to-the-minute analysis of media ethics in reporting. Journalists are often the first responders to war and terror violence, they explain, and while many are sensitive to the issues they are covering, few are victim/survivor centered. Anderson and Duerr call for new journalistic ethics to reduce harm to already vulnerable and traumatized people, particularly for the survivors of sexual violence and assault in war zones. They cite the recent cutting-edge scholarship by Foster and Minwalla,[14] whose disturbing data on victim/survivor experiences of Yazidi women reported in Western journalism is critical and overdue. As part of their thinking through ethical ways forward, they share with us information about locally developed media tool kits that offer specialized approaches when dealing with traumatized subjects. They also negotiate a path between the "systemic pressures under which journalists operate" (107), and a compassionate approach to truth telling that returns power to victims/survivors rather than exposing interviewees to further harm.

This section closes with an autoethnographic and journalist-activist account by Rouba El Helou-Sensenig who critically unpacks gender-based violence (GBV) in the Middle East and North African (MENA) region. Her chapter decenters the Global North through a metacognitive examination of her own Arab environs, and the practices of Arab media in reporting gendered violence. She produces a perceptive critique of what silencing means for victims/survivors, and highlights that finding voice is often a precarious enterprise fraught with not only danger, but judgment from within communities—"There is no easy way to be the voice of the less powerful" (130). "Intersectionality"[15] appears as a leitmotif throughout a chapter that narrates harrowing violence and equally disturbing accompanying media coverage. The aspiration of hope for change in entrenched practices is expressed through ongoing advocacy. For example, she details advocacy through the

Lebanese NGO "Fe-Male," the UN ECOSOC accredited Resource Centre for Gender Equality (ABAAD), and the development of "gender-sensitive media coverage" Code of Conduct (CoC) tool kits as part of a more honorable and compassionate way forward in terms of what is reported and how.

We opened this book with definitions and reconsiderations of shame as an inescapable companion to human existence, and interrogated correlative issues of epistemic justice and injustice through a diversity of contexts. Part 4 of our collection revisits all the themes of the book: shame, gender, violence, and ethics, through contextual appraisal of sociocultural apprehensions of shame, ecofeminism, and religious and spiritual traditions.

Vita Emery's chapter takes us on a social journey through shame and its connection to social scripts. She too references shame theorists such as Tomkins,[16] and unpacks the relationship between shame and early childhood scripting that predisposes certain attitudes to shame. She doesn't decide whether shame is an emotion or an affect but presents scholarly interpretations around definition and application in society through her section on sources of shame. She also effectively brings the tensions between "the social world we inhabit and our personal experience" (145) into her examination. Her use of Merleau-Ponty[17] on shame and the mirror phase of childhood explains clearly the notion of a child's first experience of "interest" from others and "recognition" of their own subjectivity, that gives rise to the possibilities of shaming by virtue of recognition of interest, and self. By arguing through different concepts of shame as internalized and situational, she arrives at the conclusion that shame can be dismantled to the extent it can be productively used as a therapeutic tool.

Cecilia Herles radically reconsiders transnational feminist ethical notions of responsibility and interconnectedness in relation to responses to the ecological violence and tragedies that punctuate the common age. She ably reinvigorates some of the feminist ecological scholarship from the late twentieth century, such as Susan Griffin, and provides a close read of the work by Australian ecofeminist Val Plumwood.[18] She explores how we might apply some of Plumwood's insights and projected ethics into current times, particularly Plumwood's own deconstruction of the logic behind power systems of violence toward the more-than-human and human alike. Like others in this book she renders dualistic thought (so prevalent in Western thinking) as redundant and uses the work of Plumwood as a provocation for change. In particular, she highlights her own uptake and extension of Plumwood's excellent thinking on the facets and harm of dualisms that include backgrounding, radical exclusion, incorporation, instrumentalism, and homogenization. A unique piece of ecofeminist scholarship that revives the activist/scholarship of Val Plumwood, Susan Griffin, bell hooks, Chris Cuomo, and the recent work of Sara Ahmed among others toward a renewed ethical framework that makes sense of the world, and helps us understand, as Plumwood does, "what it means to be prey." Eleanor Sanderson wraps up our book on *Shame, Gender Violence, and Ethics: Terrors of Injustice* with a meditation on the motif of the Compass Rose, as an invitation to cultivate the "manifold wisdom of God" (175). She calls for an enlivened global community, and explores different pathways of peace to achieve this, that are both practical and spiritually centered. She invites us to "be weathervanes for the blowing of God's Spirit through each other's lives" (184) from her positionality as a scholar and bishop in the Anglican church in Aotearoa/New Zealand. An "embodied and non-violent revolution of love shaped by the way of the cross" (175) forms part of her poetic and prayerful dialogue and intention. She also engages with psycho-sociological ideas around the space between post-traumatic stress, and post-traumatic growth, and her application of liberation spirituality[19] is sensitively nuanced and incorporated into the inclusive and healing way she perceives the future. There is a pneumatological tone to this chapter that gently incorporates Luce Irigaray's *The Way of Love*[20] into a theo-epistemological chapter of great beauty; a tender conclusion to a challenging collection that does critically important work. We want to conclude with expressing our sincere thanks to Sharon Labrot Crasnow and Joanne Beil Waugh for the incluson of this book into their series. We also want to thank Sydney Wedbush for all her efforts on the way towards the publication of this book.

NOTES

1. Luce Irigaray, *Sharing the World* (London and New York: Continuum, 2008), 5. We also draw the reader's attention to discourses that exceed the contents of this particular edition, but that consider how ethically and authentically the world is or is not shared. See, for example, Eve Kosovsky Sedgewick, *The Epistemology of the Closet* (Berkley: University of California Press 1990); Clifton Evers, "Hegemonic Pan-Ethnic White Australian Masculinity: Feeling Masculine During Mediated Assemblages," *Visuality, Emotions and Minority Culture: Feeling Ethnic*, ed. John Erni (Heidelberg: Springer Verlag, 2017), 147–161; Kane Race, *The Gay Science: Intimate Experiences with the Problem of HIV* (London: Routledge, 2017); Teresa de Lauretis, *Queer Theory: Lesbian and Gay Sexualities, Special Issue of Differences: A Journal of Feminist Cultural Studies*, 3: 2 (Summer 1991), iii–xviii.

2. Giorgio Agamben, *Homo Sacer: Sovereign Power and Bare Life*, trans. Daniel Heller-Roazen (Redwood City, CA: Stanford University Press, 1995), 166–80.

3. See Silvan Tomkins, *Shame and its Sisters: A Silvan Tomkins Reader*, eds. Eve Kosofsky Sedgewick and Adam Frank (Durham, NC: Duke University Press, 1995); Sandra Bartky, "Shame and Gender," in *Femininity and Domination: Studies in the Phenomenology of Oppression* (New York: Routledge, 1990); Martha Nussbaum, *Hiding from Humanity: Disgust, Shame, and the Law* (Princeton, NJ: Princeton

University Press, 2004); Bonnie Mann, "Femininity, Shame, and Redemption," *Hypatia*, 33: 3 (Summer 2018), 403. Michael Lewis, *Shame: The Exposed Self* (New York: The Free Press, 1995); Elspeth Probyn, *Blush: The Face of Shame* (Minneapolis: University of Minnesota University Press), 2005; Miranda Fricker, *Epistemic Injustice: Power and the Ethics of Knowing* (New York: Oxford University Press, 2007).

4. Giorgio Agamben, *Remnants of Auschwitz: The Witness and the Archive*, transl. by Daniel Heller-Roazen (New York: Zone Books, 2002).

5. Gabriel García Márquez, *Chronicle of a Death Foretold* (New York: Vintage International, 2003).

6. Diana E. H. Russell, "The origin and importance of the term femicide." Diana E. H. Russell, Ph. D., December 2011, http://www.dianarussell.com/origin_of_femi cide.html.

7. Judith Butler, *Frames of War. When Is Life Grievable?* (London: Verso, 2009), 3.

8. Cf. Nussbaum, *Hiding from Humanity*.

9. Lewis, *Shame*, 36.

10. Butler, *Frames of War*.

11. Fricker, *Epistemic Injustice*, 5–7.

12. Jill Locke, "Shame and the Future of Feminism," *Hypatia*, 22: 4 (2007), 149–153.

13. Probyn, *Blush: The Face of Shame*, xii–x.

14. Johanna E. Foster and Sherizaan Minwalla, "Voices of Yazidi Women: Perceptions of Journalistic Practices in the Reporting on ISIS Sexual Violence." *Women's Studies International Forum* 67 (2018): 53–64.

15. Kimberle Crenshaw, "Demarginalizing the Intersection of Race and Sex: A Black Feminist Critique of Antidiscrimination Doctrine, Feminist Theory and Antiracist Politics." *University of Chicago Legal Forum* 1 (1989): 139–167.

16. Tomkins, *Shame and its Sisters*, 133.

17. Maurice Merleau-Ponty, "The Child's Relation with Others," in *The Primacy of Perception*, ed. James M. Edie, 96–155 (Evanston, IL: Northwestern Press, 1964).

18. Val Plumwood, *Feminism and the Mastery of Nature* (London: Routledge, 1993).

19. Mary Grey, *Sacred Longings: The Ecological Spirit and Global Culture* (Minneapolis, MN: Fortress Press, 2004).

20. Irigaray, *The Way of Love* (London and New York: Continuum, 2002).

BIBLIOGRAPHY

Agamben, Giorgio. *Homo Sacer: Sovereign Power and Bare Life*. Translated by Daniel Heller-Roazen. Redwood City, CA: Stanford University Press, 1995.
_____. *Remnants of Auschwitz: The Witness and the Archive*. Translated by Daniel Heller-Roazen. New York: Zone Books, 2002.
Ahmed, Sara. *The Cultural Politics of Emotion*. Edinburgh: Edinburgh University Press, 2014, (second edition).

Bartky, Sandra Lee. *Femininity and Domination: Studies in the Phenomenology of Oppression*. New York: Routledge, 1990.

Butler, Judith. *Frames of War. When Is Life Grievable?* Verso: London, 2009.

Canadian Criminal Code, RSC 1985, C-46. Accessed May 1, 2018.

Crenshaw, Kimberle. "Demarginalizing the Intersection of Race and Sex: A Black Feminist Critique of Antidiscrimination Doctrine, Feminist Theory and Antiracist Politics." *University of Chicago Legal Forum* 1 (1989): 139–167.

Cuomo, Chris. *Feminism and Ecological Communities: An Ethic of Flourishing*. New York: Routledge, 1998.

de Lauretis, Teresa. Ed. "Queer Theory: Lesbian and Gay Sexualities," *Special Issue of Differences: A Journal of Feminist Cultural Studies*, 3: 2 (Summer 1991): iii–xviii.

Evers, Clifton. "Hegemonic Pan-Ethnic White Australian Masculinity: Feeling Masculine During Mediated Assemblages." *Visuality, Emotions and Minority Culture: Feeling Ethnic*, edited by John, N. Erni, 147–161. Heidelberg: Springer Verlag, 2017.

"Final Report. Missing and Murdered Indigenous Women and Girls." Mmiwg-Ffada. Ca. Last modified 2019. Accessed August 13, 2019. https://www.mmiwg-ffada.ca/final-report/.

Foster, Johanna E. and Sherizaan Minwalla. "Voices of Yazidi Women: Perceptions of journalistic practices in the reporting on ISIS sexual violence." *Women's Studies International Forum* 67 (2018): 53–64.

Fricker, Miranda. *Epistemic Injustice: Power and the Ethics of Knowing*. New York: Oxford University Press, 2007.

Grey, Mary. *Sacred Longings: The Ecological Spirit and Global Culture*. Minneapolis: Fortress Press, 2004.

Irigaray, Luce. *Sharing the World*. London and New York: Continuum, 2008
———. *The Way of Love*. London and New York: Continuum, 2002.

Lewis, Michael. *Shame: The Exposed Self*. New York: First Free Press, 1995.

Locke, Jill. "Shame and the Future of Feminism," *Hypatia*, 22: 4 (2007), 156–162.

Lorde, Audre. "Age, Race, Class, and Sex: Women Redefining Difference." In *Feminist Theory: A Reader*, 4th edition, edited by Wendy K. Kolmar and Frances Bartkowski, 289–293. New York: McGraw Hill, 2013.

Mann, Bonnie, "Femininity, Shame, and Redemption" *Hypatia*, 33: 3 (Summer 2018), 402–17.

Márquez, Gabriel García. *Chronicle of a Death Foretold*. New York: Vintage International, 2003.

Merleau-Ponty, Maurice. "The Child's Relation with Others." In *The Primacy of Perception*, edited by James M. Edie, 96–155. Evanston: Northwestern Press, 1964.

Nussbaum, Martha. *Hiding from Humanity: Disgust, Shame and the Law*. Princeton: Princeton University Press, 2004.

Plane Te Paa, Jenny. "Listening to the Spirit: Preparing the Way. . ." *First Peoples Theology Journal*, 4, no. 1 (2006): 64–73.

Plumwood, Val. *Feminism and the Mastery of Nature*. London: Routledge, 1993.

Probyn, Elspeth. *Blush: The Face of Shame*. Minneapolis: University of Minnesota University Press, 2005.

Race, Kane. *The Gay Science: Intimate Experiences with the Problem of HIV*. London: Routledge, 2017.

Russell, Diana. "The Origin and Importance of the Term Femicide." Diana E. H. Russell, Ph. D., December 2011. http://www.dianarussell.com/origin_of_femicide .html. Accessed March 7, 2018.

Sedgewick, Eve Kosovsky. *The Epistemology of the Closet*. Berkley: University of California Press, 1990.

Sittirak, Sinith. *Daughters of Development: The Stories of Women and the Changing Environment in Thailand*. Bangkok: WENIT, 1996.

Tomkins, Silvan. *Shame and its Sisters: A Silvan Tomkins Reader*. Edited by Eve Kosofsky Sedgewick and Adam Frank. Durham, NC: Duke University Press, 1995.

PART 1

RESPONSES TO GENDER VIOLENCE

1

"Speaking About Her Just Might Heal"

Witnessing to Canada's Missing and Murdered Indigenous Women

Jane Barter

This chapter is inspired by the courage of the family members of missing and murdered Indigenous women and girls in my city of Winnipeg, Manitoba, Canada, who never forget and who never give up. It is written with gratitude and respect for their witness.

On August 17, 2014, the body of fifteen-year-old Tina Fontaine was found in the Red River in Winnipeg, Manitoba. The duvet in which she was wrapped was weighed down with boulders to guarantee that her 33-kilogram body disappeared into the river's murky depths. Tina had been well known to the police, having run away several times from her family and from foster care—the last time from the hotel to which she was temporarily assigned by the provincial child care authority. Throughout her short life, her case was managed by six different protection agencies, usually at the same time, each with conflicting understandings of their responsibility and jurisdiction over her case.[1] Fifty-six-year-old Raymond Cormier was tried for her murder in 2018 and acquitted. Her case remains unsolved.

In June 2011, thirty-six-year-old Cindy Gladue, a mother of three, was found dead in an Edmonton hotel bathtub. She bled to death sometime in the night during a weekend in which, according to the defense lawyer of the assailant, Bradley Barton, she was contracted for sex, including "rough sex." Her death was caused by blood loss from having sustained an 11-centimeter wound to her vagina. In an unprecedented move, Alberta's chief medical examiner exhibited Gladue's severed vaginal tissue as evidence that she died of lethal force with a weapon. The court also admitted evidence on Gladue's sexual history in spite of Canada's rape shield laws. In 2015, an all-white jury acquitted Barton. After the acquittal the Crown appealed the ruling to the Alberta Supreme Court successfully and Barton currently awaits retrial for the diminished charge of manslaughter.

How are we to remember the horrific deaths of these women and the over 1,100 other missing and murdered Indigenous woman and girls in Canada? What political demands might be extrapolated from their deaths and how? Moreover, *who* is to witness to their deaths? What are the limits that should be placed, if any, on witnessing to the violent deaths of these women, especially in a moment in which the nation-state is deeply invested in somehow rectifying its colonial past in the name of reconciliation?

To be certain, these are instances of violence against Indigenous women and girls that are discrete deaths, but they are also deaths that are linked to one another by the kinds of violence they suffered, which, in turn, links them to the stories of other Indigenous women since the beginning of colonization.[2] In this chapter, I wish to examine the manner in which witnessing to Indigenous women's disappearance and murder at this moment in Canadian public life can far too easily become another form of injustice against them. In so doing, I also wish to consider as an alternative, the manner in which family members and loved ones are able to resist the current tendency to make use of the women's stories toward national redemptive ends, and thus how they enable the women's memories to remain.

THE DISPOSABLE

Feminist scholars have pointed out that what unites stories like those of Fontaine and Gladue is that the disappearance is not accidental—both cases underscore the disposability of marginalized women.[3] In Canada, the colonial project is contingent upon the erasure of Indigenous populations from the land. The erasure of Indigenous women is a particularly expedient means for it involves not only the women's removal but also their progeny's. One of the most efficient ways that Canada had in solving the "Indian Problem"[4] was to control women's reproduction, through forced sterilization and the removal of their children, whether that be through the Residential Schools, the Sixties Scoop,[5] or, later, the hypersurveillance of mothers through child welfare agencies and birth alerts.[6] This management of women's bodies involves precisely what Michel Foucault referred to as biopolitics, for it describes the manner in which the state "deals with the population as a political problem, as a problem that is at once scientific and political, as a biological problem and as power's problem."[7] The solution to the problem of the Indigenous population is at once increased surveillance and control, while it is also the abandonment and disposal of those subjects who are deemed "exceptional" and thus are to be excluded from society. Biopolitics is the power that "consists in making live and letting die."[8]

Biopower in Canada continues to function through the passive power to kill by letting die,[9] through such modern techniques and phenomena as "exposing someone to death, increasing the risk of death for some people, or, quite simply, political death, expulsion, rejection, and so on."[10] The extension of government practices over Indigenous women's daily lives holds a disciplinary function (through such phenomena as incarceration, child removal, and sterilization), but also works to divest women from political power and expelling them from their communities. Indigenous status in Canada is itself contingent upon the colonial apparatus known as the *Indian Act*.[11] Right up until 1985, women lost their status if they married a nonstatus man. Indigenous women and their children were therefore often alienated from their homes, communities, and traditional ways of living. Because of the patriarchal practices of many band councils and offices, women were often prohibited from ever returning to the reserves if their marriages ended. This double banning—by the Government of Canada and by the band—rendered Indigenous women's lives exceptional— they were neither Indigenous nor full citizens of Canada.

Such abandonment is replicated in the phenomenon of missing and murdered Indigenous women and girls. To be missing is to exist in the liminal space where one is neither dead nor alive, neither human nor inhuman. The missing are not citizens with rights; they are instead a voiceless, faceless presence whose absence marks the precise caesura of the Canadian national project. Similarly, the murder of Indigenous women often takes place in zones in which women are subject to arbitrary and shifting colonial and patriarchal power. In her analysis of the case of Pamela George, a sex-trade worker who was raped and beaten to death by two suburban white males in 1995, Sherene Razack argues that Canadian city geography itself sets up the boundaries between decent (white) and indecent (Indigenous) society. Spatialized power gives male settlers the right to be free citizens while it relegates Indigenous women like Pamela George to the Stroll:

> Two white men who buy the services of an Aboriginal woman in prostitution, and who then beat her to death, are enacting a quite specific violence perpetrated on Aboriginal bodies throughout Canada's history, a colonial violence that has not only enabled white settlers to secure the land but to come to know themselves as entitled to it. In the men's encounter with Pamela George, these material (theft of the land) and symbolic (who is entitled to it) processes shaped both what brought Pamela George to the Stroll and what white men from middle-class homes thought they were doing in a downtown area of prostitution on the night of the murder. These processes also shaped what sense the court made of their activities.[12]

In his work on the origins of sovereign power, Giorgio Agamben argues that the power to produce "bare life" (*Zoē*) is sovereignty's very hallmark.

Sovereign power is the capacity to create bodies that are bare life, or life divested from discursive and public life (*Bios*). Bare life is no less contingent upon politics even though it is rendered invisible from the public sphere; on the contrary, it is especially bound to sovereign power's coercive control to create it. The production of political life is parasitic upon the exclusion of bare life from politics, which is to say that citizenry is produced by the exclusion of those whom sovereign power deems to be an exception. Hence, those who are exceptional—in Canada, Indigenous persons whose governance is marked by the "special laws" that are the Indian Act, and Indigenous women who themselves are often excepted even from these laws—find themselves relegated to a place of noncitizenry, banned from ordinary recourse to the law, while also banned from the indeterminate and shifting colonial juridical sphere that is the band system.

The spatiality of these states of exception is notable. Like the camp that Agamben delineates as the "hidden Nomos"[13] of contemporary politics, the reserve system serves as a site where Indigenous people are separated from others and live under a juridical "state of exception," where the law conceives of them as needy and excluded bodies outside of the realm of ordinary citizenry and peoplehood. Mark Rifkin builds upon Agamben's analysis as he considers the formation of the reservation system in the United States:

> Those political collectivities whose occupancy does not fit the geopolitical ideal/imaginary of the state are left abandoned by it, exposed and threatened on the threshold of the juridical order that is made possible and validated by their exception.[14]

The abandonment of missing and murdered Indigenous women and girls is made most manifest in the kinds of violent deaths they often faced. Many of the women's bodies were found in dumpsters; their bodies were disposed of on the edge of town, in a river, or a garbage dump. Even the Crown in the Cindy Gladue case deemed it appropriate to admit portions of her severed genitalia as evidence. The use of Indigenous women's bodies and the representation of their bodies and lives as disposable are deeply embedded within the Canadian colonial imagination. But there is yet another sense in which Indigenous women are made into biopolitical objects and that is in the framing of Indigenous women's lives as peculiarly vulnerable and subject to trauma as the Canadian public attempts to come to terms with their disappearances and deaths. In her *Therapeutic Nations: Healing in an Age of Indigenous Human Rights*, Athabascan scholar Dian Million interrogates the notion of Indigenous trauma and victimhood as a device that serves the biopolitical end

of transforming Indigenous female subjects into objects requiring management, intervention, and increased jurisdiction over her "healing" and her life:

> [T]he white elephant in the room appears to me to be how the perception of
> the subject of colonial violence is indexical to comprehending the dance of
> hegemony in our times. If the institutions and discourses in place around our
> "damage" are hegemonic, what then are our relations with the mechanisms of
> "healing" in the forms in which it is most usually presented now?[15]

It is a short step from viewing Indigenous persons as traumatized subjects—
particularly sexually traumatized subjects—to the disciplining of their lives
through government programs aimed at healing. And because trauma was a
very real outcome of the genocide that Canada committed against Indigenous
peoples, it is easily manipulated in ways that further diminish Indigenous
agency. While Million does not dismiss the work of healing within and by
Indigenous communities, she does ask what tacit forces are at work that make
therapeutic culture so ubiquitous and what makes the traumatized Indigenous
subject the primary modality that settler Canadians have for viewing their
Indigenous neighbors. In the narration of colonial experience, the trope of
trauma has the effect not only of individualizing collective violence but also
of presenting the traumatized victim as a biopolitical subject—one who must
be managed, even in their disappearances and deaths.

REDEMPTIVE MEMORY

Biopolitics leaves no stone unturned in the power it extends over life. It even
mobilizes past suffering to serve its ends. By presenting trauma as an inevitable feature of Indigenous life due to Canada's colonial history, the government can at once apologize for the emotional pain that was caused in the past,
while also seeking to rectify it in the present through individual therapeutic
techniques. This enables the state to appear to be concerned with Indigenous
suffering, while also short-circuiting any claims that may be made for current redistribution of land or Indigenous sovereignty over resources.[16] Roger
I. Simon's discussion of the Truth and Reconciliation Commission[17] sounds
this word of caution:

> Rendering the people who come forward to speak to the commission as vic-
> tims living a damaged life beyond repair risks inflicting . . . wounds of mis-
> recognition. In such mis-recognition there is the danger that inter-generational
> Aboriginal life will be reduced to images of a problem-ridden, broken existence
> serving to confirm stereotypes offered as explanations for the marginalization

of native populations within Canadian society . . . Furthermore, this mis-recognition risks reducing the political to the therapeutic so that restorative justice is defined solely within support for personal healing from the wounds of colonialism.[18]

In the era of national commissions and inquiries in Canada, it is important to ask how Indigenous subjects are being represented and whether their past trauma is utilized as a barrier to their agency and self-determination. Shortly after the election of Liberal prime minister Justin Trudeau in 2016, the National Inquiry on Missing and Murdered Indigenous Women and Girls commenced its work. This federal inquiry is independent of the government; nevertheless, the government of Canada determined its mandate, which was to

> examine and report on the systemic causes behind the violence that Indigenous women and girls experience, *and their greater vulnerability to violence*, by looking for patterns and underlying factors that explain why higher levels of violence occur.[19] (Italics mine)

While there is no question that Indigenous women are materially more vulnerable to violence,[20] the government's directive to the inquiry to employ a "trauma-informed" approach[21] in hearing testimonies should be read with a critical lens.[22] Such an approach threatens to present victims and their witnesses outside the scope of ordinary public life in spite of the public nature of the inquiry. Further, the conception of vulnerability and trauma as an a priori ascription of Indigenous women connotes a subject who, while distinct from ordinary society, must also be managed by it. As victims who are intrinsically "vulnerable to violence," Indigenous women are represented as those whose deaths are tragically inevitable. In the case of those who are missing or dead, they are biopolitical subjects in the perfect sense. They are no longer able to speak; their deaths represent a final severance from language, community, and humanity, and so the state can make use of their memory easily for the sake of its own interventions. As Jenny Edkins warns, survivor testimony can be easily coopted by the state to exert further control over populations:

> Once codified . . . the traumatic experience becomes something that can be appropriated. Witnesses lose control over the interpretation of their testimony. Because testimony is highly political and if as such "it threatens the status quo, powerful political, economic, and social forces will exert pressure either to keep their silence or to revise their stories." Survivors who are marginal or isolated will be most at risk of the appropriation; if there is a powerful community a

measure of control can be retained. The pressures for conformity will be strong, precisely in reflection of the strength of the testimony itself.[23]

Throughout over 1,200 pages of the "Final Report of the National Inquiry on Missing and Murdered Women and Girls,"[24] the authors and editors worked strenuously to honor the voices of the women, and indeed they too are Indigenous women who understand intimately the nature of the stories that are being told. However, the Final Report's legal framework, its trauma-informed affective modalities, and its emphasis upon the sequential narrative from colonization to the present continues to shape the Final Report, in ways that occlude the testimonies themselves and thus it threatens to conform to the redemptive Canadian narrative that the government wishes to create and exhibit to the world.

Canada has every reason to wish to present itself in a better light on the international stage currently and is consequently deeply invested in maintaining its image as a kinder and gentler nation than its southern neighbor. Given Canada's deep dependence on resource extraction and trade for its economy, it wishes to assure its trade partners that its domestic house is perfectly in order. At the same time, it relies on Indigenous cooperation to extract resources from their lands and to set up dangerous pipelines on their traditional territories. Good relations with Indigenous communities are also good business. One of the most overt clues to the less-than-noble reasons for Canada's recent push for reconciliation can be seen in Justin Trudeau's overtures toward First Nations to allow for the extension of the Trans-Mountain Expansion Project, which seeks to carry Canadian oil from Alberta to the coast of British Columbia.[25] What better way to assure Indigenous peoples in Canada and the world that the government is concerned with the lives of Indigenous peoples, than to set up commissions? What better way to impress upon the world, and the domestic arena, Canada's benevolence? Further, by remembering Indigenous suffering as trauma, the public is trained to neglect the present colonial practices and capitalist global forces which produce social disintegration, while it turns the public gaze to the victim of these forces to try to locate trauma's source.

OTHER FORMS OF TESTIMONY

In *Remnants of Auschwitz*, Agamben points out that there are two ways of understanding testimony, according to the etymology of the term in Latin. The first term, "testis," connotes a person who in a court of law offers testimony as a third voice in the context of two rival parties ("*testis*" derives from "*terstis*," the third). In the second instance, "*superstes*" refers to a party who has survived an ordeal.[26] Here Agamben challenges the use of testimony in the first sense, its usual juridical sense in which testimony seeks to prove guilt or innocence. Instead he directs our attention to *"superstes"* as a means of thinking about witnessing in a far broader ethical sphere. This means we testify not to make a legal case for a party's guilt or innocence, but to speak to the ordeal that we have survived alongside those who have been lost. In Agamben's understanding of biopolitics, one of its chief effects is to make the subject (merely) survive, thus to reduce life to its most stripped down form, divested from political power, often segregated from community, and even from language. Agamben challenges us to testify precisely to what it means to "survive an ordeal," to be reduced to bare life within the context of a violent biopolitical order, and so to speak the unspeakable from this vantage on behalf of those who can no longer speak.

Survivors are imperfect witnesses—they are unable to speak fully to the atrocity that they witnessed both because they did not fully experience it and because the event itself resists comprehension, at least in any way that the law can address. As Agamben discusses with reference to the survivors of Auschwitz, testimony always contains within it a fundamental lacuna:

> On the one hand, what happened in the camps appears to the survivors as the only true thing, and as such absolutely unforgettable; on the other hand, this truth is to the same degree unimaginable, that is, irreducible to the real elements that constitute it.[27]

In many respects, the Final Report of the Inquiry on Missing and Murdered Indigenous Women and Girls was fully cognizant that its work was incomplete and that they were tasked with an impossible mandate. Yet testimonies themselves—the words of those who survived an ordeal—offer a fuller and more nuanced picture of the phenomenon of missing and Indigenous murdered women and girls than the Report can capture.

WITNESSING AND SISTERHOOD

The National Inquiry interviewed more than 1,400 witnesses who were usually family members. In addition, it held fifteen public hearings with communities affected by the loss of a member. Within the testimonies, the transcripts of which are documented online,[28] we certainly hear stories of trauma, but we also hear stories of resistance and stories which refuse to describe their sisters as merely vulnerable.

The sisters, loved ones, and family members bear witness to the suffering that the women experienced even though there remains an experience that can never be testified to fully, because their loved ones are now gone.

Nevertheless, they are the only ones who can speak on behalf of those who can speak no longer. This is because they, too, have survived an ordeal, which is growing up as Indigenous women in a nation-state in which they continue to be treated as disposable. These testimonies offer an account of trauma that is not subsumed into a biopolitical narrative. Indeed, what these stories offer is the connection of life to its form, to its community and relationships which speak to the existence of life beyond trauma, while they also form a lived protest which exposes the ongoing injustice which they face. In her testimony on the disappearance of her daughter, Jennifer, Bernice Catcheway recalls her initial contact with the RCMP:

> And, he [the Officer] said, "Oh, what's her name?" I said, "Jennifer. Jennifer Catcheway." "Oh, how old is she?" Like that. That's how he spoke to me. "How—how old is she?" I said, "She just turned 18 Thursday, her birthday." "Oh, give her a week. She's on a drunk." I said, "You don't even know her to talk to her [sic] like that—about her like that. You don't know her." He said, "Oh, give her a week. Give her a week."[29]

Family members resist the narrow ascriptions given to their loved ones. Their testimony corrects the tropes of traumatized victim, prostitute, addict, and alcoholic. Family members name the trauma that has been inflicted upon them and their loved ones, but the trauma does not become reduced to a moment in the redemptive narrative; it remains unreconciled. The pain and suffering that family members underwent does not serve a higher end. Jenny Edkins calls such witnessing an "encircling of trauma": "a refusal of anything that might 'heal' the pain of loss, and a demand that what happened be remembered in all its traumatic impact. This is very different from an idea of trauma as a purely individual psychological problem that should be overcome."[30]

In many cases, this kind of witness involves restoring their family members as persons with what Agamben calls a form-of-life, or a means of living which resists the logic of separation of life from its context and community:

> Form-of-life can neither recognize itself nor be recognized, because the contact between life and form and the happiness that are in question in it are situated beyond every possible recognition and every possible work. In this sense, form-of-life is above all the articulation of a zone of irresponsibility, in which the identities and imputations of the juridical order are suspended.[31]

By zone of irresponsibility, Agamben is indicating the significance of suspending juridical notions about who worthy of being remembered and how. This is a form of political witness that is beyond all statist notions of recognition. The missing are not bearers of rights; they are not emblems of a fixed identity. Instead, they simply *are*. There is no criterion which could serve to make the loved ones proper or worthy victims. They do not have to pass through juridical values in order to be remembered. Throughout the hearings, the family refused the juridical by refusing any imputation which would make their loss anything less than a profound travesty. Isabel Winning's testimony on the death of her niece, Nicole Ashley Daniels[32] is a perfect example:

> And, I think a lot of ways that we get lost in media and stuff like that is by focusing on the troubles that we have as Aboriginal people, that are not just for Aboriginal people. Those problems exist worldwide. The problem is that we suffer as addicts—I'm also a survivor as well. But, the problems that we suffer as addicts do not mean that we warrant an early death sentence because of those actions or because we have faults and because we had made mistakes.[33]

In refusing to see her and her niece's story as the inevitable consequence of life of trauma, Winning challenges those tropes that would seek to treat Indigenous populations in a systematized way as an aberrant subject. Further, Winning's testimony makes the case strongly that there is no "worthy" victim. The imputations of worth and value in judging these cases must be critically undermined. So too must the overarching narratives that would seek to harmonize the discordant, to manage the women's stories in such a way that they are a problem that needs to be solved through targeted reform of their lives.

Thus, the singularity of the women's lives is retained. It is not sacrificed for a higher, redemptive, end. The stories of the women in the testimonies themselves remain ambivalent, raw, unassimilated. This is a powerful performance, for it allows the bare life that biopolitics has created to be revealed, and in so doing, it also represents a powerful protest against it. As Jenny Edkins, following Agamben, puts it:

> The ultimate protest against sovereign power's production of subjects as "bare life" is the unconditional acceptance of that designation. Protests as bare life are the effective contestation of sovereign power. In such action, a solidarity of the shaken as Foucault calls it, protesters would accept or rather inhabit or take on their vulnerability.[34]

That there is a means of bearing witness to trauma that does not reinscribe women into the therapeutic techniques that Canadian policies often mandate where "trauma and healing is a spiral narrative from personal fragmentation to national organization"[35] is well documented in the testimonies of family members. It is within these stories that the redemptive trajectory is interrupted by the voices of the missing and those who persistently and courageously witnessed to them. While the official Report often uses the stories to offer a higher synthesis, the testimonial transcripts themselves offer a counternarrative, one of the irreducibility of a human life, even a life that is now absent. This is a life that determinedly reasserts its presence through the imperfect witness that family members speak.

I began this chapter with the stories of two very different victims of violence—Tina Fontaine and Cindy Gladue. Their deaths, and the use made of their bodies, clearly attest to the biopolitical forms of violence to which they were subjected. Their bodies were reduced to bare life, a life that was deemed less than human and so could easily be exposed and disposed of. This was true of their deaths as well as their lives, as their disposability continued in their dying as in their living. This chapter has been an articulation of a worry—one that is concerned with the manner in which the biopolitical ascriptions of Indigenous women's identity can easily continue beyond their deaths through the ways in which they are remembered nationally. The recent work of the National Inquiry into Missing and Murdered Indigenous Women and Girls is a work that has been done by extraordinary Indigenous advocates, policy makers, judges, and scholars. It is nevertheless a document that was commissioned by a colonial government with the aim to uncovering the reasons for Indigenous women's "greater vulnerability to violence." I have attempted here to interrogate the difference between loved ones' remembering and that of the nation-state. I have suggested that the narratives of families themselves make no such higher use of their memories, and as such they offer a form of politics in which reconciliation is deferred as long as women remain missing and as long as deaths like theirs continue. Through such testimony those who are witnessed to remain unassimilated and unreconciled. The wound of their loss is still palpable as are they remembered by their sisters. And as such their unreconciled memory remains the only hope that a nation such as Canada has to begin to move beyond its colonial story. It is with this in mind that I end with these words of Shayleen Goforth in relation to her sister, Kelly, who was murdered in 2013,[36] for it calls to mind the reality of her loss and the long and difficult road that just might inch toward healing:

Kelly had a positive mindset that I admired. There was nothing negative anyone can say about her. To me her strength was she had the ability to make a bad situation into a good one. She would make my sad face turn into a happy face by making me laugh. I felt she had the right words, answers for any situation. I know she's my baby sister and I'm the one who's supposed to make her feel this way, but she made me feel safe. Kelly had that loving touch like my mama that made me feel so loved and safe, and it breaks my heart knowing she had high hopes and dreams she couldn't fulfill. She had goals and ambition. She was full of life. She dreamt of becoming a model, hoped and prayed for a great future. For her and her baby. She wanted the best for her baby and for all of us.

And I know me speaking about her for the first time in public will help me deal with the situation. Nobody could ever heal my heart, but I know speaking about her just might.[37]

NOTES

1. "Manitobaadvocate.ca," last modified 2019, https://manitobaadvocate.ca/wp -content/uploads/MACY-Special-Report-March-2019-Tina-Fontaine-FINAL1.pdf.

2. According to the RCMP Report of 2011, between the years of 1980 and 2012, 1,181 cases of "police-recorded incidents of Aboriginal-female homicides and unre-solved missing Aboriginal females" were documented. "Final Report | MMIWG," Mmiwg-Ffada.Ca, last modified 2019, https://www.mmiwg-ffada.ca/final-report, 54.

3. See Sherene Razack:

"I consider the excessive violence that is meted out to Indigenous women, arguing that in the colonial imagination, the goal is to destroy the figural unity of the body of the Indig-enous person and to transform it into waste. . . . When Indigenous women's bodies are destroyed in the extreme way that we see in murdered Indigenous women, the value of their bodies in the social order is made clear. I suggest that the scopic regime of sexualized violence is key to disposability. The violence that is written on the flesh tells the colonial story of whose bodies have value."

Sherene H. Razack, "Gendering Disposability," *Canadian Journal of Women and the Law* 28, no. 2 (2016): 29, https://muse.jhu.edu/.

4. This pejorative term is used here to refer to the problems identified by Canada in the wake of Civil Rights and postcolonial movements of the 1950s and 1960s globally and Canada's efforts to improve its reputation on an international stage. Dian Million writes: "Canadians were not solely driven by a sense of altruism when they became worried about their 'Indian problem' in the 1950s and 1960s. Aboriginal peoples lived segregated and controlled under a tight colonial Indian Act bureaucracy, impoverished and suffering from a variety of social ills." Dian Million, *Therapeutic Nations: Healing in an Age of Indigenous Human Rights* (Tucson: University of Arizona Press), 89.

5. The "Sixties Scoop" refers to the mass removal of Indigenous children from their homes and into the child welfare system, usually without permission from their families or communities.

6. Birth alerts are issued by health care and child and family services agencies in order to track those considered to be high-risk pregnant women. "The alerts serve to flag certain women—largely Indigenous—in hospital, and stipulate that, if an alert has been issued, the agency may apprehend the child at birth." *Final Report*, 364.

7. Michel Foucault, *Society Must Be Defended: Lectures at the Collège de France 1975–1976*, eds. Mauro Bertani and Alesandro Fonta, trans. David Macey (New York: Picador, 1997), 245.

8. Ibid., 247.

9. When the National Inquiry published its Report in late May of 2019, it created a great stir within the public square in Canada for its unapologetic use of the word, genocide, to describe the Canadian government's policies toward Indigenous peoples. The document makes a strong argument in favor of the use of the term through legal definitions, but often words of women themselves bring the point home more clearly. In the Preface to the document, Commissioner Barb Manitowabi wrote:

"This process has changed me forever. For two years we went to the darkest places where the pain and hurt still lives. The National Inquiry has uncovered failure after failure in protecting the lives and rights of Indigenous women, girls, and 2SLGBTQQIA people. It is a system that, at its core, aims to destroy and pull families apart. Our reality is that we are watching the slow, painful destruction of Indigenous Peoples. Canada has built a system of rules and laws stemming from greed, racism, and hate; this system continues to devour our families today. Canadians cannot deny the facts, as ugly as they may seem: this is genocide."

Final Report, 25.

10. Foucault, *Society Must Be Defended*, 256.

11. The *Indian Act* is an act of Canadian Parliament, first passed in 1876, which defines "Indian" status, determines the allocation of the reserve system and its governance, and controls such various issues affecting First Nations life as health care, education, and taxation. See "Indian Act," Laws-Lois.Justice.Gc.Ca, last modified 2019, https://laws-lois.justice.gc.ca/eng/acts/i-5/.

12. Sherene Razack, "Gendered Racial Violence and Spatialized Justice: The Murder of Pamela George," in *Race, Space and the Law: Unmapping a White Settler Society*, ed. Sherene Razack (Toronto: Between the Lines, 2002), 128–129.

13. See Chapter 7, "The Camp as the 'Nomos' of the Modern," in Giorgio Agamben, *Homo Sacer: Sovereign Power and Bare Life*, trans. Daniel Heller-Roazen (Redwood City, CA: Stanford University Press, 1995), 166–180. Indigenous scholars have been quick to point out the oversight in Agamben's tracing of the phenomenon of the camp, which fails to acknowledge the reserve system as a historical precedent. See especially Mark Rifkin's "Indigenzing Agamben: Rethinking Sovereignty in Light of the 'Peculiar' Status of Native Peoples," *Cultural Critique* 73 (Fall 2009): 98.

14. Rifkin, *"Indigenizing Agamben,"* 98.

15. Million, *Therapeutic Nations*, 170.

16. In June of 2008, Conservative prime minister Stephen Harper offered a public apology to survivors of the Indian Residential Schools, decrying it as a "sad chapter on our history." In spite of his repetition of the words, "We are sorry," in the Apology, Harper went on to underfund health care, education, and housing in northern communities, while he also broke several promises to Indigenous people with respect to water protection, refused to implement any of the 94 Recommendations of the Truth and Reconciliation Commission, and refused to call a National Inquiry on Missing and Murdered Indigenous Women and Girls. "Statement of Apology to Former Students of Indian Residential Schools," Government of Canada, HYPERLINK "http s://www.aadnc-aandc.gc.ca/eng/1100100015644/1100100015649" https://www.aad nc-aandc.gc.ca/eng/1100100015644/1100100015649.

17. The Truth and Reconciliation Commission in Canada took place between 2008 and 2015 as a result of a class-action lawsuit by survivors of Canada's Indian Residential Schools (IRS). During that time, the TRC heard from 6,500 witnesses and held seven national events. Its work was concluded with the publication of 94 Calls to Action to further reconciliation between Indigenous and Non-Indigenous peoples in Canada. "Truth And Reconciliation Commission Of Canada (TRC)," Trc.ca, last modified 2019, http://www.trc.ca/.

18. Roger I. Simon, "Toward a Hopeful Practice of Worrying." In *Reconciling Canada: Critical Perspectives on the Culture of Redress*, eds. Jennifer Henderson and Pauline Wakeham (Toronto: University of Toronto Press, 2013), 132.

19. "About The Independent Inquiry," Rcaanc-Cirnac.Gc.Ca, last modified 2019, https://www.rcaanc-cirnac.gc.ca/eng/1470140972428/1534526770441.

20. *"Final Report,"* 55. (See also n 2).

21. "Government of Canada News about the Independent Inquiry," Rcaanc-Cirnac .gc.ca, last modified 2019, https://www.rcaanc-irnac.gc.ca/eng/1449870049274/1 534527666691.

22. In all this, it is vital for me as a Settler-Canadian to emphasize the fact that I do not wish in any way to undermine the vision and work of the National Inquiry, and particularly not the families and communities who contributed their stories. My critique is solely aimed at Canada's overwhelming urge and habit of transforming Indigenous suffering into stories of national redemption. It is difficult for me to imagine how a national inquiry could avoid such fate, but in spite of this impetus, the stories of the missing nevertheless manage to appear within the document, and within Indigenous-led public events in which loved ones are remembered.

23. Jenny Edkins, *Trauma and the Memory of Politics* (Cambridge: Cambridge University Press, 2003), 190. In this quote, Edkins cites Kali Tal, *Worlds of Hurt: Reading the Literature of Trauma* (Cambridge: Cambridge University Press, 1996).

24. *Final Report*, volumes 1a and 1b.

25. The Expansion Project seeks to triple the capacity for transport of oil by producing a second pipeline to the Pacific Coast of Canada. In May 2018, the Government of Canada purchased the pipeline from Kinder Morgan for $4.5 billion and is seeking partnerships with outside investors to complete the project. Due to protests by environmentalists and First Nations groups in Alberta and British Columbia, the Federal Court of Appeal overturned the expansion and directed the government to assess the potential risk to the environment and consult further with First Nations communities who were not adequately consulted. In November of 2018, the Government of Canada entered into further talks with 117 First Nations communities about the risks and benefits of this Project. In June 2019, the Trans Mountain pipeline expansion was approved by the National Energy Board, in spite of the concerns that were raised by Indigenous groups about the potential for damage to whale and salmon populations and waterways. In a sobering twist, one of the companies bidding for partnership is the Indigenous-led "Project Reconciliation."

26. Giorgio Agamben, *Remnants of Auschwitz: The Witness and the Archive*, trans. Daniel Heller-Roazen (New York: Zone Books, 2002), 17.

27. Agamben, *Remnants of Auschwitz*, 12.

28. "Transcripts and Exhibits," Final Report of the Inquiry on Missing and Murdered Indigenous Women and Girls, "Transcripts & Exhibits | MMIWG," Mmiwg-Ffada.Ca, Last modified 2019, https://www.mmiwg-ffada.ca/transcripts-e xhibits/.

29. Public Hearing, Bernice Catcheway et al. "National Inquiry on MMIWG, Testimonies," Mmiwg-Ffada.Ca, last modified 2019, https://www.mmiwg-ffada.ca /wp-content/uploads/2017/10/20171017_MMIWG_Winnipeg_Public_Vol_10_com bined.pdf.

Eighteen-year-old Jennifer Catcheway disappeared on June 18, 2008. For eleven years the Catcheways have conducted their own searches, scouring garbage dumps, rivers, lakes, and forests looking for their lost daughter.

30. Jenny Edkins, *Missing: Persons and Politics* (Ithaca, NY: Cornell University Press, 2011), 156.

31. Giorgio Agamben, *The Use of Bodies*, trans. Adam Kotsko, in *The Omnibus Homo Sacer* (Redwood City, CA: Stanford University Press, 2017), 1251.

32. Sixteen-year-old Ashley Nicole Daniels was found face down in the snow just two blocks from her Winnipeg home in April 2009. She was intoxicated and had Benzamide in her system. She was also, paradoxically according to the Coroner's Report, found with an open blouse, a jacket undone, and frozen. There were no charges laid in this case.

33. Public Hearings, Winnipeg, volume 9.Mmiwg-Ffada.Ca, last modified 2019, https://www.mmiwg-ffada.ca/wp-content/uploads/2017/10/20171016_MMIWG_W innipeg_Public_Vol_9_combined.pdf.

34. Edkins, *Trauma and the Memory of Politics*.

35. Million, *Therapeutic Nations*, 150.

36. Kelly Goforth was a twenty-one-year-old Regina woman who was murdered in 2013 by Clayton Bo Eichler, who also pled guilty to the murder of another Indigenous woman, Richele Bear. Eichler was sentenced to life in prison with no eligibility for parole for twenty years. Goforth's body was found in a dumpster on the outskirts of Regina wrapped in plastic inside a hockey bag. Richele Bear's body was never found.

37. Public Hearings, Saskatoon, volume 29. Mmiwg-Ffada.ca, last modified 2019, https://www.mmiwg-ffada.ca/wp-content/uploads/2017/11/20171122_MMIWG_S askatoon_Public_Vol_29_Goforth.pdf.

BIBLIOGRAPHY

Agamben, Giorgio. *Homo Sacer: Sovereign Power and Bare Life*. Translated by Daniel Heller-Roazen. Redwood City, CA: Stanford University Press, 1995.

_____. *Remnants of Auschwitz: The Witness and the Archive*. Translated by Daniel Heller-Roazen. New York: Zone Books, 2002.

_____. *The Use of Bodies*. Translated by Adam Kotsko. In *The Omnibus Homo Sacer*, 1011–1290. Redwood City, CA: Stanford University Press, 2017.

Edkins, Jenny. *Missing: Persons and Politics*. Ithaca, NY: Cornell University Press, 2011.

_____. *Trauma and the Memory of Politics*. Cambridge: Cambridge University Press, 2003.

"Final Report. Missing and Murdered Indigenous Women and Girls." Mmiwg-Ffada. Ca. Last modified 2019. Accessed August 13, 2019. https://www.mmiwg-ffada.c a/final-report/.

Foucault, Michel. *Society Must Be Defended: Lectures at the Collège de France, 1975–1976*. Edited by Mauro Bertani and Alessandro Fontana. Translated by David Macey. New York: Picador, 2002.

"Government of Canada News About The Independent Inquiry." Rcaanc-Cirnac. Gc.Ca. Last modified 2019. Accessed August 7, 2019. https://www.rcaanc-cirnac .gc.ca/eng/1449870049274/1534527666691.

Government of Canada. "Statement of Apology to Former Students of Indian Residential Schools." https://www.aadnc-aandc.gc.ca/eng/1100100015644/11 00100015649.

Manitobaadvocate.ca. Last modified 2019. Accessed August 10, 2019. https://ma nitobaadvocate.ca/wp-content/uploads/MACY-Special-Report-March-2019-Tina -Fontaine-FINAL1.pdf.

Million, Dian. *Therapeutic Nations: Healing in an Age of Indigenous Human Rights*. Tucson: University of Arizona Press, 2013.

Mmiwg-Ffada.ca. Last modified 2019. https://www.mmiwg-ffada.ca/wp-content/up loads/2017/10/20171017_MMIWG_Winnipeg_Public_Vol_10_combined.pdf.

National Inquiry on Missing and Murdered Indigenous Women and Girls. *Reclaiming Power and Place The Final Report*. May 29, 2019. Accessed August 10, 2019. https://www.mmiwg-ffada/ca/final-report/.

Public Hearings, Saskatoon, volume 29, Mmiwg-Ffada.ca. Last modified 2019. Accessed September 8, 2019. https://www.mmiwg-ffada.ca/wp-content/uploads /2017/11/20171122_MMIWG_Saskatoon_Public_Vol_29_Goforth.pdf.

Public Hearing, Winnipeg, volume 9, Mmiwg-Ffada.ca. Last modified 2019, Accessed August 8, 2019. https://www.mmiwg-ffada.ca/wp content/uploads/2017 /10/20171016_MMIWG_Winnipeg_Public_Vol_9_combined.pdf.

Razack, Sherene H. "Gendered Racial Violence and Spatialized Justice: The Murder of Pamela George." In *Race, Space and the Law: Unmapping a White Settler Society*, edited by Sherene Razack, 121–56. Toronto: Between the Lines, 2002.

_____. "Gendering Disposability." *Canadian Journal Of Women And The Law* 28, no. 2 (2016): 285–307.

Rifkin, Mark. "Indigenizing Agamben: Rethinking Sovereignty in Light of the 'Peculiar' Status of Native Peoples." *Cultural Critique* 73 (2009): 88–124.

Simon, Roger I. "Toward a Hopeful Practice of Worrying." In *Reconciling Canada: Critical Perspectives on the Culture of Redress*, edited by Jennifer Henderson and Pauline Wakeham, 129–142. Toronto: University of Toronto Press, 2013.

"Truth and Reconciliation Commission of Canada (TRC)." Trc.ca. Last modified 2019. Accessed August 12, 2019.http://www.trc.ca/.

"Transcripts & Exhibits | MMIWG." Mmiwg-Ffada.Ca. Last modified 2019. Accessed August 8, 2019. https://www.mmiwg-ffada.ca/transcripts-exhibits/.

2

Femicide

Another Chronicle of a Death Foretold

Danny Marrero

INTRODUCTION

In *Chronicle of a Death Foretold*,[1] Nobel Prize of Literature recipient Gabriel García Márquez re-create the events around the homicide of Santiago Nasar by the twin Vicario brothers. By committing this crime, they supposedly vindicated the honor of their family because Santiago allegedly stole the purity of their youngest sister, Angela, and, as a consequence, spoiled the arranged marriage which she was pushed to engage in. What is shameful in this story is that even though the Vicario brothers repeatedly announced their intent to murder Santiago, nobody in town tried to stop them. Femicides, understood as "the killing of females . . . because they are female,"[2] are *also* chronicles of deaths foretold.

For the purposes of this chapter, femicide is the last link of a chain of violence illustrated by this extensional definition:

> Examples of femicide include the stoning to death of females . . . , murders of females for so-called "honor;" rape murders; murders of women and girls by their husbands, boyfriends, and dates, for having an affair, or being rebellious, or any number of other excuses; wife-killing by immolation because of too little dowry; deaths as a result of genital mutilations; female sex slaves, trafficked females, and prostituted females, murdered by their "owners," traffickers, "johns" and pimps, and females killed by misogynist strangers, acquaintances, and serial killers.[3]

What all these cases have in common is the violence previous to the gender-related killing of a woman. Having this in mind, we can paraphrase García Márquez lamenting that "[t]here had never been a death more foretold"[4] than the one finishing the lives of women suffering from the violence preceding femicide.

As in the *Chronicle*, from these so-called anticipated deaths collective responsibility follows. In García Márquez's book, if someone could have intervened, stopping the Vicario brothers' plan, Santiago Nasar's homicide would have been avoided. By analogy, if some intervention is made to stop the violence preceding femicide, we could prevent at least some of the gender-related killings of women. What is shameful, though, is that neither people knowing the Vicario brothers' plan, nor societies seeing violence conducive to femicide have intervened to avoid the foretold deaths. It is inevitable for us to wonder why. My working hypothesis is that Judith Butler in *Frames of War* shows some promise in answering this question. To say it in a sentence, the problem is in "the frames through which we apprehend or, indeed, fail to apprehend the lives of others as lost or injured (lose-able or injurable)."[5] For instance, in the *Chronicle*, no one stopped the Vicario brothers because "[t]heir reputation as good people was so well-founded that no one paid any attention to them."[6] That is to say, they in turn fail to recognize Santiago Nasar's vulnerability. In this chapter, I want to explore Butler's suggestion that "[t]he epistemological capacity to apprehend a life is partially dependent on a life being produced according to norms that qualify it as a life or, indeed, as a part of life."[7] My inquiry focuses on the historical development leading to the creation of femicide as a specific offense in the Colombian Penal Code (CPC). I believe this is a good laboratory of philosophical experimentation because it shows how the epistemological capacity of Colombian judges to apprehend the violence preceding femicide depends on the normative framework that recognizes the vulnerability of women, in general, and the grievability of victims of femicide in particular. Firstly, I am going to reconstruct the relevant aspects of the historical development leading to the creation of femicide as an independent offense in the CPC. Secondly, I will show, in legal cases, how judges "apprehend or . . . fail to apprehend the lives"[8] of women victims of femicide depending upon the normativity regulating this offense. This will be an argument for the claim that "norms, [and] social and political organizations . . . have developed historically in order to maximize precariousness for some and minimize precariousness for others."[9]

THE DEVELOPMENT OF FEMICIDE
AS AN INDEPENDENT CRIME IN THE
COLOMBIAN PENAL CODE

The notion of femicide has recently been integrated to some legal systems. In Latin America, for instance, the first provisions integrating it are from

2007, when the Mexican *General Law of Women to Have Access to a Life Free From Violence*[10] defines femicide violence as "the most extreme form of gender violence against woman . . . constituted by a group of misogynist conducts that could lead to . . . impunity . . . and could culminate in a homicide or other forms of violent killing of women."[11] Two strategies have been adopted to criminalize these gender-related killings of women in Latin America, either femicide is an Aggravating Circumstance for homicide,[12] or femicide is an independent crime.[13] Colombia has used both strategies. It is worth studying these legislative movements because of two reasons. First, they are the frames leading judges to "apprehend or . . . fail to apprehend the lives"[14] of women suffering from violence leading to femicide. Second, the context in which the Colombian legislation was forced to transition from homicide to femicide illustrates how deplorable gender-related killings of women are.

Legislative Movement 1: The Gender-Neutral Provisions of Homicide

To start with, the current crime of homicide was included in the Colombian Penal Code[15] enacted in 2000 with the following wording:

Article 103. Homicide: Whoever kills another human being will be punished with imprisonment anywhere from thirteen (13) to twenty-five (25) years.[16]

The objective elements of the definition of this offense, that is, its *actus reus*, reveal its gender neutrality. Firstly, this crime is classified within the offenses against the person, specifically, it is meant to protect the fundamental right to life of all people, disregarding their gender. Secondly, the type of offender committing homicide is not qualified by gender or any other differentiation.

Thirdly, the Colombian definition of homicide does not include a description of a specific action to be performed by the offender in perpetrating this crime. Instead, all things equal, any voluntary action causing the death of another human being will be considered as a homicide. Finally, the victim of the offense is not qualified because of gender reasons either.

This apparent gender impartiality seems to be broken by the aggravating circumstances increasing the punishment of homicide in the Colombian Penal Code passed in 2000. For what matters in this chapter, these circumstances were:

Article 104. Aggravating Circumstances: The punishment will be from twenty-five (25) to forty (40) years, if the conduct described in the previous article is committed:[17]

1. against ancestors, descendants, spouses, long-term and live-in partners, siblings, adoptive parents, adopted children, or relatives up to a second degree of blood relationship.
2. to prepare, facilitate or finish the perpetration of another crime; or to hide or secure its profit or impunity for the offender or any other person taking part in it.

    . . .

6. with cruelty.
7. putting the victim in a defenselessness or an inferiority situation, or taking advantage of one of those situations.[18]

This complementary provision qualifies the offender and the victim imposing a longer period of imprisonment when he/she is a husband, a wife, or a long-term and live-in partner causing the death of his/her, ironically, "significant other." The same increased punishment should be applied when the action causing the death is cruel or renders the victim to a state diminishing his/her capability of resistance. Finally, this provision includes a subjective element of the offense (*means rea*), making a list of explicit motives that, if verified, should make the sentencing more severe.

Unfortunately, the potential that these aggravating circumstances provided to impose strong sanctions to men killing their wives and female partners was squelched by the ways in which one of the diminishing conditions for punishment was systematically applied by Colombian judges and prosecutors. I will illustrate this interpretation below, yet for now, it suffices to take a look at the respective piece of legislation to understand my point. The Colombian Penal Code states:

> Article 57. Anger and Intense Pain. Whoever performs an offense in a state of anger or intense pain, caused by another person's unjustified and serious behavior, will be punished with no less than a sixth of the lowest and no more than a half of the highest limits of the respective offense.[19]

As one can anticipate, this provision exacerbated gender stereotypes and violence against women because it was used to diminish the punishment of men killing women for futile reasons such as suspicions of cheating, jealousy, or the surprising end of a relationship. Circumstances such as these were thought to be the "unjustified and serious behavior" causing men to be in a state of anger and intense pain when killing the woman.

Legislative Movement 2: Femicide as an Aggravating Circumstance for Homicide

Fighting against stereotypes such as these, the Colombian Congress, in 2008, passed a Bill enacting provisions to "prevent, eradicate and criminalize all sorts of violence against women."[20] This piece of legislation was inspired by some instruments of international law such as the recommendations of the *UN Convention on the Elimination of All Forms of Discrimination against Women* of 1992 and the *Inter-American Convention on the Prevention, Punishment and Eradication of Violence Against Women (Convention of Belem do Para)* of 1994. But most importantly, it took into account perturbing data revealing the precarious situation of Colombian women. To illustrate, the justification of this Bill stated that the Colombian Institute of Legal Medicine and Forensic Sciences reported in 2004 that "on average, and per year, 61,000 women are taken to medical examination for crimes related to domestic violence, 38,000 for violent attacks from their partners, and 24,000 for sexual assault."[21] It also quoted the results of the National Pool of Demographics of 2005 showing that "two out of five women who have been married or have been in a long-term and live-in relationship have been physically attacked by their partners."[22] These numbers worsen if we remember the Colombian civil war that, at that time, had been going on for fifty-five years. This is why the justification of the aforementioned Bill also states that "according to the UN High Commissioner for Refugees, in 2008, Colombia was the country with more forced displacement in the western hemisphere, only surpassed by Rwanda."[23] Women and children were "75% of that displaced population, between 1,500,000 and 3,000,000 people."[24] Within this group, "52% of women who had been married or had had a long-term and live-in relationship claimed to suffer from physical violence inflicted by their partners, and 14% reported having been raped."[25] As if this were not enough, it was also recognized that "in Colombia, every two days a woman dies because of the civil war."[26]

These were some of the reasons leading the Colombian Congress to include a new Aggravating Circumstance for homicide. The new version of the Colombian Penal Code's Article 104 was:

Article 104. Aggravating Circumstances: The punishment will be from four hundred (400) months to six hundred (600) months of imprisonment if the conduct described in the previous article is committed:

. . .

11. against a woman because of the fact that she is a woman.[27]

A diligent reader will notice that this Aggravating Circumstance radically modifies the structure of the offense aggravated by it. Even though the offender and the conduct causing the death kept their gender neutrality, the victim and the motive of the offense were qualified with gender-related factors. To clarify, Aggravating Circumstance 11 does not make the killing of a general human being, but just the killing of a woman because of her woman-hood. This means that, for this condition to apply, the homicide should be consequence of an act of violence against a woman and motivated by acts of gender oppression, objectification, or discrimination. As a consequence, this condition not only is meant to protect the fundamental right of women to live, but also their right to have a secure life, and to protect their dignity, freedom, equality, and self-determination.

Legislative Movement 3: Femicide as an Independent Crime

One could expect that Aggravating Circumstance 11, and all the other provisions enacted by the Bill to "prevent, eradicate and criminalize all sorts of violence against women," would help the Colombian government to fight against femicide efficiently. However, the information found by studies following the application of this Bill was astonishing. In a period of eight years, from 2004 to 2012, it was estimated that "in Colombia four women a day were killed."[28] "Between 2010 and 2013, 5,339 women were killed."[29] Even though it was not possible to collect information from all these cases, "in 482 of them, the offenders were former husbands or long-term partners." "In 2012, 1,316 women were killed."[30] Although in 138 of the cases, the offender was a former or current partner, in 36, it was someone known by the woman killed, and in 34, it was a relative of theirs, the Aggravating Circumstance 11 was not applied one single time in 2012.[31]

The vulnerable situation of Colombian women was captured by the homicide of Rosa Elvira Cely. She was a thirty-five-year-old woman, who used to work as a street vendor, had an eleven-year-old daughter, and was finishing her high school studies. She was raped, tortured, stabbed, and left impaled in the National Park of Bogotá by one of her male classmates. Even though this seems like a gender-related crime because the perpetrator "exercise on [Cely's] body actions of oppression and control over her life's vital choices and her sexuality,"[32] the judge sentencing in this case did not apply Aggravating Circumstance 11.

In Cely's memory, and hoping to fix the problems of previous legislations, a group of NGOs and senators promoted the *Bill Rosa Elvira Cely*. In 2015, this new Bill enacted the independent offense of femicide, in the following terms:

> Article 104A. Femicide. Whoever causes the death of a woman because of her womanhood or due to gender identity motives or where any of the following circumstances have occurred or preceded, be liable to imprisonment of two hundred and fifty (250) months to five hundred (500) months.
>
> a) To have or have had a family, intimate or coexistence relationship with the victim, of friendship, companionship or of work and be a perpetrator

of a cycle of physical, sexual, psychological or economic violence that preceded the crime against her.

b) To exercise on the body and the life of the woman, acts of gender or sexual exploitation or actions of oppression and control over her life's vital choices and her sexuality.

c) To commit the crime in harnessing of the power relations exerted on women, expressed in the personal, economic, sexual, military, political or sociocultural hierarchy.

d) To commit the offense in order to cause terror or humiliation to those who are considered as an enemy.

e) That there is history or signs of any type of violence or threats at home, family, work or school sphere by the perpetrator against the victim or gender violence committed by the author against the victim, whether the act has been reported or not.

f) That the victim had been held from communications or deprived of her freedom of movement, whatever the previous time of death of the victim has been.[33]

According to the Colombian Constitutional Court,[34] one of the biggest problems for policemen, prosecutors, and judges in deciding whether what they are handling a femicide or a homicide is the identification of the motive of the conduct, verbalized in the expression "because of her womanhood or due to gender identity motives." From the Court's perspective, these motives can be interpreted as a group of circumstances from which legal agents can infer any kind of violence or threat against women. Colombian Penal Code's literals a to f, in article 104A, provide those contextual circumstances.

For instance, according to literal a, if the offender and the victim "have or have had a family, intimate or coexistent relationship," previous to the killing, it is possible to identify "a cycle of physical, sexual, psychological or economic violence." Then, it is proper to infer that the case is a femicide. Similarly, following literal b, if it is possible to verify that previous to the killing, the offender "[exercised] on the body and the life of the woman, acts of gender or sexual exploitation," then it is reasonable to conclude that the offense was femicide. The same conclusion is correctly drawn, under literal e, if previous to the killing, it is demonstrated that "there is history or signs of any type of violence or threats at the home, family, work or school spheres" inflicted by the perpetrator.

If the Colombian Constitutional Court is right, this new legislative definition of femicide, including its contextual circumstances, would facilitate the identification of the gender-related killing of women. It also would be an argument for my working hypothesis that "[t]he epistemological capacity to apprehend a life is partially dependent on a life being produced according to norms that qualify it as a life or, indeed, as a part of life."[35] Practically, from my perspective, the virtue of the contextual circumstances of femicide in article 104A is that they normatively recognize the violence previous to femicides as part of the precarious life of some women. This not only makes their vulnerability ostensible, but also potentiates the epistemological capacity of legal agents to "apprehend . . . the lives of [some women] as . . . lose-able or injurable."[36]

THE EPISTEMOLOGICAL CAPACITY TO APPREHEND THE VIOLENCE PREVIOUS TO FEMICIDE

Prima facie, one could expect that femicide, as an Aggravating Circumstance for homicide, would retool Colombian judges and other legal agents to identify gender-related killings of women and the violence previous to them. *Ultima facie*, however, this Aggravating Circumstance, as it was mentioned above, was not applied by Colombian judges one single time in a period of eight whole years. My intuition is that Colombian judges failed to recognize femicides when they were supposed to because of the norms defining this offense. I will put this hypothesis to work presenting some of the findings of an empirical research evaluating the impact of the Bill enacting femicide as an independent offense.[37] Practically, I will compare two groups of high-impact cases. The first group includes two guilty verdicts of homicide, decided after femicide was an Aggravating Circumstance, but before it was an independent offense, that is, cases decided before July 5, 2015. The second group picks up two cases decided after July 5, 2015, and in which the offender was found liable of femicide. What all these legal decisions have in common is that they match, to some degree, at least one of the contextual circumstances from which it is possible to infer that the fact-in-issue was a femicide. Nevertheless, the judges included in the first group did not apply Aggravating Circumstance 11, as they were supposed to.

SOME CASES FAILING TO APPREHEND THE VIOLENCE PRECEDING FEMICIDE

First, on October 22, 2012, Carlos A. Carrillo killed his wife Stefany B. Tafur. Even though it was proven that the victim was constantly insulted and physically attacked by the perpetrator, the judge only applied the Aggravating Circumstance 1, that is, "if . . . the conduct is committed against . . . a spouse,"[38] but he ignored the "cycle of physical [and] psychological . . . violence that preceded the crime against her."[39] This seems to be odd because when Carrillo's defendant attorney argued that this crime was perpetrated under anger and intense suffering,[40] the judge, rebuking this request, admitted that the perpetrator "was constantly threatening the victim, and always saw her as a sexual and economic object which he could attack or physically disappear from the world whenever he wanted."[41]

Second, on September 4, 2011, Duvis E. Doria was killed by her long-term and live-in partner, Jonathan J. De la Hoz, because he suspected that she was cheating on him. According to the first instance judge, "it was not an act of gender-violence against a woman, but an illegal passionate act generated by the infidelity of Doria."[42] This is why the judge applied the diminishing condition of anger and intense pain justified by the fact that De la Hoz, after killing his wife, did not run away, but waited for the police and turned himself in. The appellation judge disagreed with this diminishing condition. From his perspective, the supposed infidelity was not proven at trial, and even if that were the case, it is not a reason to kill a woman. Regardless of this gender-sensitive interpretation, the appellation judge did not apply Aggravating Circumstance 11, but 1, considering that the victim and the perpetrator were long-term and live-in partners.

Finally, on September 9, 2009, body parts of a woman were found in a plastic sack in the outskirts of a Colombian city called Ibagué. Later, the Colombian Institute of Legal Medicine and Forensic Sciences established, with a DNA test, that it was the body of Erika C. Yenerys. By a close examination of her body, they also concluded that she was tortured; the cause of death was multiple blows with a blunt instrument, and she was dismembered in such a way that her identification would be more difficult. The hypothesis of criminal investigation led to a suspect having knowledge of forensic sciences and skills in handling knives. Coincidentally, Yenerys's long-term and live-in partner, Coronel Joaquín Aldana, had the required knowledge and skills. Additionally, the police found relevant evidence in the investigation. For instance,

1. He was reluctant in helping the police to clarify the killing of his partner.
2. He moved out of the apartment that they were renting the very same day she was killed.
3. He carefully painted the apartment before giving it back to their landlord.
4. He had constant disagreements with his wife that affected his career.[43]

Furthermore, the last person seen with Yenerys was Coronel Aldana, who, when he was going to be taken into custody, escaped, but some days later turned himself in to the police. This is some of the evidence from which Coronel Aldana was found guilty for the homicide of Erika Yenerys. Given that they were long-term, live-in partners, in sentencing, the judge applied Aggravating Circumstance 1, and not 11. This decision overlooked important evidence introduced at trial such as the software Aldana secretly downloaded on Yenerys's computer to spy on her conversations, and the fact that he discovered that Yenerys was dating another man.

SOME CASES APPREHENDING THE
VIOLENCE PRECEDING FEMICIDE

Zero applications of Aggravating Circumstance 11 for eight years is a stark contrast to seventeen verdicts, finding the offender criminally liable, of femicide the first year it was enacted as an independent offense.[44] Here I present two examples. On August 18, 2015, María Y. Martínez finishing her work, met a friend, and while they were walking home, she said that it was better for her to take a taxi because her ex-boyfriend, José E. Rubiano, was following her. When the two women realized he was secretly following them, they started walking faster, but Rubiano attacked María with a knife stabbing her multiple times, while also screaming to her friend "I warned her!" At trial, some members of Maria's family testified, assuring that "Rubiano harassed her all the time, was violent with her, and used to keep an eye on her all the time to know when she was at home and at what times."[45] The judge found Rubiano guilty of femicide because "he caused the death of his ex-girlfriend" after a "history . . . of violence or threats . . . against the victim."[46]

On January 9, 2016, the police found the dead bodies of María E. Rubio and her nine-year-old son. They were stabbed to death with a machete and left at the side of a small road in a rural area of Colombia. This act was perpetrated by José H. Beltrá, who was found guilty of the femicide of his wife and homicide of his son. The former crime was justified as a femicide because of the proven fact that before this opportunity, Beltrán, out of jealousy, already had tried to kill his wife with a machete and push her down a cliff. This means that there was a "history of . . . violence . . . at home . . . by the perpetrator against the victim," as it is demanded by the Colombian Penal Code.[47]

CONCLUSION

In one interview, García Márquez,[48] revealing some of the strategies for writing the *Chronicle*, admitted that when deciding to begin his book by saying, "On the day they were going to kill him, Santiago Nasar got up at five-thirty in the morning to wait for the boat the bishop was coming on,"[49] he knew his reader is not going to stop reading the book because he/she knew Santiago Nasar was going to be killed. Indeed, García Márquez was sure that his reader "was going to be following that man until he is killed for the sake of knowing where he is going to be killed and how he is going to be killed."[50] Contextual conditions for femicide should produce the same attitude in legal agents; once they identify the violence that could lead to femicide, they should follow the woman at risk, but not to confirm when and how she is killed, but to prevent her death, instead. Then, this would not be another "chronicle of a death foretold."

NOTES

1. Gabriel García Márquez, *Chronicle of a Death Foretold* (New York: Vintage International, 2003). Originally Published in Spanish in 1981.
2. Diana E. H. Russell, "The origin and importance of the term femicide." Diana E. H. Russell, Ph. D., December 2011, http://www.dianarussell.com/origin_of_femicide.html.
3. Ibid.
4. Márquez, *Chronicle*, 50.
5. Judith Butler, *Frames of War. When Is Life Grievable?* (Verso: London, 2009), 1.
6. Márquez, *Chronicle*, 51.
7. Butler, *Frames of War*, 3.
8. Ibid.
9. Ibid., 2–3.
10. http://www.diputados.gob.mx/LeyesBiblio/ref/lgamvlv/LGAMVLV_orig_01feb07.pdf.
11. Ibid., Art. 21.
12. As in Argentina, Brazil, Costa Rica and Peru.
13. As in Bolivia, Chile, Ecuador, El Salvador, Guatemala, Honduras, México, Nicaragua, Panamá and Venezuela.
14. Butler, *Frames of War*, 3.
15. http://www.secretariasenado.gov.co/senado/basedoc/ley_0599_2000.html.
16. The punishment for this offense was increased in 2008, the current legislation is:

Article 103. Homicide: Whoever kills another human being will be punished with imprisonment anywhere from two hundred and eight (208) months to four hundred and fifty (450) months.

http://www.secretariasenado.gov.co/senado/basedoc/ley_0599_2000_pr003.html#103.
17. In 2008, this piece of legislation was modified, as follows:

Article 104. Aggravating Circumstances: The punishment will be from four hundred (400) months to six hundred (600) months of imprisonment if the conduct described in the previous article is committed: . . .

http://www.secretariasenado.gov.co/senado/basedoc/ley_0599_2000_pr003.html#104.
18. Ibid.

19. http://www.secretariasenado.gov.co/senado/basedoc/ley_0599_2000_pr001. html#57.
20. Bill 1257 (2008), http://www.secretariasenado.gov.co/senado/basedoc/ley_1 257_2008.html.
21. Corporación Sisma Mujer, *Ley 1257 sobre no violencias contra la mujer. Herramientas para su aplicación* (Corcas Editores: Bogotá, 2010), 116, http://www .arcoiris.com.co/wp-content/uploads/2016/06/Ley-1257-de-2008-sobre-no-viole ncias-contra-las-mujeres-Herramientas-para-su-aplicaci%C3%B3n-e-implementaci %C3%B3n.pdf.
22. Ibid.
23. Ibid.
24. Ibid.
25. Ibid.
26. Ibid.
27. http://www.secretariasenado.gov.co/senado/basedoc/ley_1257_2008.html#26.
28. Isabel Agatón, *Justicia de Género. Un Asunto Necesario* (Temis: Bogotá, 2013), 124.
29. Colombian Office for Women Equality. "Informe al Congreso 2013–2014. Seguimiento a la Implementación de la Ley 1257 de 2008" (2014), 6.
30. Agatón, *Justicia de Género*, 156.
31. Ibid.
32. Colombian Penal Code, Article 104A, http://www.secretariasenado.gov.co/ senado/basedoc/ley_0599_2000_pr003.html#104.
33. This translation was taken from UN Women, "Law Against Femicide." *Global Database on Violence against Women*, 2015, http://evawglobaldatabase.unwomen.o rg/fr/countries/americas/colombia/2015/law-against-femicide.
34. Colombian Constitutional Court, C-297 (2016), http://www.corteconstituc ional.gov.co/RELATORIA/2016/C-297-16.htm.
35. Butler, *Frames of War*, 3.
36. Ibid., 1.
37. Isabel Agatón, Nidia Olaya, and Carolina López, *Diagnótico sobre Potencialidades y Obstáculos para la Implementación de la Ley 1761 de 2015 por la cual se crea el tipo penal autónomo de feminicidio (Unpublished report of academic research)*. (Universidad Nacional de Colombia: Bogotá, 2017).
38. Colombian Penal Cole, Article 104, http://www.secretariasenado.gov.co/senad o/basedoc/ley_0599_2000_pr003.html#104.
39. Ibid., article 104A, literal a.
40. Ibid., article 57, http://www.secretariasenado.gov.co/senado/basedoc/ley_0 599_2000_pr001.html#57.
41. As quoted in Isabel Agatón, Nidia Olaya, and Carolina López, *Diagnótico sobre Potencialidades y Obstáculos para la Implementación de la Ley 1761 de 2015*, 174.
42. As quoted in ibid., 179.
43. As quoted in ibid., 188.
44. Ibid., 222.

45. As quoted in ibid., 227.
46. Colombian Penal Code, article 104A, literal e.
47. Ibid.
48. Gabriel García Marquez, "Gabriel García Márquez (Crónica de una muerte anunciada)," November 18, 2006, https://www.youtube.com/watch?v=Oh_sR3bKG4&index=8&list=PLD0BA7017CB06D67D
49. Márquez, *Chronicle*, 3.
50. Marquez, "Gabriel García Márquez."

BIBLIOGRAPHY

Agatón, Isabel. *Justicia de Género. Un Asunto Necesario.* Temis: Bogotá, 2013.
Agatón, Isabel, Nidia Olaya, and Carolina López, *Diagnótico sobre Potencialidades y Obstáculos para la Implementación de la Ley 1761 de 2015 por la cual se crea el tipo penal autónomo de feminicidio* [Unpublished report of academic research]. Universidad Nacional de Colombia: Bogotá, 2017.
Bill 1257, 2008. http://www.secretariasenado.gov.co/senado/basedoc/ley_1257_2008.html. Accessed July 17, 2018.
Butler, Judith. *Frames of War. When Is Life Grievable?* Verso: London, 2009.
Colombian Constitutional Court, C-297, 2016. http://www.corteconstitucional.gov.co/RELATORIA/2016/C-297-16.htm. Accessed May 15, 2018. Colombian Penal Code. http://www.secretariasenado.gov.co/senado/basedoc/ley_0599_2000.html. Accessed July 17, 2018.
Corporación Sisma Mujer, *Ley 1257 sobre no violencias contra la mujer. Herramientas para su aplicación.* Corcas Editores: Bogotá, 116. http://www.arcoiris.com.co/wp-content/uploads/2016/06/Ley-1257-de-2008-sobre-no-violencias-contra-las-mujeres-Herramientas-para-su-aplicaci%C3%B3n-e-implementaci%C3%B3n.pdf. Accessed July 17, 2018.
Colombian Office for Women Equality. "Informe al Congreso 2013–2014. Seguimiento a la implementación de la Ley 1257 de 2008," 2014.
García Marquez, Gabriel. *Chronicle of a Death Foretold.* New York: Vintage International, 2003.
_____. "Gabriel García Márquez (Crónica de una muerte anunciada)." November 18, 2006. https://www.youtube.com/watch?v=Oh_sR3bKG4&index=8&list=PLD0BA7017CB06D67D. Accessed July 26, 2018.
Russell, Diana. "The Origen and Importance of the Term Femicide." Diana E. H. Russell, Ph. D., December 2011. http://www.dianarussell.com/origin_of_femicide.html. Accessed March 7, 2018.
UN Women, "Law Against Femicide." *Global Database on Violence against Women,* 2015. http://evawglobaldatabase.unwomen.org/fr/countries/americas/colombia/2015/law-against-femicide. Accessed July 17, 2018.

3

Positions of Power

Patriarchal Considerations in Criminal Law

Melissa McKay

Laws criminalizing sexual violence have made significant strides in offering more comprehensive protections for victims, but sexual assault remains an underreported and common form of violence. The law historically treated rape as an attack against men who retained some form of ownership over a woman[1] rather than against sexual autonomy and fundamental human rights, thereby treating women as property, reducing their legal capacity, and denying recognition or recourse to the harm. Further, legal reform has generally focused on aggravated stranger rape, which fails to consider the patriarchal structures that render women's experience of violence invisible. Women[2] were treated as an afterthought, and their sexual subordination was employed as "a weapon in the struggle for power among men."[3] This chapter surveys those aspects of sexual violence, in cases of criminal law.

Patriarchy is "a model for the regulation of societal gender relations based on male privileged dominance and control,"[4] which limits women's autonomy. Laws regulating sexuality developed under patriarchal frameworks—the law has always privileged heteronormative masculinity over other genders and sexualities.[5] The patriarchy relegates victims of sexual violence, of all genders, to the private realm, where they are silenced. It is often viewed as socially inappropriate, or even offensive, for victims to vocalize the violence they face,[6] which allows for a parallel silencing to occur, to a certain extent, in the trial process,[7] as this chapter demonstrates.

Criminal trials do not adequately uphold women's sexual autonomy, because criminal law, in its current form, cannot adequately address the social issues underlying crime. A predominant focus on the content of statutes, as opposed to the process and substance of a trial, acts to restrain women's inclusion in criminal law to, primarily, the formal level.[8] For criminal law to adequately uphold the right of all individuals to be free from sexual violence, this chapter argues for a push toward greater flexibility in sexual assault proceedings, because "any rigid approach to the prosecution of sexual offences (. . .) risks leaving certain types of rape unpunished and thus jeopardising the effective protection of the individual's sexual autonomy."[9]

SEXUAL SCRIPTS

Bryana French suggests sexual scripts constitute a conceptual framework, which places sexual behavior within its cultural and relational context, to "explore the cultural norms that serve as guidelines for acceptable and accepted sexual behavior, [and] how those expectations are negotiated between individuals."[10] Sexual scripts consider gender, race, and age, among others, to assess the roles that dictate engagement in sexual activity, and how these roles develop. The sexual scripts expected from women reduce their autonomy from an early age: "[G]irls learn to look at themselves through the eyes of men."[11] Male attention remains a standard form of validation for a woman or girl's worth,[12] and female sexuality is framed so that women wait for men to decide to initiate sex, and leave women responsible to attend to men's needs.[13] Regarding "sexual agency," Burkett and Hamilton suggest this script normalizes male ownership over sexuality and reduces women's sexual autonomy.

Several common themes emerge regarding the way women's sexual scripts affect negotiations with consent and vulnerability to sexual violence. The first is that, from an early age, girls and women tend to attribute the degree to which someone is at risk for being victimized to negative personal characteristics—women and girls who lack "foresight, moral fortitude, or self-control"[14] will be assaulted, but those who are sufficiently mature and of solid moral character will not be. This deems women and girls immoral should they engage in any sexual activity: women are shamed for not being able to control their sexuality, regardless of it being a consensual act. This messaging perpetuates rape myths and drives the autonomous exploration of women's sexuality underground, by imposing a gender-specific purity requirement,[15] and creates a narrative where sexual autonomy will not be violated so long as the individual acts according to heteronormative and patriarchal ideas of sexual morality, that is, the expression of sexuality must meet masculine ideas of what is appropriate. Women and girls who express their sexuality outside this patriarchal scope are not acting morally, and it is these individuals whose autonomy is violated, hence the narrative that they must deserve this violation for their immorality.

The requirement of morality or character is inextricably linked to a second theme, wherein women and girls impose a high degree of personal responsibility on themselves to physically prevent acts of sexual violence against them.[16] Women and girls are taught what to wear, how much to drink, not to go out alone, and how to use keys as a weapon to fend off an attacker. Societies have broadly treated women's sexuality as her power, because she can wield desirability to "both arouse it and deny its fulfillment."[17] Laying this dual responsibility at the feet of women rationalizes male force in sexual experiences and blurs the lines of consensual activity.[18] Men, however, are not expected to prevent acts of sexual violence: male sexuality is viewed as "relentless and naturally aggressive (. . .) [and] inherently difficult for a man to control,"[19] and physically aggressive advances are often normalized as the means through which men display affection for women.[20] Boys and men are often framed as merely responding to the way girls and women present themselves,[21] and, women's consent, let alone enjoyment of sex, is less important, as men largely continue to become "systematically conditioned not even to notice what women want."[22]

These sexual scripts, and their continued impact on consent negotiations, were written in part by laws regulating sexual violence. Historically, in the common law, the State had to prove beyond a reasonable doubt that a woman resisted an assailant "to the utmost of her physical capacity"[23] for a finding of rape. Early American cases discussed the need to resist, finding that neither saying "let me go" only once, nor having produced only "inarticulate" screams, could amount to sufficient resistance to deter a man from having sex with her.[24] Further, a woman could not claim she had surrendered due to an "assumed superior physical force,"[25] but must continuously resist. Though the law, in many jurisdictions, has evolved from formally requiring resistance to prove rape, the application of "force" and "consent" often "make a woman's physical resistance a legal necessity."[26] These historical narratives continue to permeate the social order, particularly as it relates to women's ability to engage in meaningful sexual autonomy and negotiate consent.

Implicitly contained within women's personal responsibility is the preservation of autonomy, shaped by neoliberal and postfeminist ideologies: "Individuals are charged with making their own decisions and taking responsibility for them; negative consequences are presumed to be natural (i.e. unavoidable and deserved) consequences of faulty decisions or traits."[27] Women and girls have been taught that they must simply make the "right" choices, and unwanted sexual contact will be avoided.[28] This is further complicated by individualism, which sells "female empowerment" as a choice and removes consideration of broader societal power structures.[29] These movements flip the script on hegemonic heteronormativity: the hypersexualization of women through neoliberal individualism may mean that some girls and women engage in undesired sexual activity as an expression of women's empowerment.[30] Recent shifts in societal discourse have framed women as sexually liberated and empowered in all choices. In her aptly named article—"The Game is Rigged"—Traister suggests that "Young feminists have adopted an exuberant, raunchy, confident, righteously unapologetic, slut-walking ideology that sees sex—as long as it's consensual—as an expression of feminist liberation. The result is a neatly halved sexual universe, in which there is either assault or there is sex positivity."[31] By creating a binary between sexual assault and sex positivity, social norms mirror the binary created by the law, where there is either aggressive rape or no sexual assault at all. Such binaries ignore the underlying gendered structures that inform negotiations of consent, and render invisible the forms of sexual assault that occur within a "gray zone"—sexual activity that is unwanted, but for one reason or another was not protested, or was not interpreted by a man as having been protested in such a way that a man could recognize the assault.

By promoting this version of feminist liberation alongside liberal theories of equal autonomy, which claim a shared experience of consent negotiations between genders, the ability to point out differentiations in gendered power dynamics is lost. Without an awareness of gendered power structures, society remains blind to the conditioning of women's sexuality, which reduces women's expression of sexual autonomy, and her ability to act as a "rational agent"[32] capable of making choices as credible as those of men. This "neoliberal espousal of autonomy and its concomitant framing of sexual choices as unproblematically free masks the ongoing complexities of the process of consent."[33] The law mirrors these obfuscations by presenting consent as a "free exercise of sexual choice under conditions of equality of power without exposing the underlying structure of constraint and disparity."[34] In reality, there is a "stark difference between a woman's actual choice and what is interpreted as legal consent."[35] There are many reasons why women do not forcefully indicate what they in fact desire from a sexual encounter, which are not reflected in current legal frameworks: for example, women have reported that it would be inappropriate to not follow through with intercourse after engaging in other behaviors.[36] Many women do not take issue with engaging in these acts, as they are seen as a situation of their own making.[37] As such, the undesired sexual activity does not amount to rape or assault, but merely acquiescence. Acceptance of these situations as the norm for women's sexual experiences, and the failure to address them, has led some to describe laws governing sexual assault as a "parody of justice."[38]

I am not arguing that women have no sexual autonomy at all, that it is impossible for women to genuinely consent to sexual activity within patriarchal societies, or that all men should be tried under criminal law for every sexual encounter that occurred in a "gray zone." Complications arise when women are questioned over the decisions they make regarding their sexual autonomy—it is a lack of trust in a woman's ability to regulate her own body that historically justified men's dominion over marriage, and decisions regarding childbirth or contraception. What I would like to highlight, however, is the failure of the law to recognize how social structures inhibit the ability of women and girls to safely exercise their sexual autonomy, which disallows them from experiencing an equal level of autonomy as that held by men in heterosexual encounters.

To ignore underlying social structures is to be blind to the external factors that influence the development of human relationships, sexual or otherwise, which are carried into the negotiations and power dynamics that continually define the relationships. In all individual choices, capacity for autonomy will be limited by consideration of social, economic, and psychological factors.[39] Autonomy might be conditional, as individuals can be born with the capacity for, and the right to, self-government, yet still lack the opportunity to exercise these rights and capacities, due to circumstances outside the individual's control.[40] Autonomy might also be limited in relative terms, due to an individual's dependency on other people, conventions, and things that the individual has not created, in particular, language or a "web of discourse."[41] The "web of discourse" refers to the "network of power relations that the language we speak sets up,"[42] recognizing that underlying societal factors permeate our language and influence our interactions. The recognition of such factors on its own does not, in most contexts, mean that an environment is so coercive so as to render involuntary the choices we make.[43] Choices are often made with sufficient voluntariness. Differences in dependency and in circumstances external to the control of an individual, however, result in different expressions of autonomy, and "so a certain amount of good luck, no less than capability, is a requisite condition of *de facto* autonomy."[44] Those individuals born outside dominant social groups, be it based on their race, gender, ability, or otherwise, may operate with constraints on their opportunities, with varying degrees of "bad luck" limiting the exercise of their autonomy, and "[t]he most ubiquitous discourse, which surpasses national and cultural boundaries, is probably patriarchy."[45]

The reduction of women as fully autonomous sexual beings has created a vicious cycle: society's lack of trust in women has produced laws that further allow the marginalization of their experiences. The failure of the law to evolve in such a way that it could truly respond to the sexual scripts dictating women's experiences of consent and negotiations thereof facilitates society's distrust in women as rational decision makers. Harmful practices, including victim blaming and placing high relevance on sexual history evidence, run rampant in criminal processes,[46] thereby sowing women's distrust in the criminal justice system.[47] We cannot continue our reliance on the current framework of criminal processes while expecting justice for victims of sexual violence. Though criminal law serves as a means of determining guilt and innocence, and applying punishment, it should not remain isolated from broader considerations of our society that impact what comprises "guilt."

AUTONOMY AND CRIMINAL LAW

In domestic criminal law, a "general assumption of equal autonomy"[48] tends to exist, thus failing to take patriarchal structures into account. A survey of domestic criminal law broadly identifies three general categories for a sexual act to amount to rape:

> The sexual activity is accompanied by force or threat of force to the victim or a third party;
>
> The sexual activity is accompanied by force or a variety of other specified circumstances which made the victim particularly vulnerable or negated her ability to make an informed refusal;
>
> The sexual activity occurs without the consent of the victim.[49]

Under the Canadian *Criminal Code*, a substantive definition of consent presumes nonconsent where, among others, the accused induces the complainant to engage in the activity by abusing a position of trust, *power or authority*; or the complainant expresses, by words or conduct, a lack of agreement to engage, or to continue engaging, in the activity.[50] It is thus not required that an individual explicitly state "no" to find nonconsent. Further, the Court can infer nonconsent by considering conduct, or positions of "trust, power or authority." Judges have been progressive in interpreting what a position of trust, power, or authority entails,[51] and have additionally held that there is no defense of implied consent in Canadian law.[52] For an accused to have a defense of mistaken belief in consent, they must show that the complainant *"communicated consent to engage in the sexual activity in question. (. . .)* The accused's speculation as to what was going on in the complainant's mind provides no defence."[53] The Court has additionally clarified the definition of "consent" to mean "the complainant in her mind wanted the sexual touching to take place."[54] These interpretations affirm that each individual must choose and desire to engage in sexual activity: in theory, this reasoning safeguards sexual autonomy.

The law, however, is not all that successful in preventing these abuses, as it does not fundamentally unravel the gendered power dynamics that underlie all sexual violence. The manipulation of gendered power structures has yet to be articulated clearly as an abuse of "power or authority,"[55] and so the status quo is maintained as women continue to "consent" to unwanted sexual encounters: "the game remains *rigged*."[56] Over 80 percent of sexual assaults in Canada are not reported to police,[57] and sexual assault is not treated as seriously as other crimes in Canada: one in five sexual assault complaints across the country is dismissed as baseless, and formally labeled by the police as "unfounded,"[58] with nearly 20 percent of the total number of allegations of sexual assault over a four-year period being removed from the justice system and the overall public record at the most basic level of the system.[59] The unfounded rate for sexual assault in Canada is double that of physical assault, substantially higher than that of any other crime,[60] and further, is dramatically higher than the false-reporting rate.[61] Further worrying is that the dominant reason victims cited for not reporting was that sexual assault was viewed as a minor crime, not worth taking the time to report.[62]

Failures to change the practical treatment of sexual assault in the criminal system so that it is understood more holistically means that, despite significant formal protections, sexual autonomy is not protected equally between genders. Be it through an unwillingness in the criminal system, a limitation in the ability of judges to consider or accept broader social factors, a failure to advance more holistic argumentation before the courts, or any combination thereof, the patriarchy, which is the root cause of sexual violence, has been neglected by criminal justice, thereby allowing sexual violence to continue with relative impunity. Regardless of how far judicial interpretations go in the reconceptualization of definitions, formulas, or perspectives, the law seems to continue "devaluing sexuality."[63] In such devaluation, the law overemphasizes the idea that sex is only bad if it is compelled by blatant threats or physical injury, rather than the simple fact that it should protect "the right of every person to freely choose or refuse any sexual encounter."[64] Without consideration of gendered structures and formal inclusion of patriarchal coercion, legal amendments will continue to fail "to convince enough people that the traditional ways of thinking about rape are wrong, outdated, and unjust."[65]

THE SHIFT TO A HUMANIST CRIMINAL LAW

Decisions to engage in sexual relationships are an aspect of an individual's sexual autonomy, so consent "becomes the dividing line between legal sexual contact and punishable sexual contact."[66] The ongoing failure of criminal law to comprehend the nuances of consent severely hinders its ability to provide just sexual assault processes. A restructuring of criminal law processes can assist in unraveling power structures so that a more equitable level of autonomy is protected across gendered lines.

Legislative reform is an important first step. Formal recognition of the need to establish rather than presume consent would assist significantly in providing notice that consent can never be inferred, particularly in the face of coercive circumstances.[67] Laws assuming this more holistic quality would better protect sexual autonomy, by requiring authentic permission[68]—an absence of coercion would not be the determinative factor of whether an assault had occurred, but genuine and actual permission from all parties would be the requirement. This analysis would better situate individuals within their experiences and interactions, rather than isolating them from the social context.

Strong legislation on its own, however, is insufficient. Currently, criminal justice appears as a process upholding the State's right to convict and punish an offender, and victims are treated essentially as witnesses, with limited procedural rights. Offences are less a violation of an individual's human rights, and more an infringement of the State's laws—"strictly speaking, the state is the real victim."[69] The State thus usurps ownership over crimes, and victims become constrained in their ability to meaningfully voice their experience.[70] This allows the State to avoid "acknowledging its own responsibility for not effectively protecting the rights of an individual and for allowing victimisations to happen."[71] The perpetual silencing of experiences of sexual assault, from the lack of reporting, to failures in articulating certain coercive acts as crimes, to trial processes that retraumatize victims—each renders the current criminal system incompatible with the goal of ending impunity and creating meaningful accountability for sexual violence, thus necessitating a human rights-based approach to criminal law that treats the victims and offenders of crimes as rights holders.

The idea that criminal law should shift its emphasis to a human rights-based approach, and away from the right of a State to punish, has gained traction through the proliferation of human rights documents, international treaties and victims' rights directives, as well as within judicial reasoning in a growing number of courts,[72] which set out obligations to investigate, prosecute, convict, and punish violations "as a matter of the preventive function of criminal law."[73] The abundance of State obligations in human rights language suggests the possibility that criminal justice systems are "not entitled, but obliged to convict and punish offenders to avert the impunity of severe human rights violations and to ensure that the victims of such violations command an effective remedy."[74]

One common critique of such an approach is that the rights of accused might become lost through an overemphasis on victims. Any human rights-based approach to criminal law must clearly articulate how it will respect and uphold the rights of both victims and offenders. A legal system with reasonable apprehensions of bias inherently lacks credibility and does not offer meaningful accountability. An accused must be treated with respect for their rights, and if found criminally responsible, they must be subject to fair punishment which encourages them to develop "as an accountable person, who is able to understand the normative claims of her legal community."[75] Without engaging an accused, we will not be successful in undoing the harmful social structures that lead to sexual violence in the first place. In that aim, trial processes must maintain the basic protections of the rights of an offender, including the presumption of innocence and proof beyond a reasonable doubt.

The presumption of innocence remains compatible with a criminal system that acknowledges an individual's victimhood from the outset. In cases of sexual assault, we must recognize victims as victims, without questioning their motivations. If someone has been murdered, there is clearly a victim. If someone's house has been broken into and property is damaged or stolen, we label them a victim, despite the fact that a criminal investigation will be necessary to determine the circumstances of the robbery and to rule out any possible fraudulent claim (and certainly, any fraudulent claim would be punished). With crimes of sexual violence, however, the tendency is to question the claims. This difference is due not only to the fact that underlying patriarchal structures have molded the way that these claims have historically been viewed, but also by the uniqueness of sexual violence. Rape is a crime in a league of its own, through its marriage of sex with violence, physical force, or coercion. "It is the only crime where all cases entail physical contact (. . .) offensive physical invasion of a sexual nature contours the unique character of rape."[76] This particular violation against bodily autonomy distinguishes rape from all other violent crimes, where physical contact between individuals is not necessary—different weapons may be used to commit other violent crimes without requiring any direct contact. Sexual violence entails direct physical contact, meaning that there are necessarily at least two parties involved in the act, with conflicting versions of the encounter.

There is an apparent concern that formally acknowledging a victim of sexual violence will rebut the presumption of innocence by "taking sides." What is often forgotten, however, is that the criminal trial will determine the legality of the act against the victim. In cases of sexual violence, an individual has been harmed: they have perceived a violation of their rights, and another individual has been accused of perpetrating such harm. That harm, regardless of its legality, is real. The purpose of a criminal trial is to determine whether the accused did in fact perpetrate that harm, and the degree to which they are criminally responsible for it—recalling that, in certain circumstances, there may be no criminal culpability. When we look at the harm from a humanist approach, it is a violation of a human right—a violation against an individual, which obliges the State to take action.[77] The presumption of innocence does not mean an offence has not been committed, but rather that we cannot assume one specific person is criminally responsible.[78] We must acknowledge the distinction between the recognition or denial of an event and the presumption of innocence for the accused as a person. Calling a victim "victim" does not impute criminal responsibility but it does show the victim that they are seen—the importance of such normative messaging cannot be overstated.

Further, if the harm is a violation of a human right, and the accused is not criminally responsible, the culpability must lie with the State, for its failure to effectively undo the unequal gendered experience of sexual autonomy has led to a violation of a human right, and it will be obliged to act more effectively. This does not absolve the accused of the harmful behavior, but rather makes more visible the reasons behind our continued failure to provide meaningful accountability for sexual violence.

"Consent is supposed to be women's form of control over intercourse,"[79] and it is at the heart of criminalizing sexual assault. Consent is both an inculpatory element of *actus reus* and an exculpatory defense to prima facie criminal wrong. Laws tend to fall short by failing to explicitly state that there is no inherent presumption of consent in instances of sexual assault,[80] because such presumption is not necessary for other crimes: inherently presuming consent for murder or theft would be blatantly absurd. In all jurisdictions, consent in sexual assault, and sexual activity generally, has yet to be held to a high enough standard, where we acknowledge each aspect of coercion facing the autonomous individual. An adequate standard of consent would prioritize the rights of the victim and the accused over the rights of the State, thereby allowing victims to play more central roles in trial processes. Victims should first be consulted in their perception of the crime that has been committed against them. The role of prosecutors becomes paramount here, as judges will ultimately be restricted to consider what has been charged. Ensuring victims are consulted in framing the charges is an important first step in obtaining a judgment that speaks to their experiences, allows for a more holistic recovery, and assists in meaningful reconciliation for the broader community alongside the victim.

Where consent is at issue, victims of sexual assault should have rights to request admission of evidence, to be present at all hearings, and to ask some form of questions to the accused.[81] In a common law sexual assault trial, the accused is not obliged to testify. The victim's version of facts is put to a stringent test and their credibility is called into question, whereas a blanket denial from the accused cannot be challenged. In a human rights-based approach to criminal justice, an offender is "called upon to take responsibility for the wrong done to the victim."[82] It is clear, under the patriarchy, that it is not necessarily offenders who understand this wrong, as women and girls continue to place responsibility on themselves to prevent sexual violence, and even without aggravating factors, may consent to an undesired sexual act. The doctrine of consent continues to reinforce an "abstract and individualistic understanding of social living and self-determination."[83] Sexual assault is clearly not an individualistic event—it requires direct interaction by at least two people, as I have noted. The unique nature of crimes of sexual violence and its elements of proof necessitates greater involvement from both parties in the proceedings to allow for a factual finding that reflects the truth of the act. This may result in proceedings that appear very different from the current model, perhaps requiring both parties to submit written or oral statements of the incident. Statements from both victim and accused would provide greater clarity as to the steps that were taken in establishing consent, and thus the legality of the act at issue.

Sentencing decisions following criminal trials should also include consideration of the exploitation of patriarchal power systems. The inclusion of broader social considerations necessarily alters the scope of criminal law so that it appears to be more akin to a human rights mechanism: criminal justice still serves to provide the individual findings of guilt and innocence, but it also acknowledges that underlying causes may have contributed to the coercive aspect of these crimes. The existence of social structures does not mitigate a violent act, but a judgment addressing these structures would delineate the exploitation of gendered power dynamics, and further contribute to the notion that an offender has the "right to be treated as an accountable agent and assume responsibility."[84] Perpetrators of sexual assault should have the opportunity to become aware of the systems that they, unknowingly or otherwise, exploit. To respond to the realities underlying coercion and consent, and to address the root cause of sexual violence, consideration of broader social factors in sentencing is necessary. Such consideration would produce more holistic judgments, considering the long-standing structures of our societies, such as the patriarchy or racism, which unfairly limit meaningful access to justice. Further, judicial reasoning that considers social structures would complement formal laws where consent is not presumed, which, on their face, appear to offer strong protections against sexual assault, but in practice, continue to be found lacking.

CONCLUSION

To build more equitable conceptions of sexual autonomy between all genders, civil society education must be taken alongside criminal law reform. To use criminal law as an effective protection of an individual's right to freely choose their engagement in sexual activity, broader considerations of what it really means to consent to sex are required, along with considerations of the external influences that impact negotiations of consent. Basing criminal law in human rights would not undermine its purpose, as factual and legal findings of a violation of individual autonomy would still be central to considerations of guilt and innocence.

There will always be a fine line between moral protectionist attitudes and the promotion of autonomy as the law attempts to unpack sexuality.

Patriarchal structures have functioned to reduce women's sexual autonomy, but women should not be depicted as perpetual victims. Respect for choices to engage in sexual activity must be of utmost importance, but considerations of the legality of an act must be made with an awareness of factors that exert influence on a particular decision. It is undeniably clear that, throughout history, and across societies, heterosexual men have operated as the dominant group, and women's sexuality has been controlled. This chapter has argued that the doctrine of consent must adapt so that it reflects the social issues underpinning sexuality—its objective "should be to protect individuals from situations that restrain their autonomy, without dictating how that freedom of choice can be used."[85] This would not open a floodgate to false claims, but rather allow more comprehensive responses to issues underlying gendered crimes. The inclusion of societal structures should not be limited to gendered dynamics, but should also contemplate those of race, class, and others, to adequately address why and how crimes are committed, and how to create punishments that effectively prevent the perpetuity of various crimes.

If courts can consider coercive circumstances in the context of a conflict, or within the relationship between a drug dealer and addict, they can consider coercive circumstances that have permeated the deepest levels of society. Criminal law cannot hold singular persons responsible for underlying social systems—no single individual should be held responsible for an entire "web of discourse." No one individual is responsible for racism, just as no one individual is responsible for all sexism: these are systems we, the global community, have inherited. But these systems inherently create positions of power that degrade the autonomy of certain groups in society. The abuse of these powers must be considered within criminal processes.

The recognition of social structures does not disengage women from autonomy, but rather, it highlights the injustices throughout a given society that may limit women. Placing an individual within a context still requires an examination of the individual and their particular desires. The goal of unraveling patriarchal structures is not to tell all women that they are constantly being coerced, but to inform them of ways in which patriarchal structures might act to coerce them, that there are varying degrees to which each individual might experience this coercion, and that this might impact their negotiations with consent, their body, and sexual autonomy.

By highlighting and reinforcing the idea that sexual autonomy deserves full protection, regardless of gender, there may be greater progress in changing heteronormative power dynamics founded in hegemonic masculinity—the law may assist in changing "the ways that men treat women and the ways that men view sex in our society."[86] Criminal law must find means of broadening considerations of social conditioning, to "expand the stakes and the politics of regulating sexual harm to incorporate values of sex and gender equality, freedom, and pleasure."[87] Rather than maintaining a criminal system that overemphasizes neoliberal ideals of formal equality, a humanist approach can push the boundaries of what it means to be truly equal, and what in fact constitutes a crime, in light of all the differences that exist between individuals, due to their gender as well as other characteristics.

NOTES

1. Carley R. Kranstuber, "Equality Is Not Enough: The Importance of the Due Process Clause in Redefining Consent to a Sexual Encounter," *Capital University Law Review* 45 (2017): 765–73, 786–7.

2. Though this chapter will specifically focus on sexual violence carried out by men and boys against women and girls, traditional patriarchal power structures exist in other forms of sexual violence, including violence carried out by women, and violence perpetrated against boys or other historically marginalized genders. Stereotypes about what it means to "be a man" uphold the dominant patriarchal discourse, and deter boys and men from reporting incidences of sexual violence.

3. Kranstuber, "Equality Is Not Enough," 773.

4. John Idriss Lahai and Nenneh Lahai, "Human Rights Frameworks and Women's Rights in Post-transitional Justice Sierra Leone," in *Gender in Human Rights and Transitional Justice*, eds. John Idriss Lahai and Khanyisela Moyo (Cham: Palgrave Macmillan, 2018), 153.

5. "There is a historically grounded proclivity to give credence to male, not female, constructions." Susan Caringella, "Consent and Voluntariness: Agreement/ Nonconsent and Involuntariness, Nonagreement," in *Addressing rape reform in law and practice* (New York: Columbia University Press, 2009), 97; Kranstuber, "Equality Is Not Enough," 767.

6. Evidence of the inappropriateness of voicing experiences of sexual violence is apparent in low reporting rates, and in backlash against social movements, including #MeToo. These responses undermine the credibility of women who demonstrate the degree to which they experience coercive sexual violence, by claiming that women are attacking men, or undertaking a "witch hunt." These reactions tend to ignore the nuance of movements, and instead take on inflammatory, overgeneralized, and fatalistic tones.

7. For example, see Amanda Arnold, "3 Women on What It Was Like to Testify at Their Sexual-Assault Hearings," *New York Magazine*, September 26, 2018, https://www.thecut.com/2018/09/3-women-on-testifying-at-their-sexual-assault-hearings.html. Regarding factors considered in determining a victim's credibility, see Denise Lievore, "Victim Credibility in Adult Sexual Assault Cases," *Trends & Issues in Crime and Criminal Justice* 288 (2004): 5–6.

8. Fiona de Londras, "Prosecuting Sexual Violence in Ad Hoc Tribunals," in *Transcending the Boundaries of Law Generations of Feminism and Legal Theory*, ed. Martha Fineman (London: Routledge-Cavendish, 2010), 290.

9. *MC v Bulgaria*, ECtHR (39272/98), 4 Dec 2003, par. 166. The Court went on to state that "In accordance with contemporary standards and trends in that area, the

member States' positive obligations under Articles 3 and 8 of the Convention must be seen as requiring the penalisation and effective prosecution of any non-consensual sexual act, including in the absence of physical resistance by the victim." This has been recently affirmed in *I.C. v. Romania*, ECtHR (36934/08), May 24, 2016, par. 52, where the Court found that member states had a duty "to enact criminal-law provisions that effectively punish rape and to apply them in practice through effective investigation and prosecution."

10. Bryana H. French, "More than Jezebels and Freaks: Exploring How Black Girls Navigate Sexual Coercion and Sexual Scripts," *Journal of African American Studies* 17, no. 1 (2013): 36.

11. French, "More than Jezebels," 36–37. Sexual scripts may further reduce sexual autonomy in different and intersecting manners depending on race and class. For example, black women were historically viewed as sexual products meant to serve white male slave owners, which informed postslavery sexual scripts.

12. Melissa Burkett and Karine Hamilton, "Postfeminist Sexual Agency: Young Women's Negotiations of Sexual Consent," *Sexualities* 15, no. 7 (2012): 822–8.

13. Ibid., 827–8.

14. Laina Y. Bay-Cheng, Jennifer A. Livingston, and Nicole M. Fava, "Adolescent Girls' Assessment and Management of Sexual Risks: Insights From Focus Group Research," *Youth and Society* 43, no. 3 (2011): 1178; French, "More than Jezebels," 38; Burkett and Hamilton, "Postfeminist Sexual Agency," 817.

15. Other gendered social norms which have been instructed by patriarchy include the Madonna/whore complex, which is a description of the duality of female sexuality that hegemonic masculinity has imposed upon women, or slut shaming, which is a form of sexual harassment that functions to humiliate and stigmatize a woman.

16. Bay-Cheng, Livingston and Fava, "Adolescent Girls"; French, "More than Jezebels"; Burkett and Hamilton, "Postfeminist Sexual Agency."

17. Catharine A. MacKinnon, "Rape: On Coercion and Consent," in *Applications of Feminist Legal Theory to Women's Lives: Sex, Violence, Work, and Reproduction*, ed. D Kelly Weisberg (Philadelphia: Temple University Press, 1996), 474.

18. Ibid.

19. Burkett and Hamilton, "Postfeminist Sexual Agency," 823.

20. Stephen J. Schulhofer, "Rape in the Twilight Zone: When Sex is Unwanted But Not Illegal," *Suffolk University Law Review* 38 (2005): 416–7.

21. French, "More than Jezebels," 42–43.

22. MacKinnon, "Rape: On Coercion," 478.

23. Michelle J. Anderson, "Diminishing the Legal Impact of Negative Social Attitudes toward Acquaintance Rape Victims," *New Crim L Rev* 13 (2010): 653.

24. *Brown v State*, 106 N.W. 536, 537 (Wis. 1906), cited in ibid.

25. *Moss v State*, 45 So. 2d. 125, 126 (Miss. 1950), cited in ibid.

26. Anderson, "Negative Social Attitudes," 655.

27. Bay-Cheng, Livingston and Fava, "Adolescent Girls," 1187.

28. Kranstuber, "Equality Is Not Enough," 784–5.

29. Burkett and Hamilton, "Postfeminist Sexual Agency," 828–9.

30. The *choice* of girls and women to present themselves in a seemingly objecti-fied manner as a mode of empowerment is a *choice* that may have been informed or influenced by patriarchal discourses, to varying degrees. Rather than seeing hyper-sexualization, an apparent objectification, as a de facto objectification, a woman may see it as the liberation of all women and buy into this narrative as a form of empow-erment. A woman has every right to make such a choice, but the external gendered influences that may have facilitated this choice should be made visible.

31. Rebecca Traister, "The Game is Rigged," *New York Magazine*, October 20, 2015, https://www.thecut.com/2015/10/why-consensual-sex-can-still-be-bad.html.

32. Vanessa E. Munro, "Shifting Sands? Consent, Context and Vulnerability in Contemporary Sexual Offences Policy in England and Wales," *Social & Legal Studies* 26, no. 4 (2017): 418.

33. Burkett and Hamilton, "Postfeminist Sexual Agency," 817.

34. MacKinnon, "Rape: On Coercion," 474.

35. Kranstuber, "Equality Is Not Enough," 786.

36. Burkett and Hamilton, "Postfeminist Sexual Agency," 822–7. This is reaf-firmed by "expressive consent," where courts allow for "a woman's appearance, manner of dress, sexual history, location, or relationship to the man in question" to act as stand-ins for consent. See also Kranstuber, "Equality Is Not Enough," 785–6.

37. One woman described a night where she met a man at a bar and went home with him, where they began to "hook up." The man led her to a bedroom, where another man was waiting, and the woman and two men engaged in a threesome. The woman later expressed that she did not want to engage in that activity, but that it had been stupid of her to go home with a man she had just met, so she should just "get through it all so [she] could go home." This woman did not consider she had been raped, but described it as an unwanted sexual encounter. Burkett and Hamilton, "Postfeminist Sexual Agency," 824.

38. Kranstuber, "Equality Is Not Enough," 786.

39. Schulhofer, "Rape in the Twilight Zone."

40. Joel Feinberg, *The Moral Limits of the Criminal Law: Harm to Self* (Oxford: Oxford Scholarship Online, 1989), section 3.

41. Bert Olivier, "Foucault and Individual Autonomy," *South African Journal of Psychology* 40, no. 3 (2010): 292, 294–5.

42. Ibid., 294.

43. Schulhofer, "Rape in the Twilight Zone," 421–2.

44. Feinberg, *Moral Limits*.

45. Olivier, "Foucault," 294.

46. Liat Levanon, "Sexual History Evidence in Cases of Sexual Assault: A Critical Re-Evaluation," *The University of Toronto Law Journal* 62, no. 4 (Fall 2012): 609; Caringella, "Consent and Voluntariness"; Munro, "Shifting Sands?," 424–8.

47. MacKinnon, "Rape: On Coercion," 477; "from women's point of view, rape is not prohibited; it is regulated." Ibid., 474.

48. Wolfgang Schomburg and Ines Peterson, "Genuine Consent to Sexual Violence under International Criminal Law," *The American Journal of International Law* 101, no. 1 (2007): 126.

49. *Prosecutor v Kunarac*, No. IT-96-23-T & IT-96-23/1-T, Judgment, February 22, 2001, par. 442.

50. *Criminal Code*, RSC 1985, C-46, 273.1(2)(c), (d), and (e). Emphasis added by author.

51. See, for example, *R v Lutoslawski* (2010), 258 (3d) 1 (Ont CA), where the Court found that consent could be rendered illusory by the dynamics of a relationship and by the misuse of influence of the individual with authority. See also *R v Hogg* (2000), 148 (3d) 86 (Ont CA), where a drug addict's decision to engage in sexual activity with her dealer was not genuine due to her dependency on her dealer.

52. *R v Ewanchuk*, [1999] 1 SCR 330.

53. Ibid., par. 46. Emphasis added by author.

54. Ibid., par. 48.

55. *Criminal Code*, s. 273.1(2)(c).

56. Traister, "The Game is Rigged."

57. Shana Conroy and Adam Cotter, "Self-Reported Sexual Assault in Canada, 2014," *Statistics Canada*, July 11, 2017, http://www.statcan.gc.ca/pub/85-002-x/20 17001/article/14842-eng.htm.

58. Robyn Dolittle, "Unfounded: Why Police Dismiss 1 in 5 Sexual Assault Claims as Baseless," *The Globe & Mail*, February 3, 2017, www.theglobeandmail .com. The failure to report and the low rates of prosecution for reported rapes are problems common to other jurisdictions as well. In the United States, an estimated 5–20% of rapes are reported to the police, less than 1–5.4% are prosecuted, and less than 1–5.2% of those prosecuted result in conviction. See also Allegra M McLeod, "Regulating Sexual Harm: Strangers, Intimates, and Social Institutional Reform," *California Law Review* 102, no. 6 (2014): 1557.

59. Robyn Dolittle, "Unfounded: Will the Police Believe You?" *The Globe & Mail*, February 3, 2017, https://www.theglobeandmail.com/news/investigations/com pare-unfounded-sex-assault-rates-across-canada/article33855643/.

60. Dolittle, "Why Police Dismiss."

61. Ibid.

62. Conroy and Cotter, "Statistics Canada." Seventy-one percent of individuals in the survey provided this response. Sixty-three percent indicated that they did not report because "no one was harmed during the incident."

63. Schulhofer, "Rape in the Twilight Zone," 422.

64. Ibid., 422.

65. Caringella, "Consent and Voluntariness," 98.

66. Schomburg and Peterson, "Genuine Consent," 124.

67. Caringella, "Consent and Voluntariness," 114.

68. Schulhofer, "Rape in the Twilight Zone," 422–5.

69. Albin Dearing, *Justice for Victims of Crime* (Cham: Springer International Publishing, 2017), 7.

70. Ibid.

71. Ibid., 11.

72. Ibid., 28–30.

73. Ibid., 32–33.

74. Ibid., 365.
75. Ibid., 368.
76. Caringella, "Consent and Voluntariness," 98.
77. Dearing, *Justice for Victims*, 46–47.
78. Ibid., 378.
79. MacKinnon, "Rape: On Coercion," 473.
80. Ibid.
81. Dearing, *Justice for Victims*, 378.
82. Ibid., 368.
83. Munro, "Shifting Sands?," 418.
84. Dearing, *Justice for Victims*, 386.
85. Kranstuber, "Equality Is Not Enough," 793.
86. Schulhofer, "Rape in the Twilight Zone," 425.
87. McLeod, "Regulating," 1560.

BIBLIOGRAPHY

Anderson, Michelle J. "Diminishing the Legal Impact of Negative Social Attitudes toward Acquaintance Rape Victims." *New Criminal Law Review* 13 (2010): 644–64. Accessed May 8, 2018.

Arnold, Amanda, "3 Women on What It Was Like to Testify at Their Sexual-Assault Hearings," *New York Magazine*, 26 September 2018. https://www.thecut.com/2018/09/3-women-on-testifying-at-their-sexual-assault-hearings.html.

Bay-Cheng, Laina Y., Jennifer A. Livingston, and Nicole M. Fava. "Adolescent Girls' Assessment and Management of Sexual Risks: Insights from Focus Group Research." *Youth and Society* 43, no. 3 (2011): 1167–93. Accessed May 9, 2018.

Brown v State, 106 N.W. 536, 537 (Wis. 1906). Accessed March 7, 2018.

Burkett, Melissa, and Karine Hamilton. "Postfeminist Sexual Agency: Young Women's Negotiations of Sexual Consent." *Sexualities* 15, no. 7 (2012): 815–33. Accessed May 8, 2018.

Canadian Criminal Code, RSC 1985, C-46. Accessed May 1, 2018.

Caringella, Susan. *Addressing Rape Reform in Law and Practice*. New York: Columbia University Press, 2009. Accessed February 26, 2018.

Conroy, Shana, and Adam Cotter. "Self-reported Sexual Assault in Canada, 2014." *Statistics Canada*, July 11, 2017. Accessed April 20, 2018. http://www.statcan.gc.ca/pub/85-002-x/2017001/article/14842-eng.htm.

Dearing, Albin. *Justice for Victims of Crime*. Cham: Springer International Publishing, 2017.

De Londras, Fiona. "Prosecuting Sexual Violence in Ad Hoc Tribunals." In *Transcending the Boundaries of Law Generations of Feminism and Legal Theory*, edited by Martha Fineman, 290–304. London: Routledge-Cavendish, 2010.

Dolittle, Robyn. "Unfounded: Why Police Dismiss 1 in 5 Sexual Assault Claims as Baseless." *The Globe & Mail*, 3 February 2017. Accessed May 1, 2018. www.theglobeandmail.com.

Dolittle, Robyn. "Unfounded: Will the Police Believe You?" *The Globe & Mail*, 3 February 2017. Accessed May 1, 2018. https://www.theglobeandmail.com/news/inv estigations/compare-unfounded-sex-assault-rates-across-canada/article33855643/.

Feinberg, Joel. *The Moral Limits of the Criminal Law Volume 3: Harm to Self.* Oxford: Oxford Scholarship, 1989.

Fineman, Martha, ed. *Transcending the Boundaries of Law: Generations of Feminism and Legal Theory.* London: Routledge-Cavendish, 2011.

French, Bryana H. "More than Jezebels and Freaks: Exploring How Black Girls Navigate Sexual Coercion and Sexual Scripts" *Journal of African American Studies* 17, no. 1 (2013): 35–50.

Kranstuber, Carley R. "Equality Is Not Enough: The Importance of the Due Process Clause in Redefining Consent to a Sexual Encounter." *Capital University Law Review* 45 (2017): 765–94.

Lahai, John Idris, and Khanyisela. Moyo, eds. *Gender in Human Rights and Transitional Justice.* London and New York: Palgrave Macmillan, 2018.

Levanon, Liat. "Sexual History Evidence in Cases of Sexual Assault: A Critical Re-Evaluation." *The University of Toronto Law Journal* 62, no. 4 (2012): 609–51.

Lievore, Denise. "Victim Credibility in Adult Sexual Assault Cases." *Trends & Issues in Crime and Criminal Justice* 288 (2004): 1–6.

MacKinnon, Catharine A. "Rape: On Coercion and Consent." In *Applications of Feminist Legal Theory to Women's Lives: Sex, Violence, Work, and Reproduction*, edited by D. Kelly Weisberg, 323–36. Philadelphia: Temple University Press, 1996.

McLeod, Allegra M. "Regulating Sexual Harm: Strangers, Intimates, and Social Institutional Reform." *California Law Review* 102, no. 6 (2014): 1553–621.

Moss v State, 45 So. 2d. 125, 126 (Miss. 1950). Accessed March 7, 2018.

Munro, Vanessa E. "Shifting Sands? Consent, Context and Vulnerability in Contemporary Sexual Offences Policy in England and Wales." *Social & Legal Studies* 26, no. 4 (2017): 417–40.

Olivier, Bert. "Foucault and Individual Autonomy." *South African Journal of Psychology* 40, no. 3 (2010): 292–307.

Prosecutor v Kunarac, No. IT-96-23-T & IT-96-23/1-T, Judgment, 22 February 2001. Accessed 2 April 2018.

R v Ewanchuk, [1999] 1 SCR 330. Accessed May 1, 2018.

R v Hogg (2000), 148 (3d) 86 (Ont CA). Accessed May 1, 2018.

R v Lutoslawski (2010), 258 (3d) 1 (Ont CA). Accessed May 1, 2018.

Schomburg, Wolfgang, and Ines Peterson. "Genuine Consent to Sexual Violence under International Criminal Law." *The American Journal of International Law* 101, no. 11 (2007): 121–40.

Schulhofer, Stephen J. "Rape in the Twilight Zone: When Sex is Unwanted but Not Illegal." *Suffolk University Law Review* 38 (2005): 415–25.

Traister, Rebecca. "The Game is Rigged." *New York Magazine*, 20 October 2015. Accessed May 10, 2018. https://www.thecut.com/2015/10/why-consensual-sex-can-still-be-bad.html.

Weisberg, D. Kelly, ed. *Applications of Feminist Legal Theory.* Philadelphia: Temple University Press, 1996.

PART 2

THEORETICAL REFLECTIONS
ON SHAME

4

Reframing Anthropological Shame as Exposure

Aaron Looney

In contemporary discussions of shame in moral philosophy, shame is predominantly understood as emerging upon a violation of a norm that one, at least implicitly, acknowledges.[1] In this respect, it is a social emotion of negative self-assessment elicited in individuals for the establishment and maintenance of social norms.[2] Since Plato, however, philosophers have traced the interconnection of shame and anthropology. Although marginalized in the history of philosophy in favor of the morally more perspicuous phenomenon of guilt, the Western intellectual tradition links the phenomenon of shame with what it means to be human. Shame, in this tradition, tends to constitute the criterion for situating humanity between animality and divinity.

This anthropological frame of shame has not always had the effect of humanization, however. To the contrary. While erecting borders *within* the human being itself, it has often engendered exclusionary strategies to demarcate and enforce borders *between* human beings. Efforts to safeguard the uniquely human from the commonality of life and nature have elicited disavowals of aspects of humanity like corporeality, mortality, and vulnerability. The identification of humanity with notions like reason, autarky, autonomy, and sovereignty has served to sunder humanity in two and hierarchically separate the truly human from the subhuman. This dissection within individual human beings coincides with the association or projection of the weakness of humanity onto groups of others largely based on gender, race, or class.

The Western intellectual tradition has identified the properly human with the exercise of reason or the faculty of spirit, and it charges shame with marking the separation of the soul from the body, rationality from animality, and spirit from life. From this perspective, shame arises on the threshold between two aspects of humanity, signaling both their separation and their conjunction while safeguarding the proper from the improper. One of the basic problems with this view is that whole persons and entire groups of people are cast onto the one side of this dividing line. Whether because they are seen as lacking reason, as insufficiently embodying spirit, or as failing to demonstrate shame, they are portrayed as incapable of living up to the vocation of what it means to be human.

The insight that shame intrinsically belongs to the human condition is a powerful one, however, and we should not be so quick to dismiss it. In this chapter, I will sketch the primary anthropological frame of shame as it is been passed down throughout the history of Western thought. I will highlight the logic that connects the phenomenon of shame with the question of humanity and will demonstrate how this logic has facilitated exclusionary strategies regarding gender and race precisely by a process of immunization of the properly human from the vulnerability and contingencies of life. With this ambivalent history as a backdrop, I will endeavor to reframe anthropological shame, taking into account a more holistic conception of the human while working toward an ethics of shame based on our fundamental exposure.[3] Shame, I argue, is the affective modality of our exposure.

In Plato's dialogue *Protagoras*, the Sophist makes poignantly clear both the connection between individual shame and societal norms and the connection between shame and humanity. According to Protagoras' anthropogenesis, humans first obtained technical arts from the gods to ensure their preservation. Yet even with tools, humans were still subject to the threats from wild beasts. To protect themselves, they gathered in cities. Living in close quarters created new problems—power struggles and warring conflicts. Fearing that they might destroy themselves, Zeus had mercy on humans and gave each member of the city a sense of shame and justice (*aidos kai dike*), the principal virtues that are the basis of civic life. Zeus subsequently seals his gift of virtues with a decree to "make a law by my order, that he who has no part in shame and justice shall be put to death, for he is a plague of the state."[4] Plato's narrative underscores that every human person is capable of shame and that a demonstrative lack of shame is cause for exclusion and (divinely) sanctioned execution. Whoever is incapable of shame reveals themselves as unhuman. Aristotle crystallizes this notion, writing that to be human is to be a political animal, and anyone who acts outside of human nature is either beneath or beyond humanity, "either a beast or a god."[5]

Exploring the normative nature of humanity, Aristotle asks whether humans qua humans have a vocation. His question is largely rhetorical, for he quickly concludes that the human vocation consists in the activation of the part of the soul that is proper to humans—reason.[6] While the human soul shares living with plants and shares sense perception with animals, reason, he claims, is the highest part of the soul and is unique to humans. Beyond the nutrition, growth, and reproduction of the vegetative part of the soul and beyond the pleasure and pain of the cognitive part of the soul, the human vocation—and thus, human happiness—consists in a life of reasonable action, whether political or contemplative.[7]

Aristotle understands this function as the vocation of the human qua human, but his conception of the *polis* reveals that not everyone is equally positioned or permitted to realize his or her humanity. He famously describes the emergence of the state as "originating in the bare needs of life, and continuing in existence for the sake of a good life."[8] He links life to the body and necessity—survival and sexual reproduction—and binds corporality and necessity to the household (*oikos*). In juxtaposition to mere life, the good life is determined by and enjoyed through the activity in the *polis*.[9] Aristotle thus distinguishes between life and the good life. The latter presupposes life but transcends it. Yet, those whose place is confined to the household are kept from participating in the good life.

Informed by Aristotle, Hannah Arendt in *The Human Condition* identifies shame as "the time-honored protective dividing line between nature and the human world."[10] Arendt makes a distinction between necessity and freedom and between the private and the public, and she suggests that shame defines and protects this boundary separating human *nature* or human *life* from the human *world*. "The most elementary meaning of the two realms indicates that there are things that need to be hidden." She specifies what should be hidden: "It has always been the bodily part of human existence that needed to be hidden in privacy, all things connected with the necessity of the life process itself."[11] Quoting Aristotle's *On the Generation of Animals* (775a33), which describes the life of a woman as *ponetikos*, "laborious, woeful," Arendt observes that "women and slaves belonged to the same category and were hidden away not only because they were somebody else's property but because their life was 'laborious,' devoted to bodily functions."[12] Commenting on Arendt, Jill Locke notes that Arendt assumes that there is something "instinctive" and commonplace about what should be concealed and what may be displayed.[13] Moreover, Arendt seems to accept or, at least, to inadequately problematize the long tradition since Aristotle of excluding certain people—namely, slaves and women—from the public sphere and from participation in the good life.[14]

Bonnie Mann makes this exclusion explicit: "Women of all classes and statuses, along with men who are poor, or slaves, or colonized—so perhaps eighty percent of the humans . . . are irredeemably bound to life in the imaginary domain of the dominant class. . . . These eighty percent are given the sphere of life as their sphere of belonging and the shame of life as their inevitable lot."[15] Assigned to life, they are rendered invisible and condemned to a life of shame.

The same logic is at work in the social contract theory of Thomas Hobbes. While it seems unclear whether Hobbes represents the state of nature as a literal historical event or as a hypothetical thought construct, Charles Mills detects an implicit racial logic that resolves the tension between these two positions.[16] Hobbes explains that "there had never been any time, wherein particular men were in a condition of warre one against another." In the same breath, however, he concludes from the travel reports of the early European expeditions that "there are many places, where they live so now. For the savage people in many places of America (. . .) live at this day in that brutish manner."[17] Like wild beasts, he writes, the people of the Americas live a life of privation—without religion, without government, without cultivation, without arts, without letters, laws, and clothes. Hobbes thus suggests that the state of nature does really exist among nonwhite peoples, while it simultaneously serves as a hypothetical warning for rational, civilized, white Europeans of what would happen if the sovereign state were dissolved.

Like Hobbes, Georg Friedrich Hegel equates the wild inhabitants of the Americas with their wild, unchartered land, that is, with nature. Hegel summarizes natural life as a life without shame. For in shame, he claims, "lies the separation of the human from his natural and sensuous being. The animals, which have not progressed to this separation are, for this reason, shameless."[18] Undoubtedly, the European explorers recognized the native peoples as humans, but they did not consider them as fully human because of their privation. By failing to demonstrate shame, they could be treated as subhumans.[19] Reduced to bare life, in the terms of Giorgio Agamben, these peoples became subject to violence with impunity.[20]

The link between privation and nature has its roots in Augustine's interpretation of the Biblical scene of primordial sin. For Augustine, shame marks the difference between original nakedness and postlapsarian nakedness. He suggests that before the fall, Adam and Eve were not really nude, they were rather clothed in grace. Shameful nudity first results from the removal of the garment of grace from the human body, leaving a bare and by God abandoned nature.[21] As Giorgio Agamben observes, the relationship of nature and grace correlates with the relationship of nudity and clothing. Nature, like the naked body, is the presupposition of a grace that, like clothing, is added as a supplement to it. What emerges after the removal of grace, however, is not the presupposed nature but the fallen nature, not the natural, shamelessly nude body but the *stripped* body, corruptible and shameful.[22] According to Augustine, shame designates the awakening of consciousness to the fact that we have become "like beasts"—subject to passions and subject to death.[23] It signals the separation of and struggle between the *libido* and the will, the interval between life and spirit. In Augustine, shame *instinctively* reminds us that we are not like the other animals but were created "upright" to live according to God.[24]

This shame is existential and ontological. Augustine's account of the Biblical story of the Garden of Eden exhibits a nostalgic pattern similar to the stoic myth of the Golden Age and Aristophanes's portrayal of humans as originally perfect circular beings. Martha Nussbaum suggests that these myths articulate shame as a "longing for wholeness" accompanied and emboldened by "the sense that one ought rightly be whole."[25] This anthropological shame depends, she writes, on a "vestigial sense of an original (. . .) completeness."[26] For Augustine, anthropological shame consists in a sense for the created human nature irrevocably underlying fallen human nature. Shame, he writes, registers the sickness of our fallen condition by revealing "the pleasure of health."[27] Just as Sigmund Freud diagnoses melancholy as the unfinished process of grief, Augustine diagnoses shame as the emotive presence of a lost good.[28] Through shame, he claims, humans are able to "discern between the good they had lost and the evil into which they had fallen."[29] Referring to Paul's second letter to the Corinthians (7:8–11), Augustine characterizes shame as a "useful and desirable sorrow"—even a "godly sorrow"—"that one is as one should not be."[30] Within an anthropological frame, Augustine contrasts the shame of finite, vulnerable, and fallible life both with the insulated perfection and utter self-control of humans before the fall and humans redeemed in the afterlife, where we will be as we were created to be.

For the early-twentieth-century phenomenologist Max Scheler, shame not only reminds us of our vocation—and our failure to realize our vocation—but also propels us to our higher vocation, a life of the spirit. Adopting an Augustinian anthropology and a Hegelian dialectic, Scheler suggests that shame is the affective modality of the relation of life in the person. In Scheler's thought, shame is a uniquely human experience: "no god and no animal is capable of shame. . . . It is only because the human essence is tied up with a 'lived body' that we can get in the position where we *must* feel shame; and only because spiritual personhood is experienced as essentially independent of the 'lived body' and everything that comes from it, is it possible to get into the position where we *can* feel shame."[31] Humans, for Scheler, are middle-beings, between gods and animals, whose existence is taut in the tension between spirit and life or what he later calls *drive*. On the basis of our animality/corporeality, we have reason to be ashamed, but because of our *Geist*, we are capable of shame.

Scheler makes clear that this capacity-limitation is genuinely human, common to both men and women. At the end of his essay on shame, however, he distinguishes, according to the logic of "subordination and equivalence," between a mental or psychological shame-feeling (*seelisches Schamgefühl*) and a bodily shame-feeling (*leibliches Schamgefühl*), connecting the first to men and the second to women.[32] While both perceive the tension within human life, women, he suggests, lack "a sharp consciousness of distance . . . and of the duality . . . between person and body, the constitutive condition for psychological shame."[33] Though perceptive of the difference between how men and women experience shame, Scheler tacitly denies women the capacity to fulfill the human vocation.[34] For, he claims, "man's intention beyond himself and all life constitutes his essence . . . . He is a thing that transcends its own life and all life."[35] As "geniuses of Geist," man's shame indicates his transcendence of life, urging him toward the realization of the human vocation. As "geniuses of life," women remain immersed in the instincts of life.[36]

In *Sovereign Masculinity*, Bonnie Mann observes how the human has been pitted against life throughout the history of Western thought.[37] Whether conceived as *animale rationale, zoon logon echon,* or *imago dei,* what is properly human is identified with reason or spirit at the omission, subjection, or disavowal of the body, nature, or life. Within this tradition, shame forms a protective boundary, a bulwark against the forces of nature and the contingencies of life. As "a matter of spirit in relation to life," shame functions as a safeguard of the threshold that separates the uniquely human from life.[38] In deciding that one aspect of humanity constitutes what is proper to humanity, a line is drawn forming an inside and outside of humanity. This decision entails a rupture and a violence done within and without. In shame, we hide parts of ourselves from ourselves also by hiding those who "represent" these improper parts from the public order. Because of their association with nature, life, necessity, the body, and/or the animal, many persons, often on account of their gender or race, have been deemed incapable of fulfilling the proper human vocation and incapable of the dignity due persons.

Modern discussions suggest that shame underlies much of the abuse, exclusion, and exploitation that have dogged Western history and Western thought from the beginning. Protective shame is correlated with patterns of domination. Psychiatrists describe aggressive behavior in which persons who feel vulnerable react by projecting their own weakness onto others and subjugating others to assert their own sovereignty.[39] Stigmatization and violence based on gender, sexual orientation, race, and class can be the reactions of humankind to what Martha Nussbaum calls "primitive shame."[40] This response is rooted in a hubris that is greater than pride or arrogance.

Early philosophers were well aware of this tendency toward hubris and aggression. According to Aristotle, *hubris* means to cause shame to the victim merely for one's own gratification. "As for the pleasure in hubris, its cause is this: naive men think that by ill-treating others they make their own superiority the greater."[41] Hubris creates in humankind a desire to disgrace and humiliate others.[42] Out of shame, we put others to shame. Our sense of power and self-sufficiency is enlarged by the forced passivity and trauma inflicted on others. In his account of primordial sin, Augustine suggests that a lack of control over oneself is redirected into a desire to exert control over others.[43] What Augustine calls the *libido dominandi* is provoked by the shame of insufficiency and lack of sovereignty.

Modern, and especially feminist, philosophers have elaborated these insights, pointing out that men in most cultures have been enculturated to mask shame with activity and spontaneity that display "sovereign masculinity." In *Hiding from Humanity: Disgust, Shame, and the Law*, Martha Nussbaum highlights the consequences of this ideal of sovereign masculinity on American culture, with its emphasis on the omnipotence of the will, its denial of mortality and failure, and its propagation of the fantasy that real men are self-sufficient and lacking a deep need of others.[44] With its alienating obsession with aggression and dominance, the ideology of masculinity is unhealthy for the boys and men under its spell. In its "tendency to denigrate all parts of the personality that are viewed as female"—emotions, need, sadness, empathy, and compassion—it sets their private selves at war with their public selves.[45] The results—homophobia, bullying, and sexual violence—are catastrophic for the societies in which they live.

Shame sets up a vicious circle. Bonnie Mann writes that men who aspire to be sovereign men do not know that "such acts of disowning are never completed; they demand to be repeated again and again. (. . .) The shamed one's shame converts to rage, hostility, contempt, aggression."[46] Following Simone Beauvoir, Mann observes that "the process of fleeing intersubjective risk for the comfort of sovereignty" is "a lifelong process of self-cloaking that promises to eliminate exposure, vulnerability. . . . Sovereign masculinity has no other purpose than this display, than this cloaking. The shamed one must explode into hyperbolic self-assertion or cease to exist as a man." In Mann's analysis, "the core structure of sovereign masculinity is this shame-to-power conversion."[47]

The shame-to-power conversion has political correlations in imperialism and tyranny. Inward suppression frequently accompanies outward aggression. In ancient Athens, the imperialistic and tyrannical polity broke "the standing rules and conventions of warfare in its affairs with other Greek cities during the Peloponnesian War, even while it inculcated a rigid norm of active, male, and martial citizenship within the polity to support this imperialistic war."[48] And, in the American war on terror, Mann analyzes the "efficacy of gendered shaming in producing a morally complicit and relatively thoughtless subject, which is to say exactly the kind of subject a nation committed to a policy of preemptive war must produce, if it is not to be thwarted by the workings of its own democracy."[49]

At the same time, tyrants perhaps best underscore the difference between the moment of *recognition* and the moment of *response*. As Christine

Tarnopolsky observes in her work on the topic of shame in Plato's *Gorgias*, the figure of the tyrant in Plato is both a personality type and a regime type.[50] The tyrant is not shameless, she claims; he rather cloaks his shame in outbursts of brash self-assertion. He banishes shame from his soul, "just as he tries to banish, stigmatize, or exterminate any others who threaten to make him feel shame."[51] The tyrant wants to be like a *god*, who has no need for shame. According to Tarnopolsky, the tyrant is the person who *desires* to be shameless, and it is this tyrannical desire to be a completely self-sufficient and omnipotent person or polity that Plato criticizes.

The self is not shameless, though, because it is exposed to itself, to others, and to a world it does not control. In his book *Shame: The Exposed Self*, the pediatrician and psychiatrist Michael Lewis poses the question, "What is an exposed self and to who is it exposed?"[52] He concludes that "the self is exposed to itself, that is, we are capable of viewing ourselves."[53] He thus characterizes shame as a feeling of negative self-assessment, taking into account the emotive force of shame and the *uniquely* human capacity for self-reflection. Lewis draws from the long philosophical tradition representing shame as "unique to humans" because it springs from a capacity of the human subject to have itself as an object of reflection.[54] As Hegel suggests, this capacity is intertwined with "the separation of the human from his natural and sensuous being."[55] Shame, especially in modern philosophical conceptions, is framed as uniquely human because we are both inside and outside of nature. The separation shame emotively evokes is between ourselves as conscious subjects and ourselves as bodily objects.

Our exposure does not begin in self-reflection, however. The self is also and already exposed to itself *preflexively* in its corporality, its mortality, its insufficiency, and dependency. Moreover, this exposure is not only *intrapersonal* but also *interpersonal*. The recognition of exposure does not require a reflective act nor does the response necessarily entail a conscious decision. Before one reflects upon oneself by assessing oneself, one is implicitly aware of being exposed. The shame incurring in self-reflection and self-assessment is thus secondary to a more originary exposure.

The ethical question is how to respond to this originary exposure? Two different types of response suggest themselves. One type of response may take various forms of flight, disavowal, or concealment; the other type of response may take various forms of appreciation and responsibility. The dominant anthropological frame of shame proposes various versions of the first type of response, all too frequently resulting in exclusion and the play of projection and stigmatization. It has sought shelter in the power of reason, autonomy, and sovereignty. The second type of response embraces the exposed vulnerability of human existence that originary or primitive shame reveals. Abandoning "the drive *not to be* (human) but to master being," as the psychoanalyst Christopher Bollas puts it, entails accepting the exposition of ourselves to plurality and interdependence.[56] The process of humanization, of which Judith Butler speaks, calls for a greater appreciation for our fundamental exposure and for ethical, not violent, responses to this exposure. Vulnerability and insufficiency need to be recognized, not covered in shame. Humanization requires an increased acceptance of our own vulnerability, a more acute awareness of the vulnerability of others, and the establishment of forms of responsibility that are not reducible to guilt. Paradoxically, it is the shame felt in our dependency and vulnerability that we need to recognize and accept without shame.

The recognition of shame as part of the human condition grounds Martha Nussbaum's conception of shame. For Nussbaum, shame is "necessary and inevitable."[57] Unlike Michael Lewis, however, she suggests shame can be felt at a prereflective moment, before a person chooses to conform to social norms. "Shame," she states, "is on the scene already even before we are aware of the 'normal' perspective of the particular social value-system within which we dwell." Drawing on the insights of empirical and theoretical developmental psychologists, Nussbaum suggests that shame arises in our prereflective awareness of our insufficiency and lack of sovereignty. Beneath "any specific social orientation to norms (. . .) it is present for all of us in the infantile demand for omnipotence, for fullness and comfort—accompanied by the awareness of finitude, partiality, and frequent helplessness."[58] Consisting predominantly in a "shame at one's weakness and impotence," faced with "a world humans have not made and do not control," shame, for Nussbaum, constitutes "a basic and universal feature of emotional life."[59] Without adopting their dualistic anthropologies, Nussbaum shares with Augustine and Scheler the belief that shame "serves as a highly volatile way in which human beings negotiate some tensions inherent in their humanness."[60]

Nussbaum's approach to shame is not opposed to an approach focusing on the social norms of given cultures, however. In line with her treatment of the cognitive character of emotions, shame requires "at least an incipient sense of one's own being."[61] Seeing as it presupposes the infant's "awareness of themselves as beings both finite and marked by exorbitant demands and expectations," primitive shame is not only intrapersonal but also interpersonal.[62] Insofar as shame arises with exposure, it is rooted in our susceptibility and vulnerability to others—for good and bad. As Adriana Cavarero writes, our connections to one another are not rooted in our being capable of reason but in our being *exposed* to one another.[63]

In her book *Precarious Life*, Judith Butler writes about the interconnection between personal contacts and the acceptance of values and norms. She observes that "we are comported toward a 'you'; we are outside ourselves, constituted in cultural norms that precede and exceed us, given over to a set of cultural norms and a field of power that condition us fundamentally."[64] There is a triadic structure at work here: an "I," who is dependent on a "you," which in turn is dependent on a set of norms of recognition that exist before the "I" and the "you." This exposure to each other, to norms and social and political forces, forms what Butler calls our "common corporeal vulnerability."[65] Butler writes that recognizing our common corporeal vulnerability is "a precondition for humanization." In this process of humanizing ourselves and others, the ethical and political task is to protect bodily vulnerability without eradicating it.[66] What Butler advocates here is an embrace of our common exposure without disavowal and without exploitation.

Another philosopher who finds a basis for responsibility in our prereflective exposure to one another is Emmanuel Levinas. He writes, "Freedom is at the same time *discovered* in the consciousness of shame and is *concealed* in the shame itself."[67] The primacy of sociality in Levinas's thought illustrates how each of us is always already called into question by the other person. In Levinas's phraseology, in shame, I discover my freedom as tyranny— "arbitrary and violent"—and I conceal my freedom before the other who obliges me. For Levinas, the affective modality of shame is a check to the arbitrary freedom of sovereign masculinity, calling "in question the naïve right of (. . .) power" and "glorious spontaneity."[68] Instead of fleeing intersubjective exposure, the subject discovers in it the potential violence of his or her freedom and, at the same time, his or her responsibility for the other. To paraphrase Levinas, the consciousness of shame welcomes the other in hospitality.[69] I am exposed to her in being called into question and am responsible to her for her exposure to me and to a world of violence and need. Levinas suggests that our responsibility to come to the aid of the other is infinite, and we will always fail to satisfy it.[70] In his thought, I am never done with the other because the exposure is never ending.

Although the philosophies of Butler and Levinas differ, both recognize that "the precarity of life imposes an obligation upon us," and both, in their own ways, encourage us to refigure responsibility on the basis of exposure.[71] Historically, responsibility in ethics has been correlated with guilt and intentionality; one is responsible for what one does and does not do and is responsible for the intention behind one's actions. An ethics of shame seeks to establish forms of responsibility not based in action or intentionality but rooted in our fundamental exposure to others and our common corporeal vulnerability. As the affective modality of our exposure, the acknowledgment of shame entails the recognition of what it means to be human. Yet, even though all life is vulnerable, exposure—to what and to whom—is always contextual, and any ethics of shame must reflect on and respect the difference and inseparability of universality and singular contextuality because some lives are more exposed than others.

NOTES

1. Cf., for example, Christoph Demmerling and Hilge Landweer, *Philosophie der Gefühle: Von Achtung bis Zorn* (Stuttgart: Metzler Verlag, 2007), 219–20.

2. For a detailed philosophical analysis of shame as an emotion of negative self-assessment, see Gabriele Taylor, *Pride, Shame, and Guilt: Emotions of Self-Assessment* (Oxford: Oxford University Press, 1985).

3. In this chapter, I hope to illustrate the ambivalence of the anthropological frame of shame in Western intellectual history. For many of same sources that have facilitated exploitation and exclusion also provide critiques of power in their reflections on shame.

4. Plato, *The Dialogues of Plato*, trans. Benjamin Jowett (New York: Tudor Publishing Company, 1936), 320c–322d, chap. 26, 1206–42, 1214–5. [translation slightly modified by author]

5. Aristotle, *The Politics of Aristotle*, trans. Benjamin Jowett (Oxford: Clarendon Press 1885), bk. 1, chap. 2, 1253a28–9.

6. Aristotle, *Nicomachean Ethics*, trans. Terence Irwin (Indianapolis, IN: Hackett Publishing Company, 2. Ed., 1999), bk. 1, chap. 7, §11–6, 1097b30f.

7. Ibid., bk. 1, chap. 13, §8–19, 1102a25–1103a4.

8. Aristotle, *Politics*, bk.1, chap. 1, 1252b30.

9. Cf. Giorgio Agamben, *Homo Sacer: Sovereign Power and Bare Life*, trans. Daniel Heller-Roazen (Redwood City, CA: Stanford University Press, 1998), 2–3.

10. Hannah Arendt, *The Human Condition* (Chicago: University of Chicago Press, 1958), 324.

11. Ibid., 74.

12. Ibid., 72. See also Aristotle, *Politics*, bk. 1, chap. 5, 1254b25.

13. Jill Locke, "Shame and the Future of Feminism," *Hypatia* 22, no. 4 (2007), 146–162, 154.

14. Aristotle, *Politics*, 1254b25; Cf. Arendt, *The Human Condition*, 72, n. 80.

15. Bonnie Mann, "The Difference of Feminist Phenomenology: The Case of Shame," in *Puncta. Journal of Critical Phenomenology* 1, no. 1 (2018), 41–73, 59–60.

16. Charles Mills, *The Racial Contract* (Ithaca, NY: Cornell University Press, 1997), 66.

17. Thomas Hobbes, *Leviathan* (London: Penguin Books, 1985), Part I, chap. 13, 187. Ibid., 18

18. Georg Wilhelm Friedrich Hegel, *Werke 10: Enzyklopädie der philosophischen Wissenschaften im Grundrisse (1830). Dritter Teil: Die Philosophie des Geistes mit den mündlichen Zusätzen* (Frankfurt am Main: Suhrkamp Verlag, 2016), §24, 89: "In der Scham nämlich liegt die Scheidung des Menschen von seinem natürlichen und sinnlichen Sein. Die Tiere, welche zu dieser Scheidung nicht vorschreiten, sind deshalb schamlos." As Bonnie Mann observes, the shame of life is also perceptible in Hegel's Master/Slave dialectic. Hegel appropriates the Greek disdain of the slave who prefers life over power in contrast to the Master, who is willing to risk life for sovereignty (Mann, "Feminist Phenomenology," 59).

19. Cf. Mills, *The Racial*, 53–62.

20. See Agamben, *Homo Sacer.*

21. Augustine, *The City of God*, trans. Marcus Dods (New York, The Modern Library, 2000), 14:17.

22. Giorgio Agamben, *Nudities*, trans. David Kishik and Stefan Pedatella (Redwood City, CA: Stanford University Press, 2011), esp. 57–68. In Western culture, Agamben writes, "nudity is inseparable from a theological signature," which defines it "only negatively" as a "privation" (57).

23. Augustine, *City of God*, 13:3 and 22:24. Augustine quotes in this context Psalm 49:12.

24. Ibid., for example, 13:14, 14:27, and 22:1. Like Augustine, Sigmund Freud associates the uprightness of the human body with the emergence of shame. While Augustine adopts the Platonic view that humans are made upright because their orientation should be toward intelligible reality, Freud takes an evolutionary view. He writes, "The diminution of olfactory stimuli seems itself to be a consequence of man's raising himself from the ground, of his assumption of an upright gait; this made his genitals, which were previously concealed, visible and in need of protection, and so provoked feelings of shame in him." Although Freud admits that his theory about the emergence of shame in the human animal remains "only a theoretical speculation," it indicates, for him, the pivotal moment in the establishment of human civilization, for "the fateful process of civilization would thus have set in with man's adoption of an erect posture" (ibid., *Civilization and Its Discontents*, ed. and trans. James Strachey (New York: W.W. Norton & Company, 1962), chap. 4, n.1, 46–7).

25. Martha Nussbaum, *Hiding from Humanity: Disgust, Shame, and the Law* (Princeton, NJ: Princeton University Press, 2004), 186.

26. Ibid., 182–3. God

27. Augustine, *City of God*, 14:17.

28. Cf. Sigmund Freud, "Mourning and Melancholia," in *The Standard Edition of the Complete Psychological Works of Sigmund Freud: On the History of the Psycho-Analytic Movement, Papers on Metapsychology, and other Works, vol. XIV (1914–1916)*, trans. James Strachey (London: The Hogarth Press, 1957), 243–8.

29. Augustine, *City of God*, 14:17.

30. Ibid., 14:8.

31. Max Scheler, *Person and Self-Value: Three Essays*, ed. and trans. Manfred Frings (Dordrecht, Netherlands: Martinus Nijhoff Publishers, 1987), 5. "Kein Gott und kein Tier vermag sich zu schämen . . . Nur weil zum Wesen des Menschen ein Leib gehört, kann er in die Lage kommen sich schämen zu *müssen*; und nur weil er sein geistiges Personsein als wesensunabhängig von einem solchen 'Leibe' erlebt und von allem, was aus dem 'Leibe' zu kommen vermag, ist es möglich, daß er in die Lage kommt, sich schämen zu *können*" (Max Scheler, "Über Scham und Schamgefühl," in *Schriften aus dem Nachlass, vol. 1: Zur Ethik und Erkenntnislehre*, 2nd ed. (Bern: Francke, 1957), 65–147, 69).

32. Kari Elizabeth Børresen, *Subordination and Equivalence: The Nature and Role of Woman in Augustine and Aquinas* (Mainz: Grünewald, 1995).

33. Max Scheler, "Über Scham und Schamgefühl," 146. [trans. A.L.]

34. Cf. On the gendered differences in the lived experience of shame, see Sandra Lee Bartky, *Femininity and Domination: Studies in the Phenomenology of Oppression* (New York: Routledge, 1990), chap. 6: Shame and Gender, 83–98.

35. Max Scheler, *Formalism in Ethics and the Nonformal Ethics of Values*, trans. Manfred Frings and Roger Funk (Evanston, IL: Northwestern University Press, 1973), 289.

36. Scheler, "Über Scham und Schamgefühl," 147.

37. Bonnie Mann, "The Difference of Feminist Phenomenology," 58. Friedrich Nietzsche's critique of Western thought similarly aims at the ways we *"revenge* ourselves on life"* by emphasizing reason abstracted from history, becoming, and corporeality. According to his diagnosis, there has come to exist a powerful instinct within us "to slander, trivialize, and look down upon life" that leads to our separation from life and the positing of another, better, transcendental world (Friedrich Nietzsche, *Twilight of the Idols*, trans. Richard Polt (Indianapolis, IN: Hackett Publishing Company, 1997), 21.).

38. Anthony Steinbock, *Moral Emotions: Reclaiming the Evidence of the Heart* (Evanston, IL: Northwestern University Press, 2014), 72. Cf. Bonnie Mann's discussion of Steinbock's phenomenology of shame in "The Difference of Feminist Phenomenology," 58–61.

39. See, for example, Andrew Morrison, *Shame: The Underside of Narcissism* (New York: Routledge, 1989).

40. Nussbaum, *Hiding from Humanity*, chap. 4, esp. 177–89.

41. Aristotle, *Rhetoric*, trans. W. Rhys Roberts (Mineola, NY: Dover, 2004), 1378b.

42. Alexandra Fussi, "Aristotle on Shame," *Ancient Philosophy* 35, no. 1 (2015): 113–35, 127.

43. Augustine, *City of God*, 14:15.

44. Nussbaum, *Hiding from Humanity*, 200.

45. Ibid., 201.

46. Bonnie Mann, *Sovereign Masculinity: Gender Lessons from the War on Terror* (Oxford: Oxford University Press, 2014), 116.

47. Ibid.; cf., ibid., 111.

48. Christine Tarnopolsky, *Prudes, Perverts, and Tyrants: Plato's Gorgias and the Politics of Shame* (Princeton, NJ: Princeton University Press, 2010), 23.

49. Bonnie Mann, *Sovereign Masculinity*, 117.

50. Tarnopolsky, *Prudes, Perverts, and Tyrants*, 24–5.

51. Ibid., 25.

52. Michael Lewis, *Shame: The Exposed Self* (New York: The Free Press, 1995), 36.

53. Ibid.

54. Ibid.

55. Hegel, *Enzyklopädie der philosophischen Wissenschaften*, §24, 89 [trans. A.L.].

56. Christopher Bollas, *The Shadow of the Object: Psychoanalysis of the Unthought Known* (London: Free Association Books, 1987), quoted in Nussbaum, *Hiding from Humanity*, 194.

57. Nussbaum, *Hiding from Humanity*, 202.
58. Ibid., 173.
59. Ibid., 192; 177.
60. Ibid., 173–4; cf., ibid., 185.
61. Ibid., 184.
62. Ibid., 174.
63. Adriana Cavarero, *Relating Narratives: Storytelling and Selfhood*, trans. Paul Kottman (New York: Routledge, 2000), esp. 21 and 113.
64. Judith Butler, *Precarious Life: The Powers of Mourning and Violence* (London: Verso, 2006), 45.
65. Ibid., 42.
66. Ibid., 42–3. As Butler explains, this recognition may entail a reconceptualization of humanism or it may simply point out that "when a vulnerability *is* recognized, that recognition has the power to change the meaning and structure of the vulnerability itself" (ibid.).
67. Emmanuel Levinas, *Totality and Infinity: An Essay on Exteriority*, trans. Alphonso Lingis (Pittsburgh, PA: Duquesne University Press, 1961), 84.
68. Ibid.
69. Ibid.
70. Michael Morgan, *On Shame* (New York: Routledge, 2008), 90.
71. Judith Butler, *Frames of War: When is Life Grievable?* (London: Verso, 2016), 2.

BIBLIOGRAPHY

Agamben, Giorgio. *Homo Sacer: Sovereign Power and Bare Life.* Translated by Daniel Heller-Roazen. Redwood City, CA: Stanford University Press, 1998.
_____. *Nudities.* Translated by David Kishik and Stefan Pedatella. Redwood City, CA: Stanford University Press, 2011.
Aristotle. *Nicomachean Ethics.* Translated by Terence Irwin. Indianapolis, IN: Hackett Publishing Company, 2. Ed., 1999.
_____. *The Politics of Aristotle.* Translated by Benjamin Jowett. Oxford: Clarendon Press, 1885.
_____. *Rhetoric.* Translated by W. Rhys Roberts. Mineola, NY: Dover, 2004.
Arendt, Hannah. *The Human Condition.* Chicago: University of Chicago Press, 1958.
Augustine. *The City of God.* Translated by Marcus Dods. New York: Modern Library, 2000.
Bartky, Sandra Lee. *Femininity and Domination: Studies in the Phenomenology of Oppression.* New York: Routledge, 1990.
Børresen, Kari Elizabeth. *Subordination and Equivalence: The Nature and Role of Woman in Augustine and Aquinas.* Mainz: Grünewald, 1995.
Butler, Judith. *Frames of War: When is Life Grievable?* London: Verso, 2016.
_____. *Precarious Life: The Powers of Mourning and Violence.* London: Verso, 2006.

Cavarero, Adriana. *Relating Narratives: Storytelling and Selfhood*. Translated by Paul Kottman. New York: Routledge, 2000.

Demmerling, Christoph and Hilge Landweer. *Philosophie der Gefühle: Von Achtung bis Zorn*. Stuttgart: Metzler Verlag, 2007.

Freud, Sigmund. *Civilization and Its Discontents*. Edited and Translated by James Strachey. New York: W.W. Norton & Company, 1962.

____. "Mourning and Melancholia." In *The Standard Edition of the Complete Psychological Works of Sigmund Freud: On the History of the Psycho-Analytic Movement, Papers on Metapsychology, and other Works, vol. XIV (1914–1916)*. Translated by James Strachey, 243–58. London: The Hogarth Press, 1957.

Fussi, Alexandra. "Aristotle on Shame." *Ancient Philosophy* 35, no. 1 (2015): 113–35.

Hegel, Georg Wilhelm Friedrich. *Werke* 10: *Enzyklopädie der philosophischen Wissenschaften im Grundrisse (1830). Dritter Teil: Die Philosophie des Geistes mit den mündlichen Zusätzen*. Frankfurt am Main: Suhrkamp Verlag, 2016.

Hobbes, Thomas. *Leviathan*. London: Penguin Books, 1985.

Lewis, Michael. *Shame: The Exposed Self*. New York: The Free Press, 1995.

Levinas, Emmanuel. *Totality and Infinity: An Essay on Exteriority*. Translated by Alphonso Lingis. Pittsburgh: Duquesne University Press, 1961.

Locke, Jill. "Shame and the Future of Feminism." *Hypatia* 22, no. 4 (2007): 146–162.

Mann, Bonnie. "The Difference of Feminist Phenomenology: The Case of Shame." *Puncta. Journal of Critical Phenomenology* 1, no. 1 (2018): 41–73.

____. *Sovereign Masculinity: Gender Lessons from the War on Terror*. Oxford: Oxford University Press, 2014.

Mills, Charles. *The Racial Contract*. Ithaca, NY: Cornell University Press, 1997.

Morgan, Michael. *On Shame*. New York: Routledge, 2008.

Morrison, Andrew. *Shame: The Underside of Narcissism*. New York: Routledge, 1989.

Nietzsche, Friedrich. *Twilight of the Idols*. Translated by Richard Polt. Indianapolis, IN: Hackett Publishing Company, 1997.

Nussbaum, Martha. *Hiding from Humanity: Disgust, Shame, and the Law*. Princeton, NJ: Princeton University Press, 2004.

Plato. *The Dialogues of Plato*. Translated by Benjamin Jowett. New York: Tudor Publishing Company, 1936.

Scheler, Max. *Formalism in Ethics and the Nonformal Ethics of Values*. Translated by Manfred Frings and Roger Funk. Evanston, IL: Northwestern University Press, 1973.

____. *Person and Self-Value: Three Essays*. Edited and Translated by Manfred Frings. Dordrecht, Netherlands: Martinus Nijhoff Publishers, 1987.

____. "Über Scham und Schamgefühl." In *Schriften aus dem Nachlass, vol. 1: Zur Ethik und Erkenntnislehre, 2. Ed*. 65–147. Bern: Francke, 1957.

Steinbock, Anthony. *Moral Emotions: Reclaiming the Evidence of the Heart*. Evanston, IL: Northwestern University Press, 2014.

Tarnopolsky, Christine. *Prudes, Perverts, and Tyrants: Plato's Gorgias and the Politics of Shame*. Princeton, NJ: Princeton University Press, 2010.

Taylor, Gabriele. *Pride, Shame, and Guilt: Emotions of Self-Assessment*. Oxford: Oxford University Press, 1985.

5

Toward a Feminist Ethics of Shame

Sashinungla

While determining the significance and narrative history of shame, feminist scholarship that has emphasized the harmful effects of shame on women has also afforded weight to its different aspects. Whether it is seen as an internalized response of cultural history and normative social practice or a universal affect, shame seems integral to Being. The fact is we feel ashamed because human beings are not autochthonous creatures. Shame, according to Robert Metcalf, "is not simply a belief or the inchoate germ of a belief, but rather is a complex of belief, emotional affect, social sensitivity and self-awareness."[1] The irreducible complexities of shame then call for sensitivity to the ambiguities of shame and its affective impact on subjectivity. In tune with this exigency, the phenomenological experience of shame constitutes the critical mainstay of feminist analysis. In other words, the various conditions under which the subject is mired in shame-induced weariness and the circumstances giving rise to them, lie at the center of feminist theories and politics of shame, that retheorize earlier literature.

TWO CONTRADISTINCTIVE APPROACHES TO SHAME

A review of the shame literature across different disciplines and traditions reveals two distinguished contradistinctive views. First, I will simply offer a quick overview of the two views: (i) Shame as moral emotion: This position stresses its inherent, transformative potential that makes it possible for one to adopt a more self-critical stance and live more justly. According to Bernard Williams, shame is an extremely productive moral emotion because of the distinctive connection that it establishes between self, others, and world, through a self-evaluation that is mediated by an internalized other.[2]

Carl Schneider emphasizes the worth of shame as an "integral dimension of human experience" and as a "resource in the journey toward individuation and maturity."[3] Robert Solomon associates shame with responsibility, "including moral responsibility." "Shame is or can be a most effective tool for moral cultivation,"[4] he writes. He describes a complex web of emotions or moral sentiments that stimulate our sense of individual and social justice, and gives shame a significant role. To feel shame about not doing something we ought to do, or about something we did but ought not to have done, may contribute to our realization that an injustice must be rectified. Solomon believes, to be shameless "is a profound vice, perhaps the worst of all vices"[5] Krista K. Thomason[6] depicts shame as a sort of locus for positive moral commitments. Philosopher Aaron Ben Ze'ev recognizes that

> shame is probably one of the most powerful emotions for moral behavior. . . .
> Its emergence indicates that some of our most profound values are violated.
> Shame prevents many people from behaving immorally and from losing their
> own self-respect. . . . [Shame] expresses the fact that we care about this norm
> and this caring is commendable from a moral point of view. . . . The presence
> of shame, which expresses our basic values, is helpful in maintaining human
> dignity and integrity.[7]

(ii) Shame as negative self-assessment: This position emphasizes the pathology of shame and its authoritarian and controlling tendency that inhibit the achievement of authentic self-awareness and growth. Donald L. Nathanson describes four patterns of negative behavior involved with shame—known as the compass of shame: (a) withdrawal—for example, isolating oneself, hiding (b) avoidance—for example, denial of responsibility, neglect (c) attacking others—for example, blame others, verbal or physical aggression toward others (d) attacking self—for example, self-put-down, masochism.[8] Shame as Ralph Ellison conceives of it silences and excludes, rendering some citizens all but invisible and unheard.[9] Tangney and Dearing observe, "when people feel shame . . . they are berating themselves not just for the specific event; rather they are damning themselves—the core of their being—as flawed, useless, despicable. In this way shame experiences pose a tremendous threat to the self."[10] According to James Gilligan, feelings of "shame motivate violence."[11] Nel Nodding defines shame as a form of pain used to maintain codes of honor closely linked with violence.[12] For Silvan Tomkins, in his discussion of the Nine Affect Pairs "shame is the affect of indignity; the humiliated one . . . feels himself naked, defeated, alienated, lacking in dignity,"[13] situating shame firmly in the realm of a negative affect. Similarly, Jill Locke defines shame as a "negative global self-assessment" involving deep weariness that "readily translates into civic invisibility—a withdrawal from public life for some, a failure to engage in the first place for others."[14] "Shame can undo the self," writes Bonnie Mann, "unmake social ties, destroy the lifeworld of the one who is shamed, so that the only chance for survival seems to be a total remaking of the self and the self-world relation."[15]

I will not argue particularly against or for these viewpoints. Rather, I will review in some detail key feminist engagements with both earlier and more contemporary renditions of shame. I will then provide a reconsidered account of a feminist ethics of shame. What is of significance here is that the first position admits self-transformative experience as a necessary state of shame whereas the second position admits negative self-assessment as a necessary state of shame. Both analyses depend on some principal or core affect. It becomes a debate between pro-shame and antishame. What we get from both conceptions is not only a lopsided understanding of shame, but also two conceptual frameworks that are riddled with rigidity and insensitivity to difference (dispositional and contextual). It also turns around the question of whether such essentialist conceptions of shame are at all necessary and can be justified.

Between the two extremes, there are others who consider both sides of the shame emotion by disentangling various forms of shame from one another. Gabriele Taylor provides a first step toward distinguishing between two strands of shame, namely, "genuine" and "false."[16] Genuine shame is felt when we fail to act in accordance with our authentic values (or failure to live up to our own ideals or standards). False shame occurs when they are imposed on us from outside but not accepted by us as our own (or when we hold ourselves to some "alien" standards). According to Taylor, the experience of genuine shame is morally useful as it provides an opportunity to assess and reevaluate values and expectations. Martha Nussbaum observes that "shame can at times be a morally valuable emotion, playing a constructive role in development and moral change. . . . The person who is utterly shame-free is not a good friend, lover, or citizen." For Taylor, "false" shame occurs when imposed from outside, whereas for Nussbaum, "there are instances when the invitation to feel shame is a good thing—most often when the invitation is issues by the self, but at least sometimes when another person issues it."[17] Nevertheless, Nussbaum also argues against use in the legal system of public shame-based punishments. Following Aristotle, Nicholas Higgins stresses two kinds of shame, namely, retrospective shame and prospective shame.[18] According to him, retrospective shame is purely derived from external constraints—it is imposed upon the individual by other members of the polis, whereas the prospective shame is rooted in knowledge, and therefore power relations. For Higgins, this prospective component of shame is the one that is ethically significant. Elspeth Probyn recognizes the harmful affects of shame but on the whole views it as productive and morally useful. "Shame compels an involuntary and immediate reassessment of our-selves. . . . Shame in this way is positive in its self-evaluative role; it can even be self-transforming. . . . The things that make me ashamed have to do with a strong interest in being a good person. . . . Shame reminds me about the promises we keep to ourselves."[19]

Having mapped the broad field of shame, it becomes necessary to examine more holistically the emotion of shame in all its complexity, ambiguity, and contradictions. Hence, our understanding of it and the framing of its different dimensions should not be tied down to an essentialist and binary analysis. As Probyn further suggests, "Describing shame plugs us into . . . diversity."[20] It is ineffective to conceive of shame's affective power simply in antithetical mode—essentially in shame-induced weariness or in shame-induced sincer-ity, but moreover, in the breadth of context.

FEMINIST INTERVENTION: GENDER, POWER, AND SHAME

Until recently, major feminist concerns about women's experiences and needs were not admitted as philosophical concerns. This was primarily because the existing philosophical tools were not designed for such an investigation. This has led feminists to design new tools. Side by side feminists are in search of hitherto neglected content as there have been major omissions in mainstream philosophy. Feminist's intervention/critique adds to the search of new content as well as seeing old problems through alternative lenses. Shame has gener-ally been undertheorized within philosophy. One of the reasons attributed by feminists for this inattention is that since shame was traditionally considered a "feminine" emotion, it was seen as having little or no value within the whole gamut of moral philosophy. In his fifth lecture on psychoanalysis, Freud char-acterized shame as a "feminine characteristic par excellence,"[21] an inescapable disposition. Long before him, Aristotle had described shame as an emotion "suitable for youth." In establishing shame as *pathos* (feeling), Aristotle removes it from the realm of *hexis* (active condition) and places it in the lower part of the soul, distinct from true virtue.[22] Centuries later, Bernard Williams lamented about characterizing shame as infantile and feminine. Scholars of antiquity have maintained that moral progress means moving away from ethics associated with shame.[23] So, one of the questions this raises is, how to produc-tively critique such contained proscriptions of shame.

In her overview introduction to a special issue on shame in the *Hypatia*, Clara Fischer outlines the significance of shame to feminists: "gendered shame may form a disciplining device operating through structures of oppres-sion, such as gender, but also class, race, ethnicity, sexuality, nationality, and related intersectional categories."[24] The self-conscious emotions such as pride, shame, guilt, and embarrassment are "moral" emotions, which motivate "adherence" to social norms and personal standards, and emerge in early childhood following the development of self-awareness. Gender stereotypes of emotion maintain that women experience more guilt, shame, and embarrassment but that men experience more pride. Feminist analysis of the gendered embodiment of shame and women's sexualized body is significant here. Shame is one of the main structural components that secure the continued subordination and exploitation of women. "Shame is gendered," claims Sandra Bartky. She argues that not only do men and women not experience shame for the same transgressions, but she also claims that "the feeling itself has a different meaning in relation to their total psychic situation and general social location."[25] Gendered shame operates within the normalized social status of the feminine—the "feminine" ways of being in the world. According to Bartky, for the feminine subject, the experience of shame is not episodic, it is a species of pain or suffering that is pervasive: an environment that affectively shades the subject-world relation without reprieve. Whereas, for men, shame operates against the backdrop of a "presupposition of male power," and "is typically construed as a specific episode in the agent's history," which has an ameliorative outcome because "guilt or shame mark his investment in moral norms, these painful emotions are occasions for moral reaffirmation."[26]

In the light of Bartky's claims, I urge consideration also of the empirical study and meta-analysis which shows that blanket stereotypes about women's greater emotionality (or in this case, necessarily fixing shame experience with women and pride experience with men) are inaccurate.[27] I agree with Bonnie Mann in her reading of both Freud and Bartky, in her essay "Femininity, Shame, and Redemption."[28] Unlike Freud, she believes that shame plays an absolutely central role in masculine identity-formation, though distinct from the kind of shame she analyzes in her work. In contrast to Bartky, for Mann shame events in masculine identity-formation are also ubiquitous, and haunted by the specter of humiliation associated with failed masculinity, as much as by the promise of masculinity redeemed by power. I think both these assertions are germane as far as our vision toward a feminist theory and practice centered on collective and inclusive solidarity are concerned.

Drawing from Bartky's account of shame, Mann extends her inquiry into the role shame plays in the feminine subject-formation by categorizing shame into two distinct but related kinds. She defines "Ubiquitous shame" as "that shame-status that attaches to the very fact of existing as a girl or woman, or of having a female body. . . . It is the kind of shame that all aspiring women must negotiate, and its underside is a certain experience of pride."[29] Mann conceives of the "unbounded shame," as "a thick relentless, engulfing shame—often catalyzed by a shame-event—that snuffs out any hope for redemption, and has suicide as its logical endpoint. It is a kind of shame that many women, but not all, experience—and the threat of it is part of the thick atmosphere of danger that accompanies women's becoming."[30] Explicating the interplay between the two kinds of shame, she writes, "shamed femininity is temporally structured around its own redemptive aspirations, and that feminine shame's futural fixations are a key aspect of creating the specific vulnerabilities of emerging women/subjects to the unbounded shame."[31] The relation between the two, for Mann, hinges in that "ubiquitous shame with its promissory temporality is the 'setup' for the decisions that catalyze the events that issue in unbounded shame for some girls and women." According to her, the two forms of shame work together to secure women's vulnerability and men's power. Mann limits her account of shame to a particular manifestation of it: the power of shame in the transitional period between girlhood and womanhood, within the context of "a hypermediatized, late-capitalist social world."[32] In many ways, her theorizing goes beyond the scope of her investigation, and makes a wider call for feminists to create space for "affective investments in other kinds of self-justification for both women and men."[33]

The category of the abstract individual is not just gendered but also anthropologized. Patriarchy does not categorize all women to the "feminine" existential space. Culturally mediated images of women are often marked by two polar opposites: on the one hand as free, tough, spontaneous, and carefree *or* on the other hand as vulnerable, submissive, docile, and shy, consequently, leaving no room for a person's self-definition and authentic self-realization. To put the operation of these overlapping stereotypes or this phenomenon called gendered race/class/caste in perspective, let me instantiate from how the colonially mediated notion of modern Indian "national culture" also produced a "middle-class woman" and "common woman"[34] taxonomy in its discourse. Within such nomenclatures, middle-class woman was defined in terms of attributes such as gentility, domestic virtues, docility, and coyness. Whereas, the common woman generally belonged to the Hindu lower-caste women, tribal women, poor women, and others were considered to be lacking the superficial veneer of gentility, and due to economic compulsion, were forced to eke out an existence outside home. They were also considered to be lacking in the attributes of submissiveness and coyness which were aspired to as well as expected of in ideal Indian womanhood. Patricia Hills Collins's[35] analysis of the patriarchy's imagery of the black women vis-à-vis the white women shows a similar pattern. Also, lesbian ethicists' critique of heteronormativity highlights how they are differently implicated in chains of shame from the heterosexual women within/outside patriarchy. "Cultural representation of gays, lesbians, black, and more generally women, were never completely absent" contends Probyn, "rather, these groups were over represented in terms of pathological depictions."[36] These articulations of marginal female subjects are significant because the most powerful aspect of gendered shame has been the charges of "shamelessness" attached to (women's) expression of sexuality and desire.

As I have shown some women are *a priori* placed outside the sphere of the "feminine" (shamed femininity for Mann), therefore, Mann's ubiquitous shame cannot account for those placed outside the "futural temporal redemptive" space.[37] She emphatically argues that the ubiquitous shame "is *essentially* (emphasis added) characterized by a promise of redemption." But for such persons, there is no such possibility or experience of pride, hope, and the promise of redemption by way of the ubiquitous shame Mann is referring to.[38] Hence, in addition to the two kinds of shame, we will now need a third kind for a more in-depth understanding of how it operates to dominate, exclude, and silence. To differentiate it from shamelessness in the ordinary sense as a vice, "ubiquitous shameless shame" is the expression I am allotting to that shame-status that sticks to the very fact of existing (ubiquitous *nonfeminine* existence) as a "common woman" or as a Dalit woman, black woman, tribal woman, and so on. And placing the marginal female subjects, outside the sphere of the *feminine* existence, renders the dispossession or oppression more acceptable or supposedly inevitable.

Another key area stressed by feminist scholarship is the power dimension of shame by investigating its nature of operation in hierarchical social settings, particularly within the context of the male-female hierarchy. The scholarship highlights how unwarranted shame routinely works to the disadvantage of persons who (because of class, race, or gender) are marginalized, trivialized, demeaned, or ignored by society as inferior or defective. "Shame evolved from submission signals," writes Heidi Maibom.[39] Her evolutionary account of shame focuses on the kind of traumatic shame felt by people who are prosecuted, such as Jews or Tutsi. She associates shame with displays of submission and appeasement in nonhuman animals, which is predominantly associated with a hierarchical structure where the subordinate animal submits to the dominant one. What Maibom shows, however, is that in contrast to nonhuman animals, we humans internalize this "shaming audience":[40] we also do not simply submit to a dominant other, we submit "to a way of life, with its strictures, prohibitions, and demands."[41] Therefore, for Maibom, shame emerges when we fail to measure up "to certain standards, norms, or ideals." Because of this an audience—real or internalized—is an important aspect of shame. As demonstrated by Maibom, not everyone has the power to shame. Given the enmeshment of shame with power, shame upholds and enforces the standards, norms, and ideals of the powerful ones. In this sense, shame is coextensive with normativizing discursive regimes and iterative hegemonic practices that produce marginalized identities (nonnormative subjects).

Like Maibom, Jennifer Manion perceives an enmeshment of shame with power that she investigates within the context of the male-female hierarchy.[42] Manion shows how shame's usefulness as a moral emotion might be negatively impacted by gender. She critiques Gabriele Taylor's formulation of "false" and "genuine" types of shame,[43] which in her opinion is incomplete as it fails to account for the negative stereotype and experiences of gender which society assigns to women. As our conceptions of knowledge (femininity or ideals) are historically and culturally constructed, women or the marginalized are not always free to know—let alone reject—the validity or "truth" behind their experiences of shame. Taylor's distinction between genuine and false shame places the unwarranted burden on individuals to know the truth. Hence, Manion and other feminist critics draw attention to the fact that it is important to investigate how we have acquired these ideals because we might internalize standards that we do not agree with or are harmful to us. Although Taylor is aware of the historical situatedness of values, she is insensitive about its enmeshment in the matrices of social and political power. Her formulation of shame assumes the individual as a morally free agent and thus echoes the Kantian presumption of an autonomous self whose access to concepts of morality may somehow be detached from the context.

Nevertheless, Manion also argues that "shame can play an important positive role for the ashamed person despite its negative and potentially debilitating effects."[44] She thinks that gendered embodiment of shame does not undo shame's ethical significance *in toto*. What Manion is suggesting is an inclusion of an understanding of shame as a part of feminist's self-care/self-empathy program. In this sense, shame serves as a reminder that we are in need of some reflection to assess and evaluate one's values and expectations within a context of understanding what shames us. This deliberation is possible by giving ourselves empathy first. Yet, while empathy ostensibly creates the required distance to evaluate one's action objectively, it is not as straightforward as we might hope. This *self-concerned* reflection is however a beginning that allows us to see the influence of stereotypes on our actions that can help us recognize internalized oppression, born of debilitating stereotypes that act as a source of our shame. Manion shows that once we have moved out of shame through empathizing with ourselves, we can enter into a self-concerned reflection from an "intersubjective and impersonal perspective":[45] looking at the action/situation from another's perspective. I think Manion's self-care can also include *other-concerned* reflection, in the broader study and understanding of ethics of shame. This other-concerned reflection allows us to develop a social justice sensibility: to explore prejudice, unreflective acceptance of privilege, or other modes of belief and conduct often associated with societal patterns of injustice and inequality. In other words, it is a matter of being attentive first to our own selves—self-knowledge and self-care—then to another's well-being, and embodying willingness to continue to act toward and promote care. If we take the self to be relational, rather than autochthonous creatures, then caring for the self is unavoidably bound up with caring for the other and vice versa.

Feminist scholarship also examines shame's problematic relation with an ethic of care, empathy, and compassion. Some feminists object to the use of shame on several grounds. The central objection is that shame inhibits the development of a natural sense of connection, caring, and empathy, which they consider is necessary for living with integrity and self-respect. Since shame is often used to control, it undermines a person's development of critical consciousness and empathetic understanding. Nel Noddings observes that, as shame gets in the way of empathy, it has negative consequences, including ethical consequences, making it a "moral dead end."[46] She explicitly rejects moral relevance of shame as a form of pain, because it has been used to maintain codes of honor linked with violence.[47] As the preoccupation with shame is likely to prevent the shamed person from reaching out to others for help, the chance of establishing the empathic connection that opens up possibility for restoration and to move forward is closed. Feminist debates often question the usefulness of shame for conflict resolution as shame is positively connected with anger and the tendency to externalize blame. It is argued that shame might be useful within hierarchy-based societies, but it has no constructive role in creating a more compassionate way of living, including reducing injustice. Consistent with Noddings, shame "has great potential," writes Josina Makau, "to undermine our efforts to inculcate an ethic of love and care, of respect, and of compassion for all, and little prospect for contributing to the fulfillment of these outcomes."[48]

It is absolutely necessary to be responsive to and care for the vulnerable. But I argue, we must also consider how equally imperative it is for us to engage critically with both the social and political structures that produce such inequalities and the conceptual frameworks that help perpetuate such conditions. Care ethics (broadly understood) tell us why and how to care for the vulnerable in a general sense, but as yet, there is little provision of meaningful tools to engage with critical questions, such as why some people are rendered existentially vulnerable and their voices silenced? Nor does generalized care ethics show a way out of such situations, except by urging us to be attentive and responsive to the needs of the vulnerable. In other words, vulnerability remains underanalyzed (both locally and globally) which therefore leaves the behavior and actions of perpetrators largely unchallenged. Further, the conditions that give rise to those behaviors and actions remain underexamined as others have also alluded to in this book. It is invariably assumed that the object that needs to be responded to, cared for, reclaimed, and uplifted is the vulnerable or the oppressed. There is a tendency of placing the vulnerable in a perpetual state of being objects of care but not as agents or vehicles of knowledge. Moreover, recognition by members of their own complicity in creating and perpetuating social injustice ought to invoke a feeling of shame. All these affirm an uncanny relationship between shame, justice, and freedom. In this sense, shame is not an anathema to cultivation of an ethic of love, of respect, and of care to all.

Nonetheless, several feminists emphasize that shame should remain a valuable element in feminist ethics. As Miranda Fricker (among others) has argued, recognizing the role that privilege or power plays in the construction of "epistemic injustice" and "epistemic ignorance"[49] legitimizes the role for shame in the moral life of privileged and empowered subjects. Shame, in this sense, is a form of realizing that involves owing up to both the suffering of other women and the recognition of one's own privileged status over other women. After examining the ways in which shame and guilt have functioned to subordinate women, Elizabeth Spelman argues that shame should have a constructive role in feminist ethics. According to Spelman:

> Feminist ethics, I have been insisting, must at least address the history of woman's inhumanity to woman. . . . I do not see how women who enjoy privileged status over other women can come to think it is desirable to lose that privilege (by force or consent) unless they see it not only as producing harm to other women but also as deeply disfiguring to themselves. . . . Seeing myself as deeply disfigured by privilege and desiring to do something about it may be impossible without my feeling of shame. The degree to which I am moved to undermine systems of privilege is closely tied to the degree to which I feel shame at that sort of person such privilege makes me or allows me to be.[50]

Politicized within its racist, classist, and heteronormative contexts, we, however, should not rush to endorse in a wholesale manner the helpfulness/efficacy of the much-valorized liberal empathy or shame. Some scholars like Sara Ahmed see this kind of shame as a "form of discomfort with the comforts of inhibiting the normative."[51] The act of shame then becomes the act of my own privilege. Therefore, shame's expression in the social space can easily assume the grandeurs of self-righteousness: self-congratulatory politics of the liberal subject. I will return to this.

The call for inclusion of the self-reflection/critique dimension of shame into feminist practice from various quarters within the discipline also forms a kind of pushback against racist, classist, and other exclusions rampant in feminist theories and practices. Contending that women of color have been excluded from mainstream feminist project, Berenice Fisher emphasizes, "Judgment and shame constitute an intrinsic part of struggle as activists and intellectuals" and should be integrated more fully and usefully into feminist practice.[52] Kanchana Mahadevan's analysis follows a similar pattern. Mahadevan pointed out, "*Dalit* women in India were questioning whether the feminist movement had paid adequate attention to the caste basis of oppression. . . . The middle class 'lifestyle' feminism had, in fact, failed to understand that *Dalit* women's participation was crucial."[53] As I analyze in detail elsewhere, marginalized and disempowered women have critiqued the casteist, racist, classist, and heteronormativist exclusions endemic to feminist community (read as mainstream) in India.[54]

There must however be "uptake" of criticism, as Helen Longino rightly says, "The community must not merely tolerate dissent, but its beliefs and theories must change over time in response to the critical discourse taking place within it."[55] Audre Lourde has demonstrated how white feminists refuse to hear her anger by returning her anger in the form of defensiveness.[56] The fact of resistance within feminism to hearing the anger of some feminists is a "sign" that what "we are against" cannot be relegated to the outside.[57] As such, forms of hierarchical structures and superstructures must be spelled out and comprehensively understood to avoid assumptions about the universality of women's identity. In doing so, we should not only focus on positions of oppression and pain but should also talk about positions of privilege and power. Because (self-reflective) shame reminds one to be mindful of perspective and privilege in the activity of moral theorizing, I believe that it can serve as an instrument of conscience. Berenice Fisher rightly says, "the voices that make us most uncomfortable and the feelings that accompany them constitute a built-in critique of our ideals."[58] As Sara Ahmed argues, it is important to hear the anger of others, without blocking the anger through a defense of one's own position. She says, "such a project requires that one accepts that one's own position might anger others hence allows one's position to be opened to critique by others, according to her (it does not then, like guilt or shame, turn the self back into itself by 'taking' that anger as one's own)."[59]

Discourse about feminist solidarity and coalition has been mainly defined within the idea of a shared sense of women's oppression, which falls far too short of a plural society and reality. A valuable exercise is to form interconnections and solidarity across social, cultural, political, and gender differences so as to continually "broaden and correct the production of individual and collective knowledge."[60] Given the extent to which various axes of oppression, power, and privilege intermesh, feminists must rethink commonly held assumptions regarding the struggles, needs, and challenges faced by women in diverse subject positions, thereby providing ways to theorize about the manner in which contextually suitable feminist conceptual frameworks and praxis might be produced/achieved for all. For feminism to make a transformative difference, essentialist and individualist theories (feminist or otherwise) that value hierarchy, binarism, exclusion, and domination need to be recontextualized (if not purged) and substantially informed by our social and political realities. This reenvisioning and restructuring in both theory and praxis will need more than just sensitization and diversification. It will require the development of appropriate and relevant pedagogy in which masculinity must be also called to account.

RECONSIDERING FEMINIST ETHICS OF SHAME

There is a necessity for a critical reconsideration and examination of the shame through an integrated feminist framework. To this end, I wish to move away from both the sexist and stereotypical characterization of shame as "feminine" or "youthful," and the antithetical mode of approaching shame: primarily in shame-induced weariness or in shame-induced sincerity. I proffer shame is a *quality* rather than as a hyphenated trait: it is transgendered. In this sense, shame is associated with the nongendered, nonagized, nonanthropologized, and nonheteronormatized creative element. It is a reflection of our *being-alongsidedness*, and the fact that the world is not first ours to appropriate. Shame as I conceive of it mirrors the complexity of its latent potency. Specifically, in my view, shame is a *mean*[61] condition—like a capacity. Being a mean condition, its expression and role is variegated. In his seminal work *Rhetoric*, while examining the emotions in relation to rhetoric and their ability to affect our judgment, Aristotle investigates the nature of shame in terms of "the things that cause these feelings, and the persons before whom, and the states of mind under which, they are felt."[62] Aristotle conceives shame as a feeling, playing a crucial role as a bridge between *pathos* and *hexis*, and thus there is an ambiguity to its role.[63] Shame being a mean not only indicates it has an *excess* and *deficiency*, but primarily, it is indicative that there is an *appropriate* feeling of shame. But it also means that shame's affective power can be harnessed as an inhibitory, homogenizing agent to extort obedience and to create nonnormative subject.

By conceiving shame as a mean, a feminist account could approach shame in an integrated manner, rather than arguing about whether we are better off with or without shame. This is significant to feminist shame theory and politics in three ways: (i) for seeing how the experience of shame regulates and determines our gendered existence, particularly in terms of its homogenizing and regulatory power; (ii) for seeing shame as an alternative interventionist medium where it can be seen as a positive affect of positivity, enabling political agency and critical reconsideration of our normativized identities; (iii) for seeing the significance of the ethical material that the various articulations of the political affect, introduces in the field of our subjective realities. I believe an integrated feminist approach to ethics of shame will not only address the internal tensions constitutive of subjectivity in shame more comprehensively but also contribute to a better understanding of its relation to ethics.

Drawing from the diverse feminist conceptualizations reviewed above and by taking into consideration disparate research findings,[64] we can look at shame from a position that would allow simultaneous consideration of various factors: interactions between disposition, context, cognition, and emotion. Central to such an approach is the underlying assumption that the experience and effect of shame on subjects involves dispositional, contextual, and situational factors in complex combinations. The proposition that a defining characteristic of shame is a threat to identity highlights the individual's capacity to respond in various ways to the inconsistency between behavior and identity. In keeping with the complexity of how shame works, Bartky's advice is significant. She has said, not only shame gendered but also, "for the shame-ridden and shame-prone, it is not a penance that restores the miscreant to the proper moral equilibrium. . . . For such persons, there is no such equilibrium to which to return."[65] Hence, feminist ethics of shame ought to be sensitive to all such factors, and therefore must be committed to working toward social and political transformation, rather than to merely progress or improve in the position or suffering of women in an otherwise more or less unaltered social and political order. In other words, feminist social justice, I believe must be predicated on a philosophical vision of interrelatedness and responsibility, and a transformation of the community by linking feminist shame theory and practice with the broader vision of "creating a world that is open to the voices, dreams and imaginations of those who lie within the shadow of shame,"[66] rather than a mere cessation of shame and violence.

The essentialist idea of difference has ignored the differential power positions occupied by women, within and outside the domestic sphere, and also ignored the fact that patriarchy does not place all women within the same category. I urge that we also juxtapose the discourse on gender justice and freedom with the reality of a plural society/world in the strictest possible sense. This gains urgency particularly in the context of shame, as the feminist vision of transforming power relations and improving the material conditions of people's lives is complicated by the compulsion of an ethical involvement with others. Since representation is an exercise of power and involves speaking *for* the other, it is also an ethical act, which might better consider speaking *with* the Other. In fighting the injustices of hegemonic structures and superstructures, there is a provocation to pay attention to the tools and images we fight with, so as not to be complicit in essentializing the discourse and furthering the violence. It is important for us, as members of an epistemic community, "to actively cultivate solidarity, curiosity, and sensitivity to the fact that our public communities are unavoidably plural."[67] Let us recognize the importance of working side by side even with those we do not readily agree with, if gender justice has to move beyond superficial aspects of social change. Engaging with both women and men (and broader gender diversity) is necessary to purge ourselves of dominant notions of masculinity and femininity, to build a stronger sense of well-being and at the same time, strengthen interpersonal bonds that get eroded by sexist notions of "proper" gender relations.

For feminism, to make a transformative difference, the *reality* of the oppressive reality and its narrativization are important prerequisites. A feminist shame conception can account for both (i) the depressed positioning of women and (ii) the creative capabilities of women: agency invested in the oppressed. In other words, women as both (a) subjects implicated in shame and (b) subjects capable of experiencing self-transformation by way of shame. As the feminist project aims at disrupting *and* transforming traditional understanding and practices, freeing women from the dreadfully limiting *a priori* victim/shame/shameless/*feminine*-status assigned to their very existence is crucial.

Feminists' critique of dominant theories and practices has played a crucial role to help us see how the incorporation of viewpoints and perspectives from sections of society which remain unrepresented and underrepresented might improve the quality of our collective community. Constructive engagement with shame from feminist scholarship could create a reparative pro-social manner with and between culture that promotes self/social improvement, voices apologies for transgressions, and seeks reparative action. It is important to understand that "the act of invoking shame is itself a moral question and should be approached with moral care."[68] Emphasis should be on correcting wrongs *and* restoring social relations. Creating an affirmative world that recognizes ethical behavior and empathic association as an ongoing, dynamic responsibility of all members of the society (rather than only seeking to shame/punish), that I argue, constitutes part of the way forward.

Whether we see shame as self-regarding or social-regarding or both, all this necessitates an ethical involvement with self to self and self-other/world. Michel Foucault[69] conceives of the relation of self to self as fundamentally ethical. Ethics for him is, however, interconnected with politics. Our self-relation is shaped by the context in which it develops; in turn it reverberates when we act in the world. Foucault was however apprehensive about the possibility of self-transformation within the given context. Hence, he emphasized on working toward countering normalizing relations of power within society more broadly and promoting freedom to relate to ourselves differently. The question is how far can resistance to political power help? Can social and political articulation of shame provide us with the required impetus and freedom to constitute, understand, and relate to ourselves differently? The omissions and absences that I have shown in my analysis of the feminist intervention section above also point to the limits of the political appropriation of shame, because the social articulation of shame is invariably implicated in its historical process and thus subject to binarisms and exclusionary projects within the coercive systems of power that produce nonnormative subjects. As such, the political appropriation of shame, without being exceeded by ethics, will only continue what Levinas refer to as the drama of "being's interest," as the effort of "egoisms struggling with each other, each against all [. . .] and thus together"[70] in the commerce of rights and concessions.

I will further argue that shame's significance as a critical passion goes beyond the politics of affects and its implications for our normative social practice, for it is constitutive of our respect for others as moral agents, the recognition of our indiscretion and vulnerability: our humanity *and* inhumanity. Besides, a failure to entertain others point of view, and about who we are, and imperviousness to other's criticisms would make: any political resistance, any self or social transformation, any critical and creative examination of existing practices, any reciprocal intersubjectivity, and especially any collective and inclusive solidarity impossible. If shame (in the ethical sense) is the desire to live an honorable or noble life, then this life is and must be lived as a life with others, who themselves are expected to live well, and to recognize that that is what one is trying to do. At this point, let me return to Spelman's call to the exigency of "*seeing* (emphasis added) myself as deeply disfigured by privilege and *desiring* (emphasis added) to do something about it":[71] This "seeing" and "desiring" is only possible if I go beyond politics and move toward ethics, not only when I find myself anguished by the frailty of others who want me to re-create the world. It can only emerge in the sincerity of an ethical relation with self/other. This sincerity revealed in shame is indicative of a subjectivity (ethical consciousness to some) more fundamental and prior than its political articulation. Shame in this sense is a dissociative interruption of myself: a reminder of my alienation from my very humanity (Being) itself. Then constituting an ethic of the self, says Foucault, "may be an urgent, fundamental, and politically indispensable task, if it is true after all that there is no first or final point of resistance to political power other than in the relationship one has to oneself."[72]

To conclude, let me reiterate that our emphasis on justice—the righting of wrongs—should not eclipse the fact of our *being-alongsidedness*, where a sense of togetherness purposefully guides activities. Feminism must be cautious about the individuation tendency of the liberal justice paradigm, as: shaming, victim blaming, and self-blame, that women, particularly the victims of sexual violence experience—as all are all premised in a structure that frames gender/sexual violence as (individual) women's problem, as if dissociated from the milieus. Instead, a feminist ethics of shame might be more productively premised on values such as tolerance, defined minimally as giving the benefit of the doubt to others; empathy, "the feeling into" another person; compassion, a desire to alleviate or reduce the suffering of another; and love in its elevated form, as indispensable to social cohesion, solidarity, and transformation. All movements (theory and praxis) toward the Good need to form coalition with others, and the participation of all (including men) is absolutely necessary. Solidarity is beyond mere identity; it is a politicized/ethicized consciousness. And, when solidarity works, it emerges from a sense of mutual emancipation. But there is much for participants to learn and unlearn: to not make it about themselves, to resist prim virtue and self-congratulations, to repress the objectifying and charitable impulse, and to be consistent. Solidarity is a demanding commitment: it means listening, and opening up, and transforming. It is not facetiously ventured into.

In our pent-up frustration with injustice and violence, the disproportionate space, the idea of the role of power in social relations has come to occupy, is often underrealized within and outside of feminist theory and practice. However, this is not to reject the value of the role of power and the truth it contains, but to seek to adapt this truth with the feminist tradition on the importance of empathy and interconnectedness. Feminist practices in service of justice for the victimized and the weak are rapidly picking up pace globally, shuddering traditional hierarchies and power structures. Some of these practices, however, tend to work only on the basis of justice, which is related to the issue of power, of correcting skewed and unfair power relations, a highlighting of Equality.[73] Within an ethic of justice, emphasis is on the outcome, not the process or the route and there have been eloquent voices that have defended violence in service of justice. In closing, I ask: in such a context, should the ethic of empathy, compassion, and love, not temper the quest for justice? In Rabindranath Tagore's words, "Creative force needed for the true union in human society is love; justice is only an accompaniment to it, like the beating of tom-tom to song."[74] I have argued that there is a need for an ethic of interconnectedness and solidarity, which not only pays reverence to reason and conditions of material life, but one that bases itself on the fostering of a consciousness—that each of us is embedded with other human beings, and also connected to animate and inanimate nature, a connectedness that demands a cultivation of active empathy and collective and inclusive solidarity for all, including the self.

NOTES

1. Robert Metcalf, "The Truth of Shame-Consciousness in Freud and Phenomenology," *Journal of Phenomenological Psychology*, 31: 1 (2000), 3–4.

2. Bernard Williams, *Shame and Necessity* (Berkeley: University of California Press, 1993).

3. Carl D. Schneider, *Shame, Exposure, and Privacy* (New York: W W Norton & Co., 1977), ix–xviii.

4. Robert Solomon, *True to Our Feelings: What our Emotions are Really Telling Us* (New York: Oxford University Press, 2007), 90–100.

5. Robert Solomon, "The Emotions of Justice," *Social Justice Research*, 3: 4 (1989), 367.

6. Krista K. Thomason, *Naked: The Dark Side of Shame and Moral Life* (Oxford: Oxford University Press, 2018).

7. Aaron Ben Ze'ev, *The Subtlety of Emotions* (Cambridge, MA: MIT Press, 2000), 527–529.

8. Donald L. Nathanson, *Shame and Pride: Affect, Sex, and the Birth of the Self* (New York: Norton, 1992).

9. Ralph Ellison, *Invisible Man* (New York: Vintage Press, 1947/1995).

10. June Tangey and Ronda L. Dearing, *Shame and Guilt* (New York: The Guilford Press, 2002), 92.

11. James Gilligan, *Violence: Our Deadly Epidemic and Its Causes* (New York: Putnam Books, 1997), 111.

12. Nel Noddings, *Starting at Home: Caring and Social Policy* (Berkeley: University of California, 2002), 218.

13. Silvan Tomkins, *Shame and its Sisters: A Silvan Tomkins Reader*, eds. Eve Kosofsky Sedgewick and Adam Frank (Durham, NC: Duke University Press, 1995), 133.

14. Jill Locke, "Shame and the Future of Feminism," *Hypatia*, 22: 4 (2007), 149–153.

15. Bonnie Mann, "Femininity, Shame, and Redemption," *Hypatia*, 33: 3 (Summer 2018), 403.

16. Gabriele Taylor, *Pride, Shame, and Guilt: Emotions of Self-Assessment* (Clarendon: Oxford University Press, 1985), 34.

17. Martha Nussbaum, *Hiding from Shame: Disgust, Shame, and the Law* (Princeton, NJ: Princeton University Press, 2004), 211–216.

18. Nicholas Higgins, "Shame on You: The Virtuous Use of Shame in Aristotle's Nicomachean Ethics," *Expositions*, 9: 2 (2015), 4.

19. Elspeth Probyn, *Blush: The Face of Shame* (Minneapolis: University of Minnesota University Press, 2005), xii–x.

20. Ibid., 5.

21. Sigmund Freud, *New Introductory Lectures on Psychoanalysis: The Standard Edition* (New York: W. W. Norton, 1965), 164.

22. See Aristotle, *Nicomachean Ethics*, trans. Joe Sachs (Newburyport, MA: Focus Publishing R. Pullins Company, 2002), 21–36.

23. Williams, *Shame and Necessity*, 5.

24. Clara Fischer, "Gender and the Politics of Shame: A Twenty-First Century Feminist Shame Theory," *Hypatia*, 33: 3 (Summer 2018), 371.

25. Sandra Bartky, *Shame and Gender, in Femininity and Domination: Studies in the Phenomenology of Oppression* (New York: Routledge, 1990), 84.

26. Ibid., 84–96.

27. See Nicole M. Else-Quest, Ashley Higgins, Carlie Allison, Lindsay C. Morton, "Gender Differences in Self-Conscious Emotional Experience: A Meta-Analysis," *Psychological Bulletin*, 138: 5 (2012 September), 947–81.

28. Mann, "Femininity, Shame," 402–10.

29. Ibid., 403.

30. Ibid.

31. Ibid., 409.

32. Mann, "Femininity, Shame," 403.

33. Ibid., 415.

34. Sashinungla, "Gender, Tradition and Modernity: A Critical Feminist Analytic," in *Tradition and Modernity: Essays on Women of India*, eds., Sashinungla and Atashee Chatterjee Sinha (Kolkata, New Delhi: Jadavpur University, Suryodaya Books, 2015), 156–157. See also Suruchi Thapar, "Women as Activists; Women as Symbols: A Study of the Indian Nationalist Movement," *Feminist Review*, 44 (1993), 471–88.

35. See Patricia Hill Collins, *Black Feminist Thought: Knowledge, Consciousness and the Politics of Empowerment* (New Delhi, special Indian edition: Routledge, 2017).

36. Probyn, *Blush*, 86.

37. Mann, "Femininity, Shame," 409.

38. Ibid.

39. Heidi L. Maibom, "The Descent of Shame," *Philosophy and Phenomenological Research*, 80: 3 (2010), 21–41.

40. Ibid., 585.

41. Ibid., 587.

42. Jennifer Manion, "Girls Blush, Sometimes: Gender, Moral Agency, and the Problem of Shame," *Hypatia* 18: 3 (2003), 21–41.

43. Taylor, "Pride, Shame, and Guilt," 1985.

44. Jennifer Manion, "The Moral Relevance of Shame," *American Philosophical Quarterly* 39: 1 (2002), 73.

45. Ibid., 31.

46. Nel Noddings, *The Maternal Factor: Two Paths to Morality* (Berkley: University of California Press, 2010), 140.

47. Nel Noddings, *Starting at Home: Caring and Social Policy* (Berkeley: University of California Press, 2002), 218.

48. Josina M. Makau, "An Outcome-Based Approach to Ethical Communication," Transcript of Keynote Address at the Fifth National Communication Ethics Conference, (Michigan: Gull Lake, May 1998).

49. Miranda Fricker, *Epistemic Injustice: Power and the Ethics of Knowing* (New York: Oxford University Press, 2007); See also Jose Medina, *The Epistemology of Resistance: Gender and Racial Oppression, Epistemic Injustice, and Resistant Imaginations* (New York: Oxford University Press, 2013).

50. Elizabeth Spelman, "The Virtue of Feeling and the Feeling of Virtue," in *Feminist Ethics*, ed., Caludia Card (Lawrence: University press of Kansas 1991), 228–229.

51. Sara Ahmed, *The Cultural Politics of Emotion* (Edinburgh: Edinburgh University Press, 2014, second edition), 121.

52. Berenice Fisher, "Guilt and Shame in the Women's movement: The Radical Ideal of Action and its Meaning for Feminist Intellectuals," *Feminist Studies*, 10: 2 (1984), 205.

53. As quoted in D. Karthikeyan, "Exploitation of Women is Complex in Nature," *The Hindu*, April 27, 2008.

54. Sashinungla, "Feminist Theory, Politics of Sovereignty and Epistemic Injustice," *Journal of Indian Council of Philosophical Research*, New Delhi. (forthcoming).

55. Helen Longino, *The Fate of Knowledge* (Princeton, NJ: Princeton University Press, 2002), 129.

56. Audre Lorde, ed., "Age, Race, Class, and Sex: Women Redefining Difference," in *Sister Outsider: Essays and Speeches* (Freedom, CA: Crossing Press, 1984), 124, 114–24.

57. Ahmed, *The Cultural Politics*, 178.

58. Fisher, "Guilt and Shame," 206.

59. Ahmed, *The Cultural Politics*, 178.

60. Medina, *The Epistemology of Resistance*, 29–43.

61. In his first mention of shame in *Nichomachean Ethics*, Aristotle also refers to shame as a "mean condition." However, it is important to note that Aristotle articulated his definition of shame within the context of his applied pragmatics of political rhetoric. Also, I do not agree with his presentation of *aidos* as "fitting only in the young." I'm only referring to his presentation of shame as a "*mean* (emphasis added) condition [. . .] involving the feelings": indicative of its complex and paradoxical nature. (See Aristotle, 2002, 21–78).

62. Aristotle, *Rhetoric*, trans. W. Rhys Roberts (New York: Routledge, 2004), 72.

63. Aristotle, 2002, 21–36.

64. See Steven A. Murphy, and Sandra Kiffin-Petersen, "The Exposed Self: A Multilevel Model of Shame and Ethical Behavior," *Journal of Business Ethics*, 4 (2017), 657–675; See also Nathan Harris, "Shame, Ethical Identity and Conformity: Lessons from Research on the Psychology of Social Influence," in *Emotions, Crime and Justice*, eds. Susanne Karstedt, Ian Loader and Heather Strang (Oxford: Hart Publishing, 2011), 193–209.

65. Bartky, *Shame and Gender*, 96–97.

66. Locke, "Shame and the Future," 148.

67. Medina, *The Epistemology of Resistance*, 1–13.

68. *Shame*, in S. N. Terkel and R. S. Duval eds., *Encyclopedia of Ethics* (New York: Facts on File, 1999), 248.

69. See Michel Foucault, *The Hermeneutics of the Subject*, ed. Frederic Gros. trans. Graham Burcheel, (New York: Palgrave, 2005).

70. Emmanuel Levinas, *Otherwise than Being: Or Beyond Essence*, trans. Alphonso Lingis (Pittsburg: Duquesne UP, 1998), 4.

71. Spelman, "The Virtue of Feeling," 228–29.

72. Foucault, *The Hermeneutics*, 252.

73. The famous slogan of the French Revolution, now a universal aspiration: Liberty, Equality, Fraternity. It is interesting to note that fraternity, brotherhood, has become completely muted if not sidelined in contemporary discourse.

74. See Sisir Kumar Das, ed. *The English Writings of Rabindranath Tagore: A Miscellany*, Vol. 3 (New Delhi: Sahitya Akademi, reprint, 2006), 315.

BIBLIOGRAPHY

Ahmed, Sara. *The Cultural Politics of Emotion*. Edinburgh: Edinburgh University Press, 2014, (second edition).

Aristotle. *Nicomachean Ethics*. Translated by Joe Sachs. Newburyport, MA: Focus Publishing R. Pullins Company, 2002.

———. *Rhetoric*. Translated by W. Rhys Roberts. New York: Routledge, 2004.

Bartky, Sandra. "Shame and Gender." In *Femininity and Domination: Studies in the Phenomenology of Oppression*. New York: Routledge, 1990.

Ben Ze'ev, Aaron. *The Subtlety of Emotions*. Cambridge, MA: MIT Press, 2000.

Collins, Patricia Hill. *Black Feminist Thought: Knowledge, Consciousness and the Politics of Empowerment*. New Delhi (Special Indian edition): Routledge, 2017.

Das, Sisir Kumar, ed. *The English Writings of Rabindranath Tagore: A Miscellany*, *Volume Three*. New Delhi: Sahitya Akademi (reprint), 2006.

Else-Quest, Nicole M; Ashley Higgins; Carlie Allison; Lindsay C. Morton. "Gender Differences in Self-Conscious Emotional Experience: A Meta-Analysis." *Psychological Bulletin*, 138: 5 (2012 September), 947–81.

Ellison, Ralph, *Invisible Man*. New York: Vintage Press, 1947/1995.

Fischer, Clara. "Gender and the Politics of Shame: A Twenty-First Century Feminist Shame Theory." *Hypatia*, 33: 3 (Summer 2018), 371–383.

Fisher, Berenice. "Guilt and Shame in the Women's Movement: The Radical Ideal of Action and its Meaning for Feminist Intellectuals." *Feminist Studies*, 10:2 (1984), 185–212.

Freud, Sigmund. *New Introductory Lectures on Psychoanalysis: The Standard Edition*. New York: W. W. Norton, 1965.

Fricker, Miranda. *Epistemic Injustice: Power and the Ethics of Knowing*. New York: Oxford University Press, 2007.

Foucault, Michel. *The Hermeneutics of the Subject*. Edited by Frederic Gros. Translated by Graham Burcheel. New York: Palgrave, 2005.

Gilligan, James. *Violence: Our Deadly Epidemic and its Causes*. New York: Putnam Books, 1997.

Harris, Nathan. "Shame, Ethical Identity and Conformity: Lessons from Research on the Psychology of Social Influence." In Susanne Karstedt, Ian Loader and Heather Strang, eds. *Emotions, Crime and Justice*. Oxford: Hart Publishing, 2011, 193–209.

Higgins, Nicholas. "Shame on You: The Virtuous Use of Shame in Aristotle's Nicomachean Ethics." *Expositions*, 9: 2 (2015), 1–15.

Karthikeyan, D. "Exploitation of Women is Complex in Nature." In *The Hindu*, April 27, 2008.

Levinas, Emmanuel. *Otherwise than Being: Or Beyond Essence*. Translated by Alphonso Lingis. Pittsburg: Duquesne UP, 1998.

Locke, Jill, "Shame and the Future of Feminism," *Hypatia*, 22: 4 (2007), 156–162.

Longino, Helen. *The Fate of Knowledge*. Princeton: Princeton University Press, 2002.

Lorde, Audre, ed. "Age, Race, Class, and Sex: Women Redefining Difference," In *Sister Outsider: Essays and Speeches*. Freedom, CA: Crossing Press, 1984. 114–24

Maibom, Heidi L. "The Descent of Shame." *Philosophy and Phenomenological Research*, 80: 3 (2010), 21–41.

Makau, Josina M. "An Outcome-Based Approach to Ethical Communication." Transcript of Keynote Address at the Fifth National Communication Ethics Conference. Michigan: Gull Lake, May 1998.

Man, Bonnie, "Femininity, Shame, and Redemption" *Hypatia*, 33: 3 (Summer 2018), 402–17.

Manion, Jennifer. "Girls Blush, Sometimes: Gender, Moral Agency, and the Problem of Shame." *Hypatia* 18: 3 (2003), 21–41.

———. "The Moral Relevance of Shame." *American Philosophical Quarterly* 39:1 (2002), 73–90.

Medina, Jose. *The Epistemology of Resistance: Gender and Racial Oppression, Epistemic Injustice, and Resistant Imaginations*. New York: Oxford University Press, 2013.

Metcalf, Robert. "The Truth of Shame-consciousness in Freud and Phenomenology." *Journal of Phenomenological Psychology*, 31: 1 (2000), 1–18.

Murphy, Steven A. and Sandra Kiffin-Petersen. "The Exposed Self: A Multilevel Model of Shame and Ethical Behavior." *Journal of Business Ethics*, 4 (2017), 657–675.

Nathanson, Donald L. *Shame and Pride: Affect, Sex, and the Birth of the Self*. New York: Norton, 1992.

Noddings, Nel. *Starting at Home: Caring and Social Policy*. Berkeley: University of California, 2002.

———. *The Maternal Factor: Two Paths to Morality*. Berkley: University of California Press, 2010.

Nussbaum, Martha. *Hiding from Shame: Disgust, Shame, and the Law*. Princeton, NJ: Princeton University Press, 2004.

Probyn, Elspeth. *Blush: The Face of Shame*. Minneapolis: University of Minnesota University Press, 2005.

Sashinungla and Atashee Chatterjee Sinha, eds. "Gender, Tradition and Modernity: A Critical Feminist Analytic." In *Tradition and Modernity: Essays on Women of India*, 150–163. Kolkata, New Delhi: Jadavpur University, Suryodaya Books, 2015.

———. "Feminist Theory, Politics of Sovereignty and Epistemic Injustice," *Journal of Indian Council of Philosophical Research*, New Delhi. (forthcoming)

Schneider, Carl D. *Shame, Exposure, and Privacy*. New York: W.W Norton & Co., 1977.

Shame, in S. N. Terkel and R. S. Duval eds. *Encyclopedia of Ethics*. New York: Facts on File, 1999.

Solomon, Robert. *True to Our Feelings: What Our Emotions are Really Telling Us*. New York: Oxford University Press, 2007.

———. "The Emotions of Justice." *Social Justice Research*, 3:4 (1989), 345–374.

Spelman, Elizabeth. "The Virtue of Feeling and the Feeling of Virtue." In *Feminist Ethics*, Caludia Card ed., Lawrence: University Press of Kansas, 1991, 213–232.

Tangey, June and Ronda L. Dearing. *Shame and Guilt*. New York: The Guilford Press, 2002.

Taylor, Gabriele. *Pride, Shame, and Guilt: Emotions of Self-Assessment*. Clarendon: Oxford University Press, 1985.

Thapar, Suruchi. "Women as Activist; Women as Symbols: A Study of the Indian Nationalist Movement." *Feminist Review*, 44 (1993), 471–88.

Thomason, Krista K. *Naked: The Dark Side of Shame and Moral Life*. Oxford: Oxford University Press, 2018.

Tomkins, Silvan. *Shame and its Sisters: A Silvan Tomkins Reader*. Edited by Eve Kosofsky Sedgewick and Adam Frank. Durham, NC: Duke University Press, 1995.

Williams, Bernard. *Shame and Necessity*. Berkeley: University of California Press, 1993.

6

Epistemic Injustice, Shame, Humility, and Sharing the Epistemic Space with Others

An Investigation of Epistemic Justice as a Virtue

Vojko Strahovnik

This chapter has three broad aims. The first one is to suggest a possible positioning of epistemic justice within a specific framework of epistemic virtues that distinguishes between core and ancillary epistemic virtues. According to this account, epistemic justice is to be understood as an ancillary epistemic virtue. The second aim is to examine the hybrid nature of epistemic justice encompassing both epistemic and moral aspects and do this in a way that smoothly figures in with the previously developed view on epistemic justice. The third aim is to relate such an understanding of epistemic justice to (epistemic) humility.

EPISTEMIC INJUSTICE AND THE
VIRTUE OF EPISTEMIC JUSTICE

The discussion about epistemic justice as an epistemic virtue gains intense momentum after the seminal work by Miranda Fricker, in particular her book *Epistemic Injustice: Power and the Ethics of Knowing* (2007). In pursuing the three aims mentioned above, I will follow her initial characterization of the phenomena of epistemic injustice and virtue of epistemic justice closely, despite being fully aware that her work faced both important criticisms and amendments, in particular concerning the inclusion of the dimension of social institutions and other types of epistemic injustice.[1]

The debate on epistemic justice followed an initial unearthing of the phenomenon of a specific form of injustice that is distinctively *epistemic* in its nature and cannot be reduced to other forms, for example, to particular forms of moral injustice (e.g., injustice concerning matters related to knowledge whereby an unequal and unjust distribution of wealth leads to significantly diminished educational opportunities for those at the lower end of such distribution). Epistemic injustice as a distinctively epistemic kind of injustice can be best characterized by appeal to a specific form of wrong(ness), meaning that "any epistemic injustice wrongs someone in their capacity as a subject of knowledge, and thus in a capacity essential to human value,"[2] and hampers an individual's self-understanding and self-development. Epistemic injustice can befall an individual or a group in their capacity as epistemic agents. In order to aptly understand epistemic injustice, we must turn our attention to the epistemic practices of epistemic agents as situated within the community or society, their social identity, and social and power relations. Fricker underscores the methodological primacy of epistemic injustice, which thus precedes considerations about epistemic justice, since by focusing on the manifest forms of epistemic injustice, it is easier to understand its essence than to focus attention only on gaps and to understand epistemic *injustice* as a lack of epistemic *justice*.

Epistemic injustice occurs in two main forms, namely, in *testimonial* and *hermeneutical* injustice. Testimonial injustice is a form of epistemic injustice that typically arises in situations when the speaker is given less credibility by the hearer than otherwise, and this is caused by the prejudice on the hearer's part. In this case, a specific epistemic wrong occurs because the speaker is *wronged* in their capacity as a possessor and giver of knowledge—as an informant. Hermeneutical injustice is a form of epistemic injustice that stems from a gap in collective hermeneutical resources—a gap, that is, in the shared tools of social interpretation—where it is no accident that the cognitive disadvantage created by this gap impinges unequally on different social groups. The disadvantaged members are

> hermeneutically marginalized—that is, they participate unequally in the practices through which social meanings are generated. This sort of marginalization can mean that our collective forms of understanding are rendered structurally prejudicial in respect of content and/or style: the social experiences of members of hermeneutically marginalized groups are left inadequately conceptualized and so ill-understood, perhaps even by the subjects themselves; and/or attempts at communication made by such groups, where they do have an adequate grip on the content of what they aim to convey, are not heard as rational owing to their expressive style being inadequately understood.[3]

The epistemic wrong or harm implicated here is that such situated hermeneutical inequality prevents the victims of such epistemic injustice from making sense of an experience which is strongly in their interests to render intelligible. In this regard, the victims are wronged in their capacity as subjects of social understanding.

After this initial setup with the brief presentation of the phenomenon of epistemic injustice, we can move on to the discussion about the virtue of epistemic justice as a pertinent remedy. As Fricker extrapolates, *epistemic justice* can thus be considered an epistemic *virtue* (or a set of virtues) that enables us to surmount epistemic injustice on our part, for example, as the hearers in the case of testimonial injustice. *Testimonial justice* is an epistemic virtue (in fact, hybrid, i.e., epistemic and moral) that enables the hearer to be in a shared epistemic space in such a way that the influence of identity prejudice on the hearer's credibility judgment is detected and corrected for. Fricker emphasizes testimonial sensibility as a form of rational sensitivity.[4] One can develop it through attention to testimonial practices, adequate or reliable attribution of credibility, careful perception and perception of cognitive status, etc. *Hermeneutical justice* is an epistemic (in fact, hybrid) virtue that enables the hearer to exercise a reflexive critical sensitivity to any reduced intelligibility incurred by the speaker, owing to a gap in collective hermeneutical resources. This brief exposition of the critical phenomena in the debate leads to a broader framework for thinking about our epistemic agency and epistemic virtues and then turns to the issues concerning a comprehensive understanding of the virtue of epistemic justice.

EPISTEMIC AGENCY AND
EPISTEMIC RESPONSIBILITY

One of the suppositions that enables the development of the comprehensive approach to epistemic injustice and the virtues that remedy it is a recognition of *epistemic agency*, since *virtuousness* is a feature of agents, and is a matter of exercising their agency in specific ways and being disposed to exercise it in those ways. There are several possible ways to think about the epistemic agency and what it relates to, and my proposal will be quite wide ranging in respect to which epistemic practices are included into the domain of exercising agency.[5]

Belief fixation, that is, the formation and maintenance of beliefs, surely is at the heart of our epistemic endeavors and practices and establishing an epistemic agency, for it then enables extending agency to other aspects as well, at least to the ones that presuppose beliefs (e.g., judgment, reflection, deliberation). Frequently, there is a certain skepticism associated with belief fixation concerning it being agentive since it is presupposed that we do not have *voluntary control* over beliefs we form.[6] According to such views, genuine agency can merely be attributed to actions that precede or accompany belief fixation such as focusing our attention to various bits of evidence, looking through a window, turning our head in order to see what is around the corner, etc.

There are several characteristics of *agency in general* (from the experiential perspective), but one that is perhaps most problematic concerning the epistemic agency is thus voluntariness, which belief fixation seems to lack. However, although episodes of belief formation are experienced as *non*-voluntary, they are not experienced as *in*-voluntary (as a polar opposite of voluntariness). Such experiences are *agentive* in a broad sense, because of the important similarities they bear to experiences of ordinary voluntary agency. Belief fixation shares with ordinary practical agency other important experiential aspects, which are briefly presented in what follows.

First, belief fixation involves an appreciation of reasons *qua* reason, that is, *epistemic* reasons as considerations experienced as evidentially favoring a belief. Second, there is a sort of *motivational pull* or *grip* involved, in which we are pulled-toward-*believing* by our evidence-appreciation and this grip is experienced as desire-independent and *categorically* imperatival. Epistemic reasons figure here as authoritative and call for forming a particular belief at hand in response to them, leaving aside any of our preexisting desires or interests.[7] Third, the phenomenology of belief fixation resembles voluntary agentive phenomenology by involving a reasons-related "rational becausal" aspect. This is not an aspect as-of passively experiencing one's state of evidence-appreciation state-causing the onset of one's belief. Instead, it is an experience as-of *autonomously* (albeit nonvoluntarily) exercising one's epistemic agency and competency, that is, one's capacity to appreciate epistemic reasons, to be pulled-toward-believing by such appreciation, and to be gripped into belief because of being so pulled. Fourth, experiencing oneself being thus *autonomously gripped*—gripped into belief by one's appreciation of the evidential force of one's reasons—has the phenomenological aspect of *self as source*. Self-sourcehood is experienced as the aspect as-of *purposively* exercising one's rational epistemic agency, where the reason for which one adopts the belief, for example, the epistemic "purpose" for thus believing, is one's appreciation of one's evidence for it. Fifth, some of the mentioned aspects, for example, reasons appreciation, can be present only implicitly in the conscious experience of forming a belief and operate from the rich and dynamic cognitive background. Sixth, belief fixation phenomenology features a distinctive kind of means-ends teleological structure—with beliefs aiming at truth—similar to the one concerning practical agency, when one acts, for example, in response to a desire.[8]

The above-described experiential aspects are tightly *intertwined* in the experience of epistemic agency. From the perspective of epistemic agency and epistemic agent, we can use the metaphor of being situated in the *space of reasons*[9] and being responsive to these reasons. This experiential context includes aspects of being able to appreciate epistemic reasons and being in the grip of the authority of epistemic reasons ("being gripped into believing"), recognizing and experiencing oneself as believing in light of these reasons and being able to respond to queries regarding beliefs formed in this manner. Such an extended conception of epistemic agency that sees us as responsible for how and what we believe is entirely in line with Fricker's conception of epistemic agency and epistemic agents that also emphasizes the aspect of responsibility.

CORE AND ANCILLARY EPISTEMIC VIRTUES

In this next step, the discussion will move from epistemic agency to epistemic virtues. An intermediate step in this exposition will be a discussion about *epistemic rationality*. I take beliefs to be psychological commitment-states of a certain kind. In believing that the cat is sleeping on the mat, I am psychologically committed to this being the case. A belief is a commitment to the world's actually being this way. In the words of Bernard Williams, a belief "*aims*" at truth.

When I say that beliefs aim at truth, I have particularly in mind three things. First:

> that truth and falsehood are a dimension of an assessment of beliefs as opposed to many other psychological states or dispositions. (. . .) [T]o believe that p is to believe that p is true. To believe that so and so is one and the same as to believe that that thing is true. This is the second point under the heading of "beliefs aim at truth. (. . .)" The third point, closely connected with these, is: to say "I believe that p" itself carries, in general, a claim that p is true.[10]

Because this is the nature of belief, believing thus has a constitutive *telos*: to believe only what is *true*, and to do so via a *reliable belief-forming process*. I will call this the *truth telos*.[11]

Humans are *perspectivally situated*, as epistemic agents, with respect to (i) their available *evidence* and (ii) their own deep *epistemic sensibility* regarding makes-likely-true relations. This situatedness, together with the fact that belief constitutively has the truth telos, generates a nested hierarchy of constitutively connected epistemic means and ends, with the final end (the top level in the hierarchy) being believing only what is true by deploying a reliable process of belief fixation. At the bottom of this hierarchy is the end of forming our beliefs as based on *epistemic seemings*, that is to say, to believe on *our best take* given what seems to us true in a given case. (I consider an epistemic *seeming*, vis-à-vis a proposition p, to be a state of mind consisting in p's seeming to be true.) In the middle ground, there are other levels of rationality, which also include one's subjective epistemic sensibility and objective rationality, where we believe what is subjectively or objectively highly likely to be true. One can be fully *rational* at the top level (perhaps by deploying a process that is entirely reliable by pure chance), without being rational at the lower levels. However, when it comes to epistemic *virtuousness*, one cannot be virtuous at a higher level without also being virtuous at the lower levels as well, since virtue cannot be a matter of pure chance. Aligning our beliefs to the truth as much as possible is what I will call *epistemic virtuousness*, which includes *core epistemic virtues* representing the mentioned levels of the hierarchy. Possessing a core epistemic virtue is a matter of consistently forming one's beliefs in a manner that exhibits the features definitive at a specific level in that hierarchy. Beliefs that are formed in a way that exhibits these features thus qualify as being virtuously formed. The modifier "core" is intended to indicate two things about these virtues: first, they are constitutively linked to the truth telos, and second, they concern one's best means for synchronically pursuing the truth telos. Since successive levels of core epistemic virtue are embedded each within the next, one cannot synchronically improve the overall quality of one's belief fixation.

Nonetheless, there is a host of ways that various *ancillary epistemic virtues* can improve the overall quality of an epistemic agent's belief fixation, thereby rendering the agent more effective in the pursuit of truth. I call these further virtues "ancillary" not because they are of secondary importance vis-à-vis the truth telos, but because they *enhance*—rather than displace—belief fixation. These include epistemic virtues that are usually discussed in virtue epistemology literature, virtues such as impartiality, intellectual sobriety, and intellectual courage, perceptiveness, synoptic grasp, intellectual honesty, sense for alternative points of view both perceptual and theoretical, salience recognition and focus, practical wisdom, creativity, epistemic conscientiousness, self-awareness, self-scrutiny, inquisitiveness, reflectiveness, contemplativeness, curiosity, impartiality, intellectual perseverance, diligence, etc.[12]

There are several (nonexclusive) categories of ancillary epistemic virtues. In the first category are virtues that help us, over time, to be better epistemic agents in the sense that we form our belief in close alignment with the top level of core epistemic virtuousness (attaining the truth). Also, there is a category of ancillary epistemic virtues that help us attain the so-called power of beliefs, which is that we form and maintain a significant number of beliefs worth having, that is, beliefs relevant and useful for us. There is also a category of ancillary epistemic virtues that help us in attaining other epistemic goals, like understanding or wisdom. Not all ancillary epistemic virtues will be relevant in all epistemic situations. Some situations, but not others, call for epistemic courage. Different situations, but again not others, call for epistemic integrity—or for epistemic humility, or for inquisitiveness, etc. The more one exhibits such ancillary virtues, the more likely it is that one's epistemic seemings will align with one's epistemic sensibility, and the more likely it is that both one's epistemic seemings and one's epistemic sensibility will align with objective rationality and reliably form true beliefs—all of which will tend to counteract any prejudice and implicit bias that one might otherwise exhibit in one's belief fixation.

Before moving on, I wish to highlight another dimension of the proposed account of believing, the teleological structure of belief and epistemic virtuousness. The distinction between the top level where truth as the telos of belief is in the forefront and the lower level of experiential epistemic rationality where our epistemic seeming, responsiveness to reasons, and epistemic sensibility are in the foreground, enables this view to account for both *teleological* and *deontological* epistemic evaluation. In ordinary life, and also in epistemological theorizing, epistemologically evaluative concepts are employed in ways that exhibit both deontological and teleological aspects. When one's epistemic-evaluative purposes are oriented more closely to the *telos* itself (attaining the truth), the teleological aspect looms large. When one's epistemic-evaluative purposes are oriented more closely to the lower levels and to exercising one's epistemic agency in a duly responsible way, the deontological aspect looms large. Such a deontological aspect is a deeply ingrained aspect of the ordinary epistemic-evaluative practice, which includes having and expressing epistemic reactive attitudes toward others and/or toward oneself. For example, when one realizes one has made some reasoning blunder or has failed to appreciate the now-fairly-obvious import of one's available evidence, one doesn't just wish that one's belief-forming processes had operated in a more reliable way; rather, one feels ashamed of oneself for having exercised one's epistemic agency poorly.

EPISTEMIC JUSTICE AS AN ANCILLARY EPISTEMIC VIRTUE

Given the framework of epistemic virtuousness presented above, epistemic justice is to be understood as an ancillary epistemic virtue. This means that it assists us to align our beliefs with truth. It is thus a virtue that operates *diachronically*. That is to say, it enables us to improve over time and increase our epistemic sensibility, in particular to evidence or reasons that have to do with assigning proper credibility to ourselves and others, including overcoming of prejudice (testimonial epistemic justice), and to be more sensitive to possible gaps in communicative intelligibility and other phenomena that could be incurred due to particular social identities and a gap in hermeneutical resources.

Both, testimonial and hermeneutical justice thus occupy a corrective role, and such a role fits well with the above-presented framework since attaining epistemic justice could be seen as one possible epistemic goal or a moral goal (or both). In the first case, one could label this as a mixed epistemic goal that consists of two aspects, namely (i) the purely epistemic goal of believing only what is true and (ii) the epistemic goal of attaining epistemic justice. In the second case, one could label this as a hybrid *epistemic-cum-moral* goal that consists of epistemic goals and a moral goal of justice. The apt pursuit of epistemic justice thus involves not only core epistemic virtuousness alone, but rather the interaction of core epistemic virtuousness, ancillary epistemic virtues, and moral virtues.

Again, this is fully in line with Fricker's basic idea of epistemic justice being a *hybrid* virtue, having both truth and justice as an ultimate end, while at the same time one can still think of, testimonial epistemic justice as having a more immediate end of neutralizing prejudice in one's credibility judgments. "The hybridity of the virtue stems from the fact that negative identity prejudice—the thing whose impact on judgement the virtue neutralizes—is both an intellectual and an ethical offence. With this in mind, it seems entirely fitting that the virtue which guards against it should turn out to be both ethical and intellectual in character, at once a virtue of truth and a virtue of justice."[13]

This overall proposal is also one possible answer to the challenge of how to relate discussion about epistemic injustice to more traditional approaches in epistemology. This also aligns with the worry that Fricker is exposing in relation to postmodernism and reduction of knowledge to relations of power.

> Suspicion of the category of reason per se and the tendency to reduce it to an operation of power actually pre-empt the very questions one needs to ask about how power is affecting our functioning as rational subjects; for it eradicates, or at least obscures, the distinction between what we have a reason to think and what mere relations of power are doing to our thinking. If one has an interest in how questions of justice might present themselves in relation to our epistemic practices, then the reductionist tendency obscures essential distinctions between, say, rejecting someone's word for good reason and rejecting it out of mere prejudice.[14]

This is not to say that one can understand epistemic injustice without reference to social identities and power relations, but that such understanding must include traditional epistemic categories. The interpretation of epistemic justice as an ancillary epistemic virtue in relation to mixed or hybrid epistemic goals enables us to situate the discussion about epistemic injustice within such a context.

EPISTEMIC JUSTICE AND EPISTEMIC HUMILITY

In this concluding section, I will relate epistemic justice with the virtue of *epistemic humility*. Humility is a multifaceted concept and cannot easily be captured within a one-dimensional or straightforward theoretical model. James Kellenberger identifies seven elementary dimensions that we generally associate humility with. These are: (i) having a low opinion of oneself, (ii) having a low estimate of one's merit, (iii) having a modest opinion of one's importance or rank, (iv) lack of self-assertion, for example, in cases where one has made a contribution or has merit, (v) claiming little as one's desert, (vi) having or showing a consciousness of one's defects or proneness to mistakes, and (vii) not being overly proud, haughty, condescending, or arrogant.[15] A conception of relational humility emphasizes that humility is closely associated with behavior within a particular relationship that demonstrates that as a humble person we have an accurate perception of the evaluation of ourselves, and that in being humble we are other-oriented in the sense that we consider the well-being of the other at least as much as one's own and that this engenders trust in others. Humility includes intrapersonal, interpersonal, and motivational dimensions or aspects.[16]

Many definitions of humility explicitly include both *moral* and *epistemic* aspects. Cole Wright and colleagues define humility as the inherent psychological position of oneself or toward oneself, which includes cognitive and moral alignment, calibration, or situatedness.[17] From an epistemic point of view, this means that it is the understanding and actual experience of ourselves as a limited and fallible being, which is part of a larger creation and thus has a limited and incomplete viewpoint and the perception of the whole that surpasses this being. Humility in this sense also restricts our tendency to experience exceptionality, unique distinction, or superiority, as well as restricting giving priority to our beliefs (it also restricts the claims of special recognition or commendation and the establishment of supremacy over others). Intellectual humility is both a virtue and a stance that involves having appropriate, modest, and nonhaughty view of our intellectual abilities, advantages, and disadvantages, that we can adequately consider and evaluate various ideas and positions in a way that includes respect for others who disagree with us, etc. It enables us to establish an apt relationship to ourselves as epistemic agents, which among other things includes that we are open to new facts and insights, an ability to integrate new knowledge into our existing knowledge, an ability to assess the relevance of this knowledge, etc. At the same time, it puts us into an epistemic space with others in a way that allows nonhaughty, noncondescending, and solidary participation in the common pursuit of truth—as in public discourse. Understood in this way we can understand intellectual humility as an epistemic virtue.

One can also point out a close connection between humility and *moral shame*. Kellenberger puts forward a suggestion that humility can be understood in terms of two distinct core contrasts, the first being the contrast between humility and pride and the second the contrast between humility and what he calls the pride-shame axis.[18] According to the first understanding, humility is seen as the opposite of pride, arrogance, egotism, smugness, vanity, and this is reflected in the fact that we often simply equate humility with the absence of pride. According to the second contrast, humility is the opposite of pride-shame axis. Both pride and shame are closely connected with our self-image, self-concern, and our centeredness on ourselves. On the other hand, humility is in a sense not marked with an exclusive focus on the self; quite the contrary, it rejects such a focus and thus cannot be placed on the mentioned axis.

> If humility and the pride–shame axis of self-concern are operative as core contrasts, so that humility in this expression excludes both pride and shame, then shame would not be the response to a failure in humility or to other failures. Failure in exterior or interior behaviour would instead result in dismay, sadness, down-heartedness, guilt, or an awareness of having sinned, of having violated one's relationship to another or to God, none of which must by its nature be tied to self-concern and a pride ideal.[19]

Humility in this sense is thus associated with a kind of *eradication of the self*, and such a view was most decidedly stated by Simone Weil: "True humility is the knowledge that we are nothing in so far as we are human beings as such, and, more generally, in so far as we are creatures."[20] We can gain important insights by focusing our attention on the relationship between humility and (moral) shame. I specifically underscore two aspects of shame, namely, reflective situatedness aspect and status aspect. Reflective situatedness aspect enables one to relate a given action or a given part of one's character to the self as a whole. This is what Bernard Williams pointed out when arguing that shame (as opposed to guilt) affects our whole personality, for example, by implying a certain feeling in which our whole personality is revealed to ourselves as diminished, weakened, lessened, or damaged. Furthermore, shame helps us understand our relationship to our (wrong) actions or lapses; proper, reflective cultivation of shame can disclose this relationship and establish or rebuild our personality and identity, both at the individual level and at the level of community.[21]

Shame focuses on ourselves. It calls for confrontation with ourselves, for improvement and for progress that must be achieved and also establishes a relationship between us and the other(s). If one transposes this reflective situatedness aspect to intellectual humility, one must thus focus first on the relationship between a belief, a set of beliefs, or a part of our epistemic system and the epistemic self as a whole. This enables an overall framework for the epistemic appraisal that relates both mentioned parts. The second aspect of rank also closely associates shame and humility. After a given wrongdoing (either by an individual or by a group), what a proper cultivation of moral shame and humility must establish is a recognition, in the form of truthful moral responsiveness and humble attentiveness, of the other (in this case victim(s) of the wrongdoing) as fully equal to us, as having a full human status.[22] Shame and humility impose such leveling of statuses and ranks, recognizing others as being our equals. If one understands epistemic or intellectual norms, standards, and ideals as social norms, which function to direct, adjust, and control our intellectual endeavors, then humility and shame can function as part of such a system of regulation. Promoting intellectual humility fosters overall recognition of our epistemic limitations, stimulates overcoming of our intellectual flaws, and motivates us to achieve epistemic ideals and to flourish intellectually. Just as moral virtues, emotions, and reactive attitudes can play the role of promoting pro-social, moral behavior, the idea is that one can draw parallels for intellectual virtues and epistemic reactive attitudes, including intellectual humility and shame. Intellectual correlates of shame and humility also play an important role in leveling out the public discourse field by emphasizing participants' equal status in the sense that impedes *preexisting biases, prejudices, stereotypes*, and so on.

The virtue of intellectual humility is one of the epistemic virtues, which also plays a particularly important role in overcoming epistemic injustice. I have already highlighted two central aspects of humility, namely, self-situatedness in a given (moral or epistemic) space, and status, which we ascribe to ourselves and to others in this space. Humility includes an accurate view of self and an awareness of my limitations, our interpersonal stance is other-oriented, rather than self-focused; it is characterized by respect for others, rather than superiority or arrogance and an ability to restrain egotism (i.e., self-oriented emotions such as pride or shame). It situates us in *epistemic space* with others in a way, which enables nonarrogant and solidary cooperation in the search for the truth. Promoting intellectual humility fosters overall recognition of our epistemic limitations, stimulates overcoming of our intellectual flaws, and motivates us to achieve epistemic ideals (including epistemic justice) and to flourish intellectually. Intellectual humility reveals itself as an important facet of epistemic justice.

Such understanding of humility also goes beyond the framework of virtue or character traits, and it already, among other things, stands in the domain of attitudes, gestures, practices, and traditions. Humility, compassion, or other similar responses in the light of good are not emotional responses in the sense of something that accompanies our beliefs about the suffering of the other, but a form of recognition of this suffering,[23] just as epistemic justice is not merely a *response* to epistemic injustices, but also *a form of recognition* of them. As such it enables us to confront three important and interrelated challenges that modern times are pressing on us, namely, the question of: how do we position ourselves in relation to others in epistemic space (as possible authorities or sources of knowledge), how do we assign proper credibility (the problem of testimonial epistemic injustice), and how do we cultivate apt understanding both of ourselves as well as others (the problem of hermeneutical epistemic injustice).

NOTES

1. Cf. Rachel McKinnon, "Epistemic Injustice," *Philosophy Compass* 11, no. 8 (2016): 43746; Elizabeth Anderson, "Epistemic Justice as a Virtue of Social Institutions," *Social Epistemology* 26, no. 2 (2012): 163–73.

2. Miranda Fricker, *Epistemic Injustice. Power and the Ethics of Knowing* (New York: Oxford University Press, 2007), 5.

3. Ibid., 6–7.

4. Ibid., 69.

5. An outline of such a view was developed in Terry Horgan, Matjaž Potrč and Vojko Strahovnik, "Core and Ancillary Epistemic Virtues," *Acta Analytica* 33, no. 3 (2018): 295309.

6. Hilary Kornblith claims that

"the appeal to epistemic agency seems to be nothing more than a bit of mythology. A demystified view of belief acquisition leaves no room for its operation. Epistemic agency does not seem to be a feature of belief acquisition generally. But any attempt to tie agency to reflection seems doomed, since our agency is involved only in actions which provide input to our belief-forming processes, not in the formation of belief itself. And this therefore provides us with no more reason to speak of agency in the case of belief acquisition than the fact that eating is undertaken voluntarily gives us reason to speak of digestion as a manifestation of our agency." (Hilary Kornblith, "Epistemic Agency," in *Performance Epistemology: Foundations and Applications*, ed. Miguel Ángel Fernández Vargas [New York: Oxford University Press, 2016], 177.)

7. William Tolhurst defends a view, similar to this. Epistemic seemings have the feel of truth, the feel of a state whose content reveals how things really are. Their felt givenness typically leads one to experience believing that things are as they seem as an objectively fitting or proper response to the seeming. "Seemings are mental

states in which the subject experiences a felt demand to believe the content of the state" (William Tolhurst, "Seemings," *American Philosophical Quarterly* 35, no. 3 (1998): 298).

8. For elaboration of these phenomenological aspects of belief fixation, see Horgan, Potrč and Strahovnik, "Core and Ancillary Epistemic Virtues." For epistemological relevance of some of these aspects, see Terry Horgan and Matjaž Potrč, "The Epistemic Relevance of Morphological Content," *Acta Analytica* 25, no. 2 (2010): 155–73.

9. Such a use of the notion "the space of reasons" is Sellarsian in spirit. Sellars related it to the notion of knowledge in stating that "in characterizing an episode or a state as that of knowing, we are not giving an empirical description of that episode or state; we are placing it in the logical space of reasons, of justifying and being able to justify what one says" (Wilfrid Sellars, "Empiricism and the Philosophy of Mind," in *Science, Perception, and Reality* (London: Routledge and Kegan Paul, 1956), §36).

10. Bernard Williams, *Problems of the Self* (Cambridge: Cambridge University Press, 1973), 137.

11. Some virtue theorists, invoking one common mode of usage in ancient philosophy, sometimes use the term "skopos" for the immediate target of a specific act, while reserving "telos" for a general aim of "doing well." Cf. Julia Annas, "The Structure of Virtue," in *Intellectual Virtue: Perspectives from Ethics and Epistemology*, ed. Michael DePaul and Linda Zagzebski (New York: Oxford University Press, 2003).

12. James Montmarquet, "Epistemic Virtue," *Mind* 96, no. 384 (1987): 482–97; Juli Eflin, "Epistemic Presuppositions and their Consequences," *Metaphilosophy* 34, no. 1/2 (2003): 48–68; Jason Baehr, *The Inquiring Mind. On Intellectual Virtues and Virtue Epistemology* (New York: Oxford University Press, 2011), 21.

13. Fricker, *Epistemic Injustice*, 124.

14. Ibid., 3.

15. James Kellenberger, "Humility," *American Philosophical Quarterly* 47, no. 4 (2010): 321–322.

16. Davis et al., "Humility and the Development and Repair of Social Bonds: Two Longitudinal Studies," *Self and Identity* 12 (2013): 61.

17. Cole Wright et al., "The Psychological Significance of Humility," *Journal of Positive Psychology* 12, no. 1 (2016): 4.

18. Kellenberger, "Humility," 324–31.

19. Ibid., 330.

20. Simone Weil, *Gravity and Grace* (London: Routledge, 1952), 40.

21. Bernard Williams, *Shame and Necessity* (Berkeley: University of California Press, 1993), 94.

22. Raimond Gaita, *A Common Humanity: Thinking about Love and Truth and Justice* (Abingdon: Routledge, 2000), 102.

23. Raimond Gaita, "Morality, Metaphysics, and Religion," in *Moral Powers, Fragile Beliefs: Essays in Moral and Religious Philosophy*, ed. Joseph Carlisle, James Carter and Daniel Whistler (New York: Continuum, 2011), 11.

BIBLIOGRAPHY

Anderson, Elizabeth. "Epistemic Justice as a Virtue of Social Institutions." *Social Epistemology* 26, no. 2 (2012): 163–73.

Annas, Julia. "The Structure of Virtue." In *Intellectual Virtue: Perspectives from Ethics and Epistemology*, edited by Michael DePaul and Linda Zagzebski, 15–33. New York: Oxford University Press, 2003.

Baehr, Jason. *The Inquiring Mind: On Intellectual Virtues and Virtue Epistemology.* New York: Oxford University Press, 2011.

Cole Wright, Jennifer, Thomas Nadelhoffer, Tyler Perini, Amy Langville, Matthew Echols and Venezia Kelly. "The Psychological Significance of Humility." *Journal of Positive Psychology* 12, no. 1 (2016): 3–12.

Davis, Don E., Everett L. Worthington Jr., Joshua N. Hook, Robert A. Emmons, Peter C. Hill, Richard A. Bollinger and Daryl R. Van Tongeren. "Humility and the Development and Repair of Social Bonds: Two Longitudinal Studies." *Self and Identity* 12 (2013): 58–77.

Eflin, Juli. "Epistemic Presuppositions and their Consequences." *Metaphilosophy* 34, no. 1/2 (2003): 48–68.

Fricker, Miranda. *Epistemic Injustice: Power and the Ethics of Knowing.* New York: Oxford University Press, 2007.

Gaita, Raimond. *A Common Humanity: Thinking about Love and Truth and Justice.* Abingdon: Routledge, 2000.

Gaita, Raimond. "Morality, Metaphysics, and Religion." In *Moral Powers, Fragile Beliefs: Essays in Moral and Religious Philosophy*, edited by Joseph Carlisle, James Carter and Daniel Whistler, 3–28. New York: Continuum, 2011.

Horgan, Terence, Matjaž Potrč and Vojko Strahovnik. "Core and Ancillary Epistemic Virtues." *Acta Analytica* 33, no. 3 (2018): 295–309.

Horgan, Terry and Matjaž Potrč. "The Epistemic Relevance of Morphological Content." *Acta Analytica* 25, no. 2 (2010): 155–73.

Kellenberger, James. "Humility." *American Philosophical Quarterly* 47, no. 4 (2010): 321–36.

Kornblith, Hilary. "Epistemic Agency." In *Performance Epistemology: Foundations and Applications*, edited by Miguel Ángel Fernández Vargas, 168–83. New York: Oxford University Press, 2016.

McKinnon, Rachel. "Epistemic Injustice." *Philosophy Comp*ass 11, no. 8 (2016): 437–46.

Montmarquet, James. "Epistemic Virtue." *Mind* 96, no. 384 (1987): 482–97.

Sellars, Wilfrid. "Empiricism and the Philosophy of Mind." In *Science, Perception, and Reality*, 129–194. London: Routledge and Kegan Paul, 1956.

Tolhurst, William. "Seemings." *American Philosophical Quarterly* 35, no. 3 (1998): 293–302.

Weil, Simone. *Gravity and Grace.* London: Routledge, 1952.

Williams, Bernard. *Problems of the Self.* Cambridge: Cambridge University Press, 1973.

Williams, Bernard. *Shame and Necessity.* Berkeley: University of California Press, 1993.

PART 3

GENDER VIOLENCE IN THE MEDIA

7

Obligations to Expose and the Responsibility to Protect

Journalistic Ethics for Reporting on Wartime Sexual Violence

Janet H. Anderson and Benjamin Duerr

The work of journalists has revealed the invisible pain of large-scale sexual violence in wars, but victims are raising their voices against inappropriate interview questions, sensationalist reporting, and the life-threatening exposure of their personal stories. As practitioners, we want to shed light on the tension between our ambition to uncover injustices and the need to protect victims from further harm. We have the power to expose violence and its perpetrators. But by shaming the perpetrators, media are often shamed themselves.

In the first section of this chapter, we explain the role of the media in revealing the realities of sexual violence, which has always been surrounded by a culture of silence. We examine the tensions between the obligation to expose and the responsibility to protect. We then explain how current ethics codes have been developed and show the specific gaps which have led journalists to not take the needs of sexual violence survivors into consideration. We also look at the small grassroots initiatives from journalists embedded in or closely working in survivors' networks and consider how they deal with ethical issues. Finally, we argue that the global media system, based on inequalities between the local and the international level, creates a thirst for sensation, leads to selective reporting, and incites inappropriate behavior. While journalists have individual moral responsibilities, we highlight the systemic pressures under which they operate: a system which transfers the pressure to attract attention at the international level to the victims on the ground, who are forced to tell stories of intimate violence for the sake of creating a shock effect for a global audience. We highlight the power of ethics in media and demonstrate how written and unwritten codes can give power back to victims. We argue that the introduction of a new journalistic ethic of respect and compassion is necessary to avoid greater harm for victims of sexual violence and assault. Our analysis is grounded in the extensive work on both sides: as and with journalists, as well as with victims of sexual violence.

The case of Luvungi, a village in the outmost east of the Democratic Republic of the Congo (DRC), illustrates the tensions we seek to explore in this chapter. At the end of July 2010, rebels moved into the village and raped several persons.[1] Aid workers who treated the victims told international media how the rebels engaged in the "systematic raping of women."[2] In the days following the attack, major international outlets, including global news agencies, covered the mass rape. The *New York Times* ran a story on its cover page.[3] For several weeks, reporters and photographers traveled to Luvungi to interview the victims.[4]

The media reports about Luvungi shifted international attention to the curse of wartime rape. As Laura Heaton noted, the events caused not only an influx of journalists into the village, but also of high-level dignitaries who put the issue on the political agenda.[5] Around the time of the Luvungi attack, sexual violence was emerging as a "hot topic" on the international agenda.[6] The Office of the Special Representative of the Secretary-General on Sexual Violence in Conflict had been created just a few months earlier,[7] and, while it is hard to draw causal relations, the attention on Luvungi raised by media reports might have helped to focus and keep the attention of the international community on the broader issues of wartime rape. In other situations, the impact of global media appears to have been even more direct: in the former Yugoslavia, there are indications that an increase in media attention led to a decrease in systematic rape.[8] A UN report highlighted the increase in news stories in 1992 and the beginning of 1993, and a dramatic decline of the number of registered cases in the months following the media attention, thus suggesting a correlation and the power of the commanders to halt the use of rape, as they were shamed publicly.[9] The power of the media to expose and to shame the perpetrators also elevates large-scale sexual violence to an issue of international concern; journalists played a crucial role in revealing this hidden aspect of war and shaping the response of the international community.

In the process of shaming others, however, the media were shamed themselves in the former Yugoslavia, Luvungi, and beyond. In the former Yugoslavia, the growing media attention forced women to repeatedly tell their story. Many experienced severe traumatization and feared awakening bad memories, some felt exploited, others attempted suicide after interviews.[10] In Luvungi, news reports included accounts with pornographic undertones. The French glossy *Paris Match* produced a report published under the headline "Les femmes violées de Luvungi" ("The Raped Women of

Luvungi"), including a two-sided group photo of women and children, which appears insensitive to stigmatization and the vulnerability of children.[11]

In Iraq, a recent study revealed widespread unethical reporting practices. In their research with Yazidi women survivors, Johanna E. Foster and Sherizaan Minwalla found inappropriate and unethical behavior of journalists on a wide scale, including the exposure of women and girls which put them at risk of reprisals, and emotional consequences resulting from telling their stories many times.[12] Yazidi women recounted interviews in which journalists pressured them to speak, asked deeply intimate questions, or took pictures against the will of the women. Interestingly, however, Foster and Minwalla also describe how women felt the worth and usefulness of telling their story to a global audience, in the hope the media reports could lead to political support. They found that "women who survived captivity were almost twice as likely as otherwise displaced Yazidi women to state the importance or value in telling the world what happened to them through journalists."[13] The frustration the women interviewed felt about a lack of response from the international community, however, returned to the media because of unfulfilled expectations or, in some cases, unfulfilled promises by journalists. Sixty percent of the women interviewed in the study "expressed serious dissatisfaction with the global response to the crisis in the wake of what they understood to be widespread media attention," Foster and Minwalla wrote.[14] According to the researchers, women who had been in captivity felt particularly betrayed: "Not only did they, personally, receive little to nothing in return for sharing their stories, but they believed that nothing useful has come for the Yazidis in captivity and displacement as a result of the disclosure of their personal traumas."[15] The study with Yazidi women and girls shows the highly complex and multilayered processes between journalists and survivors of wartime sexual violence. More generally, the examples of the former Yugoslavia, DRC, and Iraq highlight the fine line between shaming perpetrators and being shamed as reinforcing the emotional violence experienced by survivors.

In the next sections, we describe the development of journalistic professional codes, and we reflect how relatively little attention is paid to training ethics in the broader sphere of international media support and training. We will argue that a new journalistic ethic of respect and compassion could help to address several structural deficiencies.

Journalistic ethical codes have traditionally derived from the debates around the role of the media in Western democracies and how journalists provide a counter to power. Writing for the United Nations Educational, Scientific and Cultural Organization (UNESCO) on how the media can self-regulate, Andrew Puddephatt, for example, links debates around regulation of the media with journalists' rights: "freedom of expression has long been regarded as a fundamental right, one which is important in itself and also helps to defend other rights and freedoms."[16] The Media Development Indicators of UNESCO reinforce this framework which judges the diversity and efficacy of a media ecosystem based on the space provided for freedom of expression. Puddephatt further synthesizes a number of reports into media freedom to argue against regulation of media spaces by the state, because of the close linkages between the right to freedom of expression and free media. But he also asks: how then is the media's own accountability to be achieved? He argues that self-regulation by the media itself is the answer because it "preserves independence of the media and protects it from partisan government interference." He further argues that self-regulation is more efficient, cheaper, and may also encourage more compliance through peer pressure.[17] Thus, the development of media ethical codes is inherently connected to the media making its own rules about how it should operate, in order to protect its role as a space for free expression.

The earliest attempts to draft a code of journalistic ethics date back nearly a century to one adopted by the first Pan-American Press Conference held in Washington in 1926.[18] The first International Federation of Journalists, also established in 1926 adopted a professional "honor code" and after its refoundation in 1952, developed a professional ethical code for journalists and adopted a declaration of journalists' duties in 1954.[19]

A range of national media institutions in subsequent years have also developed their own codes of conduct. These codes have in common a focus on basic common journalistic principles which are widely taught in journalism schools—a respect for truth and for the right of the public to truth; the right to fair comment and criticism; factual and objective reporting; the use of fair methods to obtain information; the willingness to correct mistakes; respecting the confidentiality of sources. In an example of a standard teaching text, quoted by Puddephatt,[20] these definitions are considered essential elements in any journalistic ethical code:

- Journalism's first obligation is to the truth.
- Its first loyalty is to the citizens.
- Its essence is discipline of verification.
- Its practitioners must maintain an independence from those they cover.
- It must serve as an independent monitor of power.
- It must provide a forum for public criticism and compromise.
- It must strive to make the news significant, interesting, and relevant.
- It must keep the news comprehensive and proportional.
- Its practitioners must be allowed to exercise their personal conscience.

A sampling of these lists through a range of sources shows that they have traditionally nothing to say about how journalists should cover sexual and gender-based crimes during conflict. They are focused on the role of the press and the nature of freedom of expression. Other limitations also apply. Their very voluntary nature suggests they are difficult to uphold: sanctions are limited, with unions or professional bodies having the potential to punish or expel members, but there would still be no prohibition against anyone continuing to work as a journalist.

These gaps in journalistic codes and their lack of relevance to the current situations faced by journalists have not gone unexamined by academics. Stephen J. A. Ward has termed[21] current journalism ethics as "parochial," and sees these codes as mainly based on a highly practical approach which "no longer serves journalism, the study of journalism, or the public of journalism," because they lack connection to the full range of new media in which journalists work and the global nature of communication. Jane B. Singer has also been arguing that journalism is undergoing such rapid and dramatic structural change that traditional ethical guidelines need to be reconsidered.[22] She situates her analysis in a study of the practical changes that journalism has been undergoing with the rise of digital and social media—the collapse of previously reliable business models, restructuring of newsrooms, and new formats being experienced by journalists. She suggests that the ethical reconsiderations will be needed in the light of the new relationship being forged between journalists and "the people formerly known as the audience,"[23] using the influential terminology developed by New York University professor Jay Rosen in his combative manifesto which called on mainstream media organizations to recognize the power-shift inherent in the change in consumption and more especially production patterns constituted by the rise of social media platforms. According to these academics and practitioners, journalist codes of ethics—as encoded over the last 100 years—are feeling relatively limited, irrelevant, and powerless.

If the encoded versions of ethics are proving outdated, are new sets of ethics nevertheless being inculcated within the journalism profession, via those concerned with professional development of journalists and teachers of journalism? In particular are issues of gender, power, and sexual violence—whether in conflict or outside—being taught?

One example comes from Louise North who finds that in Australian undergraduate journalism courses, no programs offer a unit that specifically addresses the portrayal of women in the media or, importantly, the gendered production of news and gendered newsroom culture.[24] She acknowledges that there are increased numbers of women in newsrooms, but says "[t]he increased presence of women in newsrooms hasn't encouraged the substantive changes in newswork practices that many scholars and journalists had predicted." She further believes that "many of those educators currently teaching journalism curriculum are not aware of, interested in, or informed about gender issues in relation to journalism production and media content."

Such a sweeping claim requires further study. She acknowledges herself that straightforward "content analysis does risk missing the overall sense of a body of communications, if we do no more than offer quantitative summaries of content."[25] A more detailed research to uncover the way that gender issues are taught in journalism schools and how students are being encouraged to conceptualize media's role in supporting meta-narratives and how media reflects dominant culture—which may well be gendered critiques—could offer different insights in pedagogy. Other courses within a university may be offering gender studies which students then apply in their journalism classes. On the other hand, the choice not to use the word gender in titles or descriptions of courses may also be a strong indicator of resistance within journalism educators to acknowledging inequalities or the legitimacy of gendered approaches.

Nevertheless, there is journalistic interest in, and consistent coverage of stories of violence against women. As Pamela Mejia has suggested, small studies of the actual coverage of sexual violence by journalists have shown that the majority of stories are linked to criminal justice milestones such as a trial or an arrest.[26] And the framing of such news regularly perpetuates "rape myths." Rarely do journalists look for new sources or angles. Rarely do they explore areas where change is needed. By focusing mostly on themes of process and punishment, they fail to cover "efforts to stop sexual violence before it starts."[27]

Media toolkits produced by local organizations such as the Chicago Taskforce on Violence against Girls & Young Women[28] have offered specialized approaches to addressing the sexual and gender violence lacunae evident in journalist ethical practice. The efforts are focused on challenging language, providing positive examples of reportage, and enabling journalists to consider how they too perpetuate issues of stigma around rape and sexual violence. The regularity with which these toolkits are created indicates the problems are not easy to eradicate and, to some degree, may be structural in nature.

The violations of ethical codes and moral norms described earlier are committed by individual journalists, but the problem lies deeper than in the behavior of individuals. As Majid Tehranian has pointed out, the individual journalist works within the context of institutional cultures,[29] which are in turn part of national and international regimes. Their behavior is influenced and guided by the forces of the system.

Unequal power relations between the local and the global translate into reporting behavior and are particularly strong in reports on sexual violence. International media hold the power to shape discourses and set the agenda, often with little involvement of and engagement with the survivors and local communities. Often, through our research, we have noted that international media can struggle to reflect the long-term impact of war on *ordinary* citizens, and even more on marginalized groups, including women and girls. The plight of thousands of women who have been raped over the past decades in the DRC goes largely unnoticed. Except for a few incidents, such as Luvungi, Walikale, and Kavumu, large-scale sexual violence in the DRC rarely receives the attention of the global media.

Journalists operate in an environment in which they are often forced to play according to the rules of the system. News is not an objective, independent reflection of reality, but a social construct influenced by the history and interests of a society.[30] Unless a war, or a particular aspect of a conflict, is of national interest to a country, chances are slim the media will pay critical attention to it. The dominance of Western news media—American, British, French, and German—leads to a narrow focus as these media primarily serve the population in these countries and therefore take Western-centered angles.[31] They tend to focus on major events of a conflict,[32] such as the outbreak, a major battle, and the signing of a peace agreement. The complexities, underlying causes, historical contexts, and social structures—in the case of large-scale sexual violence in the DRC, for example, the patriarchal society and the normalization of violence[33]—are overlooked in the explanations and analyses.

The dynamics of power inequality and selective reporting influences journalistic practice on the ground. The need to create a story that reaches the threshold of international attention and to "sell" the news to far-away audiences and advertisers forces journalists to focus on certain, particularly gruesome features of a conflict.[34] War, as Teresa Joseph put it, needs to be a "spectacle."[35] Journalists, therefore, tend to tell stories of mass rape in sensational and trivial ways. As we have tried to convey in this chapter, survivors regularly appear in narrow, stereotypical roles as disempowered victims.

The work of journalists has advanced the knowledge about and the investigation of wartime sexual violence, facilitated the pursuance of justice of the victims and, through reporting, created a climate of naming and shaming. But without a shift in the way international media perceive conflict, the bitter dynamics of ignorance, selectivity, and international dominance over local survivors will continue to stimulate unethical journalistic practice.

NOTES

1. "Final Report of the Fact-Finding Missions of the United Nations Joint Human Rights Office into the Mass Rapes and Other Human Rights Violations Committed by a Coalition of Armed Groups along the Kibua-Mpofi Aix in Walikale Territory, North

Kivu, from 30 July to 2 August 2010, July 2011," United Nations Office of the High Commissioner for Human Rights (OHCHR), https://www.refworld.org/docid/4e15 99bc2.html.

2. Michelle Faul, "Some 200 Women Gang-Raped Near Congo U.N. Base," *AP*, August 23, 2010, https://www.cbsnews.com/news/some-200-women-gang-raped-near -congo-un-base/. The number of victims has been heavily disputed between humanitarian organisations, the United Nations, and observers, and ranged from 6 to 387. See Laura Heaton, "What Happened in Luvungi?" *Foreign Policy* 199 (March/April 2013); Micah Williams and Will Cragin, "Our Experience in Luvungi," *Foreign Affairs*, May 3, 2013, https://foreignpolicy.com/2013/03/05/our-experience-in-luvungi/.

3. Jeffrey Gettleman, "Mass Rapes in Congo Reveals U.N. Weakness," *The New York Times*, October 3, 2010, https://www.nytimes.com/2010/10/04/world/africa/04 congo.html.

4. Laura Heaton, "The Risks of Instrumentalizing the Narrative on Sexual Violence in the DRC: Neglected Needs and Unintended Consequences," *International Review of the Red Cross* 96, no. 894 (June 2014): 627.

5. Heaton, "The Risks of Instrumentalizing the Narrative," 628.

6. Anette Bringedal Houge and Kjersti Lohne, "End Impunity! Reducing Conflict-Related Sexual Violence to a Problem of Law," *Law & Society Review* 51, no. 4 (2017): 757.

7. "About the Office – United Nations Office of the Special Representative of the Secretary-General on Sexual Violence in Conflict," Office of the Special Representative of the Secretary-General on Sexual Violence in Conflict, https://www .un.org/sexualviolenceinconflict/about-us/about-the-office/.

8. Todd A. Salzman, "Rape Camps as a Means of Ethnic Cleansing: Religious, Cultural, and Ethical Responses to Rape Victims in the Former Yugoslavia," *Human Rights Quarterly* 20, no. 2 (May 1998): 357.

9. "Final Report of the Commission of Experts Established Pursuant to Security Council Resolution 780 (1992)," par. 237, http://www.icty.org/x/file/About/OTP/un_ commission_of_experts_report1994_en.pdf.

10. "Rape and Abuse of Women in the Territory of the Former Yugoslavia: Report of the Secretary-General, E/CN.4/1994/5," par. 13. https://documents-dds-ny.un.org/ doc/UNDOC/GEN/G93/141/36/PDF/G9314136.pdf?OpenElement.

11. Mariana Grépinet and Alvaro Canovas, "Les femmes violées de Luvungi," *Paris Match*, 10 September 2010, https://www.parismatch.com/Actu/International/ Les-femmes-violees-de-Luvungi-151296.

12. Johanna E. Foster and Sherizaan Minwalla, "Voices of Yazidi Women: Perceptions of Journalistic Practices in the Reporting on ISIS Sexual Violence," *Women's Studies International Forum* 67 (2018): 56.

13. Ibid., 58.

14. Ibid.

15. Ibid.

16. Andrew Puddephatt, "The Importance of Self Regulation of the Media in Upholding Freedom of Expression," *UNESCO, Communication and Information Debate Series*, N. 9, BR/2011/PI/H/4, February 2011.

17. Ibid., 12.
18. Cees J. Hamelink, "Media Ethics and International Organizations," in *The Handbook of Global Communication and Media Ethics*, ed. Robert S. Fortner and P. Mark Fackler (Hoboken: John Wiley & Sons, 2011), 441.
19. Ibid.
20. Puddephatt, "The Importance of Self-Regulation," 13.
21. Stephen J. A. Ward, "Philosophical Foundations for Global Journalism," *Journal of Mass Media Ethics* 20, no. 1 (2005): 3–21.
22. Jane B. Singer, "Journalism Ethics amid Structural Change," *Daedalus* 139, no. 2 (2010): 89–99.
23. Press Think, "The People Formerly Known as the Audience," http://archive.pressthink.org/2006/06/27/ppl_frmr.html.
24. North, Louise, "The Gender 'Problem' in Australia Journalism Education," *Australian Journalism Review* 32, no. 2 (2010): 103.
25. Ibid., 105.
26. Pamela Mejia, Alisha Somji, Laura Nixon, Lori Dorfman and Fernando Quintero, "What's Missing from the News on Sexual Violence? An Analysis of Coverage, 2011–2013," *Berkeley Media Studies Group*, http://www.bmsg.org/resources/publications/issue-22-sexual-violence-news-analysis-2011-2013.
27. Ibid., 18.
28. Chicago Taskforce on Violence Against Girls & Young Women, "Reporting on Rape and Sexual Violence: A Media Toolkit for Local and National Journalists to Better Media Coverage," http://www.chitaskforce.org/wp/wp-content/uploads/2012/10/Chicago-Taskforce-Media-Toolkit.pdf
29. Majid Tehranian, "Peace Journalism: Negotiating Global Media Ethics," *The Harvard International Journal of Press/Politics* 7, no. 2 (April 2002): 58.
30. Teresa Joseph, "Mediating War and Peace: Mass Media and International Conflict," *India Quarterly* 70, no. 3 (2014): 232.
31. Mel McNulty, "Media Ethnicization and the International Response to War and Genocide in Rwanda," in *The Media of Conflict: War Reporting and Representation of Ethnic Violence*, ed. Tim Allen and Jean Seaton (London: Zed Books, 1999): 269.
32. Joseph, "Mediating War and Peace," 23.
33. See, for example, Sara Meger, "Rape of the Congo: Understanding Sexual Violence in the Conflict in the Democratic Republic of Congo," *Journal of Contemporary African Studies* 28, no. 2 (April 2010): 130.
34. Joseph, "Mediating War and Peace," 234.
35. Ibid.

BIBLIOGRAPHY

Bringedal Houge, Anette and Kjersti Lohne. "End Impunity! Reducing Conflict-Related Sexual Violence to a Problem of Law." *Law & Society Review* 51, no. 4 (2017): 755–89.

Chicago Taskforce on Violence Against Girls & Young Women. "Reporting on Rape and Sexual Violence: A Media Toolkit for Local and National Journalists to Better Media Coverage." Accessed September 9, 2019. http://www.chitaskforce.org/wp/wp-content/uploads/2012/10/Chicago-Taskforce-Media-Toolkit.pdf.

Faul, Michelle. "Some 200 Women Gang-Raped Near Congo U.N. Base." *AP*, August 23, 2010. Accessed September 29, 2019. https://www.cbsnews.com/news/some-200-women-gang-raped-near-congo-un-base/.

Foster, Johanna E. and Sherizaan Minwalla. "Voices of Yazidi Women: Perceptions of Journalistic Practices in the Reporting on ISIS Sexual Violence." *Women's Studies International Forum* 67 (2018): 53–64.

Gettleman, Jeffrey. "Mass Rapes in Congo Reveals U.N. Weakness." *The New York Times*, October 3, 2010. Accessed September 22, 2019. https://www.nytimes.com/2010/10/04/world/africa/04congo.html.

Grépinet, Mariana and Alvaro Canovas. "Les femmes violées de Luvungi." *Paris Match*, 10 September 2010, Accessed April 17, 2019. https://www.parismatch.com/Actu/International/Les-femmes-violees-de-Luvungi-151296.

Hamelink, Cees J. "Media Ethics and International Organizations." In *The Handbook of Global Communication and Media Ethics*, edited by Robert S. Fortner and P. Mark Fackler, 434–451. Hoboken: John Wiley & Sons, 2011.

Heaton, Laura. "The Risks of Instrumentalizing the Narrative on Sexual Violence in the DRC: Neglected Needs and Unintended Consequences." *International Review of the Red Cross* 96, no. 894 (June 2014): 625–639.

———. "What Happened in Luvungi?" *Foreign Policy*, no. 199 (March/April 2013): 32–36.

Joseph, Teresa. "Mediating War and Peace: Mass Media and International Conflict." *India Quarterly* 70, no. 3 (2014): 225–240.

McNulty, Mel. "Media Ethnicization and the International Response to War and Genocide in Rwanda." In *The Media of Conflict: War Reporting and Representation of Ethnic Violence*, edited by Tim Allen and Jean Seaton, 268–286. London: Zed Books, 1999.

Meger, Sara. "Rape of the Congo: Understanding Sexual Violence in the Conflict in the Democratic Republic of Congo." *Journal of Contemporary African Studies* 28, no. 2 (April 2010): 119–135.

Mejia, Pamela, Alisha Somji, Laura Nixon, Lori Dorfman and Fernando Quintero. "What's Missing from the News on Sexual Violence? An Analysis of Coverage, 2011–2013." *Berkeley Media Studies Group*. Accessed September 8, 2019. http://www.bmsg.org/resources/publications/issue-22-sexual-violence-news-analysis-2011-2013.

North, Louise. "The Gender 'Problem' in Australia Journalism Education." *Australian Journalism Review* 32, no. 2 (2010): 356–373.

Office of the Special Representative of the Secretary-General on Sexual Violence in Conflict. "About the Office – United Nations Office of the Special Representative of the Secretary-General on Sexual Violence in Conflict." Accessed April 21, 2019. https://www.un.org/sexualviolenceinconflict/about-us/about-the-office/.

Press Think. "The People Formerly Known as the Audience." Accessed September 8, 2019. http://archive.pressthink.org/2006/06/27/ppl_frmr.html.

Puddephatt, Andrew. "The Importance of Self Regulation of the Media in Upholding Freedom of Expression." *UNESCO Communication and Information Debate Series* 9, BR/2011/PI/H/4 (February 2011).

Salzman, Todd A. "Rape Camps as a Means of Ethnic Cleansing: Religious, Cultural, and Ethical Responses to Rape Victims in the Former Yugoslavia." *Human Rights Quarterly* 20, no. 2 (May, 1998): 348–378.

Singer, Jane B. "Journalism Ethics amid Structural Change." *Daedalus* 139, no. 2 (2010): 89–99.

Tehranian, Majid. "Peace Journalism: Negotiating Global Media Ethics." *The Harvard International Journal of Press/Politics* 7, no. 2 (April 2002): 58–83.

United Nations Office of the High Commissioner for Human Rights (OHCHR). "Final Report of the Fact-Finding Missions of the United Nations Joint Human Rights Office into the Mass Rapes and Other Human Rights Violations Committed by a Coalition of Armed Groups along the Kibua-Mpofi Aix in Walikale Territory, North Kivu, from 30 July to 2 August 2010, July 2011." Accessed April 6, 2019. https://www.refworld.org/docid/4e1599bc2.html.

United Nations Security Council. "Final Report of the Commission of Experts Established Pursuant to Security Council Resolution 780 (1992)." Accessed April 14, 2019. http://www.icty.org/x/file/About/OTP/un_commission_of_experts_rep ort1994_en.pdf.

———. "Rape and Abuse of Women in the Territory of the Former Yugoslavia: Report of the Secretary-General, E/CN.4/1994/5." Accessed April 14, 2019. https://documents-dds-ny.un.org/doc/UNDOC/GEN/G93/141/36/PDF/G9314136.pdf?OpenElement.

Ward, Stephen J. A. "Philosophical Foundations for Global Journalism." *Journal of Mass Media Ethics* 20, no. 1 (2005): 3–21.

Williams, Micah and Will Cragin. "Our Experience in Luvungi." *Foreign Affairs*, May 3, 2013. Accessed September 29, 2019. https://foreignpolicy.com/2013/03/0 5/our-experience-in-luvungi/.

8

A Voice of Our Own

Retelling the Stories of Gender-Based Violence in the Lebanese Media

Rouba El Helou-Sensenig

INTRODUCTION

This chapter considers the current state of discourse on media coverage of GBV in the Middle East.[1] It begins with a brief portrayal of the most recent training tools and teaching programs on GBV for media practitioners in Lebanon, and will be followed by a theoretical overview of the relationship between this author and cases of violence in society today. As a journalist, trainer, educator, and researcher in the field, I am personally affected by the topic on a variety of levels. The reflections offered in this chapter are attempts to demonstrate the interrelatedness between reporting, power, and the experiences of male and female victims and perpetrators.

Although Lebanese media, when dealing with GBV, has as a rule maintained a superficial level of professional decorum, many of these reports ended up leaving the recipients perplexed, unable to construct a proper gendered understanding of the context, the culture, and the signs of the produced language. Therefore, and in order to address gendered topics made silent and invisible through centuries of tradition in the MENA, a uniquely adapted approach is necessary, which is not dependent upon the predominant codes in the Global North. I will examine two extreme cases of GBV as portrayed in the Arab media, in which I reflect on how those cases may be perceived by the public, and how I, as a researcher have been impacted by this topic within my own family, with respect to my adopted stepdaughter. Further, I explain how auto-ethnography is a powerful methodological tool when dealing with such complexity.

Up until this point in time, gendered topics and gender mainstreaming (GM) were rarely seen as an integral part of communication and journalism in the MENA. On the one hand, training and awareness-raising on socially salient topics in Lebanon were generally carried out by journalism, media studies, or communication schools. On the other hand, training and awareness-raising on gendered topics specifically has remained the prerogative of feminists and women's rights advocacy organizations. This meant that both sectors were working parallel to each other, seldom pooling their resources and as a result were often disconnected from each other. In this context, it is important to mention that the Lebanese Journalists Union (LJU) (which is supposed to include all workers in the various media sectors in Lebanon), and the Press Order (comprised of the owners of daily newspapers), have never mentioned, let alone tackled, these important topics.

Gender matters, whether it is related to citizens, immigrants or refugees, the workplace, organized religion, the home or the public sphere. It matters because people reflect upon their lives differently; they recall memories and events differently.[2] Accordingly, V. Spike Peterson specifies gender as "a socially imposed and internalized lens through which individuals perceive and respond to the world."[3] Peterson maintains that gender shapes "concepts, practice and institutions in identifiable gendered ways."[4] These distinctions are not only socially different. Female activities are generally represented as inferior to male-dominated activities, such as paid work. In the following, I approach the gender perspective from the viewpoint of an activist and as a researcher. The questions and inquiries raised here are underpinned by my long-standing activist and scholarly motivations, both personally and professionally.

In October 2016, after a two-and-a-half year interim period, the Lebanese parliamentarians finally elected the thirteenth president of the republic Michel Aoun, ending a long-standing political impasse.[5] Immediately thereafter a new government was formed leading to a new development for the country. The new cabinet for the first time included a ministry of state for women's affairs. However, and in an unexpected twist, the appointed head of this ministry turned out to be a man. One of the declared objectives of the new ministry was a campaign to increase and promote women's participation in politics. "While Lebanon may seem liberal from the outside, it is shockingly behind when it comes to the implementation of women's rights."[6] Since 1963, a mere fourteen women have been able to enter the parliament in Lebanon. Since its founding as an independent state in September 1920, Lebanon has witnessed many extraordinary and unsettling times. Lebanon distinguished itself from other countries in the Middle East through its strong tradition of press freedom and a culture of media pluralism, in addition to its vibrant civil society which played a major role in promoting women's issues and gender equality. However, and despite all of the above, Lebanon is considered to be a highly discriminatory country when it comes to women's rights within the religious courts, citizenship laws, workplace issues, and domestic violence.[7] Feminist organizations and journalism schools worked parallel to each other on freedom, equality, and social justice issues for decades. Eventually, bridging the knowledge gap between the NGO sector and academia regarding gender dynamics became a crucial need. The examples to be dealt with at the end of this chapter represent just a few cases in which this divide was bridged.

In the following, I will portray the current situation in Lebanon focusing on the needs in the field of media and education. I will also reflect on how these topics have influenced me personally and shaped the way I processed knowledge and recognized the need for social change. I hope to illustrate how the personal is not only political, but how science and knowledge are power and that ignoring, that is, being silent and blind, on this interrelatedness has dire consequences for the progress of gender equality.

VISIBLE DARKNESS

Now resting, bless'd and hallowd the Seav'nth day,
As resting on that day from all his work,
But not in silence holy kept; the Harp
Had work and rested not, the solemn Pipe,
And Dulcimer, all Organs of sweet stop,
All sounds on Fret by String or Golden Wire
Temper'd soft Tunings, intermixt with Voice
Choral or Unison; of incense Clouds
Fuming from Golden Censers hid the Mount.[8]

John Milton's poems have always provided me with profound inspiration; works of art which demonstrate how fragile our world is, how obsessed one becomes by fighting or trying to destroy the other, and most importantly what it means to be free in a mortal world like ours. In *Paradise Lost*, Milton retells a Biblical story: the one of Adam and Eve, along with Satan and his followers. Full of uncontrollable pride, Satan decided to revenge a silent God. Through this poem, Milton infiltrated metaphorical images and paradoxical symbolism of light/darkness, good/evil, and silence/music as a chaotic and unclear world where silence and darkness are enveloped by evil. The idea of "speaking silences" can be applied to stories and narratives of survivors and victims of GBV not only in Lebanon or in the MENA region but all over the world—an issue which I critically consider as a feminist and an activist-scholar.

At the time of this writing, a shocked Arab and international media were following the murder of a young Palestinian woman, Israa Gharib, by her family members. She was brutally beaten by her male relatives leading to a serious spinal injury.[9] The reason for this violent attacked turned out to be a post she had made on her Instagram account, a picture with a young man in a coffee shop who had earlier asked Israa's family for her hand in marriage. The Gharib family immediately attempted to challenge the narrative of the killing by blaming her death on a heart attack and that she was supposedly possessed by an evil spirit.[10] As a response, numerous hashtags spread on social media platforms calling for justice. #WeAreAllIsraa and #JusticeforIsraa trended for weeks. Civil society human rights activists and feminists, along with many other nongovernmental organizations, called for not only an investigation into the occurrence surrounding Israa's death, but also for just due process and convictions condemning the numerous crimes committed. Rashida Tlaib, the Palestinian American U.S. congresswoman, tweeted "Isra's death illustrates an ever-present toxic masculinity and control over women's bodies and lives."[11] Many also rejected the media term "honour killing," which they considered to be a travesty and the result of an unjust societal infrastructure and an imbalance of power that undermines women's rights and interests.[12]

Israa's death is not a singular event. It is, however, a case that caught the media's attention in a unique way. One of the most shocking aspects of this murder was the revelation of a voice message exchange via WhatsApp between Israa and her female cousin Riham. The latter's accusations in a WhatsApp message were reported in the media to be the reason behind the family's rage against their daughter. The conversation between the two female cousins was massively shared on social media and in news coverage on the incident. In it we could hear Riham telling her cousin that her conduct, her life style, and makeup is against their tradition, but her father and brothers are bribed and placated through the money she was earning as a successful makeup artist.

Traditionally, the superior positions and dominance experienced by males in their families were due to their control of the means of production, whether historically in primitive hunting and gathering or feudal societies or more recently during the industrial period and up until the present. Women were portrayed as being silent and invisible with a lack of voice in their families, as well as within the public social and economic structures. As opposed to the silent and invisible women of the past, Israa had a voice and was seen earning money for her family, which however still attempted to retain control over her newly established resources. Srilatha Batliwala, the Indian social activist and scholar, analyzes the rise of power structures which create injustice, inequality, exclusion, discrimination, marginalization, and violence in her latest publication *All about Power.* Batliwala wonders if activists realize that when they tackle all forms of injustices in society they are "actually trying to change power equations."[13] She argues that economic empowerment for women and awareness campaigns on the rights of girls "have helped to some extent"; however, these strategies focusing on the means of production seem to address "the symptoms, not the root causes."[14] Might combating silence and invisibility in the public and private spheres be as important as accessing economic resources?

Referring back to Milton in his *Paradise Lost* below is an excerpt from his poem describing hell:

At once as far as angel's ken he views
The dismal situation waste and wild,
A dungeon horrible, on all sides round
As one great furnace flamed, yet from those flames
No light, but rather darkness visible
Served only to discover sights of woe,
Regions of sorrow, doleful shades, where peace
And rest can never dwell, hope never comes
That comes to all.[15]

Milton presents here a compelling vision of hell. Satan is observing his new surroundings in a visible silent darkness—a realm in which voice and light have been banned, which is reminiscent of the world in which Israa's family—both male and female—hoped she would live if she wanted to stay alive. Unlike Satan, Israa's hell is not of her own making, but reinforced by her family through the visible darkness of structural oppression and ultimate subjugation to the will by the family-clan.

Analyzed with a gendered lens, this poem has often been highly criticized by feminist scholars who argue that Eve's representation in the poem lacks intellectual powers.[16] By giving her an invisible voice—and thus making her silent and invisible—her essence of being and discourse is shaped and created by a patriarchal authority. She is thus, like Israa, a victim and not a subject able to act in her own right. However, Matthew Jordan sees the opposite in this female character. "Eve is in significant respects an equal, a companion for Adam with considerable powers of reasoning and, while a beautiful, sexual being, is by no means the hollow temptress whose presence in earlier accounts of the fall renders them so inconsistent."[17] According to the scholar William Shullenberger, "to read Milton well becomes a trail of identity for the reader,"[18] as Milton's texts change based on the generations and the readers' assumptions. Shullenberger considers it absurd to criticize Milton from a feminist perceptive "for the way of feminist thinking was at best obscure and marginal in the seventeenth century."[19] Therefore, an assumption of Milton's understanding of the significance of gender identity will continue to be developed based on a variety of intersectional perspectives that were hardly accessible in Milton's time of writing.

From her hospital bed, a few days before she was killed, Israa posted a picture declaring that she was fine and strong. Did she really think that she could win out over patriarchy? Would she have attempted to narrate her own story if she had been allowed to survive? Did she realize the overwhelming dominance of the layered power structures working together against her? Didn't she know that "visible silent darkness" was destined to be her fate? How normal is it in our part of the world for people to witness the fall of a patriarchy, to see the "dungeon horrible, on all sides round" be effectively challenged, indeed, to hear a subaltern speak loudly? Can things be put back together in a way that the reality of those who are suffering can be changed?

In his early masterpiece *Things Fall Apart*, Chinua Achebe, the renowned Nigerian novelist, identifies different forms of oppression and patriarchal hegemony against men and women in the Umuofia village (today's Nigeria) at the end of the nineteenth century, at a time when the missionaries encountered the Igbo people for the first time. Early on in the narration of the novel we are introduced to Okonkwo, the protagonist of the novel, who is a warrior, a powerful and successful wrestler. He is a thoughtful man, but extremely violent trying to demonstrate a masculine identity, whose image of supreme power is that of a person who beats his wives, kills his adoptive son "Ikemefuna" in a ritual ceremony, and ignores his biological son "Nwoye" because he reminds him of his lazy father.[20]

The layers of cultural codes in the novel demonstrate a male-centered gendered discourse of character, identity, and social class. This novel is significant to the research at hand since women were excluded from the story, marginalized, silenced, and largely invisible. It is an important early message on power in the private and public spheres in and from the Global South and deals with these issues in the precolonial period. Perhaps this is Achebe's overarching view of how "things can really fall apart" once one gender is overly empowered over the other, thus making truth speaking almost impossible for both men and women. For this reason, this chapter aims at exploring and narrating the possibilities and changes of the social structure of a fragile world. It speaks with both Milton and Achebe to make some basic points. Therefore, I am traveling with the readers through intertextual passages, narrating the life of an "Other" in the pursuit of the "roots" of injustice, with a proliferation of the various dimensions of gender, differences, and identity. The travel route will be narrated via landing points adopting an auto-ethnographic production technique. The key to this approach will be provided to the traveler in following.

THINGS FALLING APART: IN SEARCH
OF AN AUTO-ETHNOGRAPHER

"I want to understand the world from your point of view. I want to know what you know in the way you know it. I want to understand the meaning of your experience, to walk in your shoes, to feel things as you feel them, to explain things as you explain them. Will you become my teacher and help me understand?"[21] James Spradley in his foundational study guide *The Ethnographic Interview* suggests how best to bridge the gap between the researcher and the subject of research within complex social environments.

The examples presented below are difficult to deal with. They are particularly overwhelming when a journalist, author, or researcher attempts to link reporting events to changing the world for the better. This becomes even more difficult when the stories being investigated awaken recollections of similar events in one's own history. This section will therefore link two extreme cases of reporting on GBV in the media to the selected methodology for this chapter, auto-ethnography. The study of culture and diversity is one of the objectives of an ethnographer. This technique follows a systematic approach in order to provide readers with a deeper understanding of the studied question, and thus "putting oneself in someone else's shoes" when conducting a participatory research. It does not differ significantly from the work and skills of journalists, who are required to be empathetic when unpacking human rights violations. It is always advisable for the media narrative to follow professional ethics and a CoC.[22] More significant, however, is that journalists, authors, and scholars could ultimately empower and encourage their recipients to become citizens who can break the chains of silence and invisibility and boldly speak truth to power.

Example 1
Time: February 4, 2014
Place: Beirut

"Please cover me sister, I am cold." These were the last words Manal Assi (thirty-three years old) uttered that day.[23] Manal is another victim of GBV who was tortured for hours before her husband Mohammed Al Nahaily informed her mother on the phone to come and witness her daughter's death. In fact, by the time her mother, brother, and sister arrived, Manal's head had been bashed with a pressure cooker. Media reports in Lebanon revealed that Manal had been the victim of domestic violence for more than sixteen years. The mother of two girls did not seek a divorce, even though her husband got married to a second wife and had a son from her. That day Mohammed Al Nahaily justified his brutality against Manal on the grounds that he was

angry and that he was protecting his reputation after he discovered that she
had a lover.

Example 2
Time: November 28, 2018
Place: *Aatel Aan El Horiye* ("Without Freedom" or "Unfree") program on
    MTV Station—Lebanon.[24]

In it is sixth season the program hosted the perpetrator Mohammed Al
Nahaily who is interviewed from his prison where he was sentenced for
eighteen years after being convicted of the murder of his first wife Manal
Assi. This episode was highly criticized by women's rights organizations,
feminists, and civil society in general for sharing the point of view of a murderer who declared that he initially had no intention to kill his wife, and that
he did not want to beat her but his feelings were hurt when he discovered
her betrayal. As a result of this shocking revelation, Mohammed got angry
and lost his mind that day, so he claimed. This justification of his behavior
was supported in the TV program by an interview with a female psychiatrist
who maintained that from her professional perspective Mohammed went to a
"dark point in his consciousness," not believing that his wife could do what
she did. A further supporting explanation for Mohammed's defense was also
given as an expert opinion regarding the bruises on Manal's body by the
male medical examiner, who did not consider these injuries to be the result
of domestic violence. A clear objective was showed through the program: it
is empathy toward the murderer and indirect apathy toward the victim, thus
killing her twice.

    The distribution of power in the case of Manal Assi and her husband
Mohammed Al Nahaily goes beyond the personal relationship toward complete ownership and control. The "intersectional"[25] form of power between
gender and religion in this particular tragedy emphasized a deep masculinist
ideology, a patriarchy of exclusion and violence, a toxic patriarchal approach
which perpetuates privileged hegemonic masculinity. The TV program
exploited the traditions-based situation and expectations in Lebanon and
Palestine and favored a notorious system of power and institutionalized
patriarchal domination. Mainstreaming male-controlled values, patriarchal
structures, and practices of gendered power in the public space thus goes
hand in hand with those in the private space. Media coverage cannot be seen
as impartial, informative, fair, or balanced in this case, simply because the
program showed the point of view of a killer while justifying his act. The
relationships between Manal and Mohammed, between Israa Gharib, her
cousin Riham, and the entire Gharib clan, and ultimately, in an analogous
sense, between Achebe's fictional warrior Okonkwo and his entire tribe, are

reproduced within the media portrayals in Middle Eastern TV. Through the way the program is structured, the interviewees discoursed, and the message provided, a systematically biased view emerges, a perspective which the Glasgow University Media Group calls a "systematic ideological bias."[26]

The argument here is that media produces textual codes by constantly negotiating meanings, collective context in addition to individual functions of terms within a given language. Media is part of and helps shape power relationships based on control of meaning and the shaping of social roles. The *Aatel Aan El Horiye* program, facts are presented in a particular way aiming to validate a certain aspects over the others. The predominant claim of the program is that they are trying to show the other side of the story and to provide insights to the audience, in that regard, news is no longer neutral but it is a "manufactured production of ideology."[27] I argued in an article titled "Dissonance and Decorousness: Missing Images of Syrian Women Refugees in the Lebanese Media" that most of the coverage in Lebanese media relies on human suffering as a subject of media scoops, reframing news according to "specific and sometimes biased political, gender, or ethnic view." I end the article by stating the following: "meanwhile, the never-ending discussion around creating an ethical code of conduct, with the support of professional journalists, heads of unions, and the support of the state, is still overdue."[28] At the end of this chapter, we will return to this issue of codes of conduct, education, and field training for journalists and the tools which have been developed to serve these purposes.

Reporting is evidence based, and the prima facie of the truth is a burden which needs to be validated and achieved. Below, I share the experience of how my initial idea in structuring this chapter has been completely altered during the process of researching and drafting it. I wanted it to serve as an overview of what has been achieved regarding gender equality in Lebanon, reflecting on my work and contributions in the field, in addition to my learning experience through this process, as an activist-scholar, whether with nongovernmental organizations, academic institutions, media, or youth. However, I found that I was self-reflecting on such stories and on a personal one which my husband and I have kept private for the longest time. I also found myself for the first time writing publicly as an auto-ethnographer about my adopted stepdaughter. As an academician, I have been trained to cherish objectivity, and the positivist traditions that go with it, while conducting any research process. The foundational traditions of this method have no room for a subjective reflection of the world. As an activist-scholar I have always been concerned in producing knowledge for a purpose and in connecting the personal with the social, in other words through adopting the second-wave feminism slogan *the personal is political.* "Being curious takes energy"[29] as American feminist theorist Cynthia Enloe reveals to us. For her lack of curiosity is "dangerously comfortable." She writes: "What is distinctive about developing a feminist curiosity? One of the starting points of feminism is taking women's lives seriously. 'Seriously' implies listening carefully, digging deep, developing a long attention span, being ready to be surprised."[30] With respect to the cases being studied here, the curious question would be the following; how to inter-link experiences and incidents deeply ingrained in Middle Eastern traditions based on a structure of social power and control leading to oppression based on class, race, religion, and gender without seriously skewing the results of our work? How can one narrate personal involvement as an author/researcher by trying to take action against inequality in the community without being affected in a way which distorts the process?

During my recent work on the topic of gender in the Middle East, but particularly on media coverage of GBV in the private sphere in Lebanon, I realized that the notion of neutrality when trying to embrace social justice and change will lead nowhere. It is an attempt to delink the researcher, the research topic, and those being researched and is itself of form of silencing and blindness. Inversely, and as stated by the Brazilian pedagogue Paulo Freire, "people have a universal right to participate in the production of knowledge which is a disciplined process of personal and social transformation. In this process, people rupture their existing attitudes of silence, accommodation and passivity, and gain confidence and abilities to alter unjust conditions and structures."[31] As stated at the outset of this section, when dealing with "things falling apart" auto-ethnography seemed an effective tool for dealing with this complexity. Therefore, to better serve the purpose of a free world leading to justice, and to engage readers in subjective methodological concerns, the researcher is engaged in the subject, the researcher is also the subject, the researcher is the auto-ethnographer, and the reader goes along on the journey.

"What is auto-ethnography?" writes the leading American scholar Carolyn Ellis in the preface of her book *The Ethnographic I*, and continues: "You might ask. My brief answer: research, writing, story, and method that connect the autobiographical and personal to the cultural, social, and political. Autoethnographic forms feature concrete action, emotion, embodiment, self-consciousness, and introspection portrayed in dialogue, scenes, characterization, and plot. Thus, autoethnography claims the conventions of literary writing."[32] Auto-ethnography is considered by many anthropologists as a creative model which allows the author/researcher to contribute in a dialogical interchange between the self and the community, leading to a commitment toward social justice.

According to the anthropologist David Hayano, auto-ethnography emerged as a research method, allowing us to examine events with an observer-participant eye, or what Carolyn Ellis and Arthur Bochner describe as linking "the personal to the cultural"[33] in a conceptual social framework. Although

Hayano explained in his article "Auto-Ethnography Paradigms, Problems, and Prospects" that auto-ethnography "encompasses a wide range of studies, as it includes the works of other social scientists who have done intensive participant-observation research in natural field settings,"[34] he also emphasized that this approach does not merely encompass either studies, methods, or theories, but rather covers "all three as they are employed in fieldwork." It is important for auto-ethnographers to seek meaning in cultural representations, to be able to understand the nuances and the variety of communication paradigms in the everyday practice. Therefore, and to borrow from Stuart Hall's understanding of what is "essential to meaning,"[35] to seek the essence of meaning we must be able to "connect the autobiographical and personal to the cultural and social."[36]

Hayano writes that he was introduced to the term auto-ethnography for the first time in 1966 by Sir Raymond Firth, during his structuralism seminar in the London School of Economics (LSE). Many researchers criticized this subjectivity-based approach and considered that it would bias the results of the research process. Therefore, it is important to explain the conditions in which this method is used, especially in the context of this chapter.

To analyze the situations and incidents from an analytical auto-ethnographic perspective one should be a member of a research group, committed to publish her/his story in an analytical perspective with an aim to improve the understanding of a crisis or of the issue at hand as a societal phenomenon. This method of research illustrates a personal experience following an analytical modus operandi, in order to determine and further understand the first, the influence of the personal experience on the research process, and second the impact of cultural and societal experiences on the research process and oneself. In other words, this form of self-narrative involves multiple layers of a conscious self, connecting the personal experience to a larger sociocultural experience and interaction or what Andrew Sparkes, a researcher in physical education and sport, defines it as "highly personalized accounts that draw upon the experience of the author/researcher for the purposes of extending sociological understanding."[37] In the case of the interface between GBV, media education, and communications research in the MENA, the nascent partnership within civil society between NGOs and the education sector and finally the life experience of media practitioners, activists, and scholars themselves, the auto-ethnographic approach can help to grasp this complexity, or at least not try to silence and blind it by assuming it doesn't exist.

In the last part of the chapter, I will focus on how communication if well strategized can help in freeing women and men from tyranny. More than forty years ago, the American sociologist Gaye Tuchman considered that the portrayal of women in media had more often than not been trivialized, omitted, or condemned by focusing on men's activities. For her, such portrayals had a negative effect on women in comparison to the way men are portrayed, which led to distorted images of gender and contributed, according to her to the "symbolic annihilation"[38] of women in public discourse. These unequal power dynamics, in addition to my personal experience, motivated engagement with ongoing research relying on a gendered auto-ethnographic approach.

FINDING OUR VOICES: MAKING A DIFFICULT DECISION

There is one common denominator between Israa, Manal, and my stepdaughter referred to at the outset of this chapter. In all three cases, the perpetrators forced the victims to be still, under their control or silent. More ambiguous is the role of friends and family members, bystanders, and the audience. When perpetrators have based their actions on assumed and generally accepted traditions and social norms, "third parties" often find themselves unable to take a position, confused and almost frozen. With respect to my stepdaughter I am confronted with the situation in which Sharia Law is utilized to the detriment of a child. I, as a "third party," am torn between various notions which all seem to be bad, and I can thus sympathize with how some of the family members of Israa and Manal must have felt.

There is no easy way to be the voice of the less powerful—to adopt analytical and sensitive attitudes to a story in a dialogical context when it is not a fictional setting. There are indeed moral obligations and pressing responsibilities to give voice to the invisible suffering of a marginalized group or individual. I grew up assuming that real-life dichotomies are black and white, between good and evil. As a child, evil was always portrayed as an ugly creature, while goodness is beauty; this naïve approach between the good and the bad was also emphasized in the fairytales we read. However, the layers of lived dichotomy are indeed infinite, and so too our actions and the feeling of confusion and pain. In my sympathy and suffering, whether with the tragedies I read about, or in my own situation, I am constantly on mobility mode in my mind whether in time or space trying to find a solution to an immobile and intersectional structure. My mind is the practiced space where I retell the story of my stepdaughter, where my imagined feelings are receptive in a constant state of movement, where the pain of separation is abolished. According to Madison, her ethnographic dilemma "is not the absence of the Other who cannot be there to see the show but how and by what means I can make the audience who is there feel a sense of being present with the Other in the Other's actual absence."[39]

Returning to the need to bridge the knowledge gap between the civil society and academia, I will wrap up this chapter by briefly describing three steps taken to bring activists and scholars together in order to make "the audience feel absence of the Other" in the field of GBV in the media. These include firstly, the drafting of a CoC and a resulting media practitioner's toolkit; secondly, the university-based launching of these tools, and thirdly a training program for investigative journalists on how to report on GBV, built on this experience. The CoC and the simultaneously developed "toolkit" on gender-sensitive media coverage in conflict/postconflict situations for women and girls survivors of GBV were unique in that they not only responded to the articulated need of journalists in the field, but also integrated for the first time the goals and principles of the United Nations Security Council Resolution 1325, as a GM tool for the media, within the Lebanese context. As the person responsible for the gender, communication, and the global mobility studies unit at Notre Dame University (NDU), I was contacted by colleagues from the Lebanese NGO "Fe-Male" concerning an ongoing project being carried out in cooperation with the Beirut-based and UN ECOSOC accredited "Resource Centre for Gender Equality" (ABAAD) and funded by the Dutch Ministry of Foreign Affairs. This project was designed and implemented with my academic input under the leadership of Fe-Male. In order to highlight the cooperation between academia and the NGO sector and to accentuate the need to further develop this unique partnership within civil society, a university setting was selected for the launching of both. The CoC and toolkit were presented to the public during a gala event and workshop on May 29, 2018. This full day event included a series of panels and an NGO fair.

By cohosting the May 2018 event ABAAD and Fe-Male teamed up with the Gender, Communications and Global Mobility (GCGM) studies unit in the Faculty of Law and Political Science at NDU, not only were we able to introduce the newly developed tools and their bridging function within civil society, but also to highlight the need for an intersectional and subjectivity-based approach to journalism, training, and research. Titled "A Voice of Our Own: Retelling the Stories of Gender Based Violence"[40] this one-day conference aimed primarily to fill the long-standing gap in the MENA and in Lebanon in particular. It brought together professors, NGO activists, members of the diplomatic core, the International Labor Organization (ILO), students, international developmental organizations, media practitioners, and owners of media outlets in addition to the youth network "My Fair Home," which supported domestic workers rights in cooperation with ILO, the International Domestic Workers Federation, and Fe-Male. Following the event, a national training campaign for the toolkit was launched throughout Lebanon in summer and fall of 2018. Simultaneously, I was part of the training process and establishment of feminist clubs in the peripheral regions of Lebanon. The participants, both young men and women, acquired knowledge related to gender, history of feminism, and important theories in the field. Based on the training rooted in the CoC and toolkit, they produced media content that reflected gender equality for use in their regions. The culmination of this process was a six-month piloting phase in which Lebanese journalists were trained on investigative journalism coverage of GBV.

CONCLUSION

The literary work of Milton and Achebe has been an eye-opener to many international readers, over time and place. Be it via poetry or through the prose retelling stories, their sociological and cultural impact has detached the frame around the human conscience and helped drop the distorted stereotypical images of the "Other." I argue that the two thinkers, even though centuries separate them, wrote not to transform the political sphere nor to challenge it, but rather in the hope that people can learn and try to change themselves, resist tyranny, and fight injustice. Personally, I wonder why we define things by opposing them, thus necessitating the existence of an "Other." For hundreds of years *Paradise Lost* was read and interpreted based on the assumption of its misogynistic character structures, for its Otherness and gendered alienation. However, my reading—as presented here—is related to patriarchy as a whole; to the dichotomic opposites which need each other as much as night and day, evil and good, male and female, Global North and Global South. I am reading these literary works in the twenty-first century, as an Arab woman applying a Southern gendered lens, thus viewing that Adam and Eve are an inseparable whole and complete being. In an interview with the *Paris Review* in 1994, Achebe revealed that he grew up enjoying reading adventures stories, but that he always took the side of the white man. He realized that this might not be right, but primarily because his people had not written their own stories, he saw no other alternative. He stated: "There is that great proverb—that until the lions have their own historians, the history of the hunt will always glorify the hunter. That did not come to me until much later. Once I realized that, I had to be a writer. I had to be that historian. It's not one man's job. It's not one person's job. But it is something we have to do, so that the story of the hunt will also reflect the agony, the travail—the bravery, even, of the lions."[41]

When it comes to media coverage of GBV it is essential that we attempt to be as accurate as possible. This means allowing both the hunters and lions to have their say. Representation of violence and oppression is always a tricky business and it is not easy for reporters to find their place in this complex constellation. It also becomes harder, however, when the reporters themselves are not gender sensitive, are not savvy enough to resist the temptation to blind and silence the participants in conflict.

In Lebanon today, and as I mentioned earlier, the LJU does not provide professional training to media workers. In a country with a gradually collapsing media sector, media enterprises primarily use financial arguments to explain why reporters are not properly trained. I realized this growing need early on in my career as a journalist and built on it when I started my academic career. This is why I deemed it important to not only bridge the gap between academic institutions and NGOs, but to also work on research and tools that can also communicate gendered media skill to professionals. In September 2018, I worked as an expert consultant with Fe-Male and ABAAD to further develop and disseminate the above-mentioned toolkit, as well as more advanced techniques for journalists. The concept was to equip media practitioners during an intensive three-day training program with the practical knowledge and comprehension of legal perspectives necessary to grasp gender-related power relationships and GBV in Lebanon. The participants had to commit to work on a gender-sensitive media production related to GBV, to be published on Fe-Male's feminist news website in Arabic "sharikawalaken."

I engaged the help of my colleague Walid Al-Saqaf, a senior lecturer at Södertörn University in Stockholm, whose field of research is how to use the Internet and media technology to enhance journalists' capacity to debunk misinformation. Walid prepared three course modules on how to use and verify online news, advanced fact checking and data journalism, linking all of them to gender. Walid is a Swedish and Yemeni dual-citizen. As such he developed "Alkasir," a program that allowed users to circumvent web censorship. Since 2012, the program has been widely used by activists in the Arab world in particular. Having Walid as a trainer sent two messages: (1) advancing in the field of reporting should run parallel with an increase of knowledge in the latest technological skills; (2) Walid's symbolism of an Arab man who is fighting against injustice, caring for a better world without oppression and annihilation of the "Other," thus advancing on the road to gender equality.

The training session was followed by a six-month process of investigative journalism, working with mid-career journalists in Lebanon. I worked on and followed up on two controversial topics for Arab language media. The first was related to gendercide in Iraq titled "Deadly Gender Identity in Iraq."[42] It showed how the LGBTQ community is included in a hit list just because they do not adhere to the cultural codes of the Iraqi society. Two survivors were filmed in Beirut after their rescue, while their identity was kept anonymous. The second story was related to Lebanese women's rights when it comes to religious courts. With the title "Life on Hold: Stories of Women in Lebanese Religious Courts"[43] the investigative piece featured stories of divorced women in fifteen different courts, showing that the common denominator among all sects in Lebanon is putting women's life on hold. Many of them were forced to wait for more than a decade to get a divorce approval, receive child custody, or rights for visitations. Many are also still waiting for their alimony. The implementation phase of the training program was emotionally significant for me because it highlighted personal involvement with this topic and how it is necessary to factor a trainer/researcher's subjectivity into this process. This also highlighted for me the pressing need to liberate family status issues from the control of the religious courts.

Back to the article research and drafting process, the journalist trainee spent hours in the respective Sunni and Shia Islamic family status courts. She used a questionnaire to access the Evangelical Protestant and Maronite Catholic Christian courts. Her article concluded that there is no equality for women and men in a sectarian system, in which the freedom of many women has been taken away and divorce often delayed just because a spouse had political or religious backing, or because of traditions and administrative bureaucracy. It also mentioned that people prefer to have their sisters, mothers, or friends "on hold" so to speak and not to be divorced, which is still considered a societal stigma in Lebanon.

It's been quite a journey, from the outset of the research for this chapter until its completion; I am still working with an auto-ethnographic eye. I am still working on developing new techniques and forms of measurement which will enable me and others to better cover sensitive topics in the media with a subjective auto-ethnographic "I." Testing my findings in the classroom, in the field training context, and in the research process has sharpened my perspective. I believe it is my duty to equip people with the ability to properly reflect on their difficult and joyful moments. The art of communication should be a way to empower the marginalized and the mainstream, it should be a way to allow people to speak truth to power and thus make it easier for people to be good.

NOTES

1. This chapter is dedicated to my stepdaughter whose presence nourishes joy and turns darkness into light.

2. Isabelle D. Cherney and Brigette Oliver Ryalls, "Gender-Linked Differences in the Incidental Memory of Children and Adults," *Journal of Experimental Child Psychology* 72, no. 4 (1999): 305–28, doi:10.1006/jecp.1999.2492.

3. V. Spike Peterson, "Transgressing Boundaries: Theories of Knowledge, Gender and International Relations," *Millennium: Journal of International Studies* 21, no. 2 (1992): 183–206, doi: 10.1177/03058298920210020401.

4. Ibid., 194. Also see V. Spike Peterson, "Feminist Theories Within, Invisible To, and Beyond IR," *The Brown Journal of World Affairs* 10, no. 2 (2004): 35–46, http://www.jstor.org/stable/24590519.

V. Spike Peterson has developed a complex critical method by which she established an interdisciplinary approach to international relations (IR) with respect to more equitable gender relations. She also questions power relationships in order to specify the category of "insider-outsider" in the feminist sphere. The interdisciplinary nature of Peterson's approach in the field of IR brings significant insights to this chapter which can be applied in fields of study such as communications, literature, and combating GBV.

5. Martin Chulov, "Iran ally Michel Aoun elected as president of Lebanon," *Guardian*, October 31, 2016, https://www.theguardian.com/world/2016/oct/31/mich el-aoun-elected-president-lebanon-iran-tehran-saudi-arabia.

6. "Lebanon Let's Talk: Tackling Sexual Violence Requires a Shift in Mentality," *Executive Magazine*, no. 221, February 1, 2018, accessed September 7, 2019. https://www.pressreader.com/lebanon/executive-magazine/20180201/282050 507543827.

7. See Human Rights Watch, "World Report 2019," *Lebanon Events of 2018*, https://www.hrw.org/world-report/2019/country-chapters/lebanon. See also, William Robert Avis, *Gender Equality and Women's Empowerment in Lebanon*, K4D Helpdesk Report 175 (Brighton, UK: Institute of Development Studies, 2017).

8. Milton, John. "Paradise Lost," *The John Milton Reading Room*, ed. Thomas H. Luxon, bk. 7, lines 592–600, https://www.dartmouth.edu/~milton/reading_room/ pl/book_7/text.shtml.

9. BabyFist, "Isra Gharib's Murder Exposes Issues of Power We Can't Ignore," August 31, 2019, https://baby-fist.com/get-inspired/isra-gharibs-murder-exposes-st ories-of-power-we-cant-ignore.

10. Tamara Abueish, "Palestinian Officials Confirm Israa Ghareeb Died from Physical Assault Wounds," *Al Arabiya English*, September 12, 2019, http://english. alarabiya.net/en/News/middle-east/2019/09/12/Palestinian-officials-confirm-Israa -Ghareeb-died-from-physical-assault-wounds.html#.

11. Rashida Tlaib, "Isra's Death Illustrates," *Twitter* account @RashidaTlaib, September 2, 2019, accessed September 5, 2019, https://twitter.com/RashidaTlaib/st atus/1168310469809119232.

12. Yara Hawari, "Israa Gharib's Murder Has Nothing to Do with Honour," *AlJazeera Indepth Opinion*, September 5, 2019, https://www.aljazeera.com/indepth/o pinion/israa-gharib-murder-honour-190904131045999.html.

13. Srilatha Batliwala, *All about Power: Understanding Social Power & Power Structures* (New Delhi: Creating Resources for Empowerment in Action (CREA), 2019), 10.

14. Ibid., 11.

15. Milton, "Paradise Lost," bk. 1, lines 59–67.

16. Fredson Bowers, "Adam, Eve, and the Fall in 'Paradise Lost'," *PMLA* 84, no. 2 (1969): 264–73, accessed August 28, 2019, doi:10.2307/1261283.

17. Matthew Jordan, *Milton and Modernity: Politics, Masculinity and Paradise Lost* (Hampshire and New York: Palgrave, 2001).

18. William Shullenberger, "Wrestling with the Angel: 'Paradise Lost' and Feminist Criticism," *Milton Quarterly* 20, no. 3 (1986), 69–85.

19. Ibid.

20. Chinua Achebe, *Things Fall Apart* (New York: Anchor Books. 1994).

21. James Phillip Spradley, *The Ethnographic Interview* (New York: Harcourt Brace Jovanovich College Publishers, 1979), 34.

22. In this context Janet Anderson and Benjamin Duerr deal with this issue in the article *Obligation to Expose and the Responsibility to Protect: Journalistic Ethics for Reporting on Wartime Sexual Violence* contained in this volume. Furthermore, Johanna Foster and Sherizaan Minwalla deal with the impact of field research and journalism with populations in conflict under threat and the necessity to incorporate respect for their needs in journalistic and research-based codes of conduct, in: "Voices of Yazidi Women: Perceptions of Journalistic Practices in the Reporting on ISIS Sexual Violence," *Women's Studies International Forum* 67 (2018): 53–64.

23. Aya Balaa and Rayane Abou Jaoudel, "Manal Assi's Family Demands Justice," *Daily Star*, February 8, 2014, accessed September 5, 2019, https://www.dailystar.com.lb/News/Lebanon-News/2014/Feb-08/246764-manal-assis-family-demands-justice.ashx.

24. Samir Youssef, "Mohammed Al Nahaily," *Aatel Aan El Horiye*, season 6, documentary series, MTV Lebanon, Beirut, November 28, 2018, accessed September 7, 2019, https://www.mtv.com.lb/vod/en/video/194927.

25. In 1989, Kimberlé Crenshaw coined the term intersectionality by addressing the marginalization, and intersection of gender and race in the United States within the larger women's movement. She particularly elaborated on institutionalized discourses, such as those common in the legal sector, which narrowed down the social justice agenda around racism, sexism, and patriarchy to its constituent parts—a system that doubly marginalized certain women. Since then, the scope of studies based on intersectional methodological approaches has taken on an international dimension, thus assisting various movements to progress toward a better understanding of power dynamics and their structures in multiple fields. The twenty-first-century application of intersectionality questions a variety of social structures in order to change them. The aim of using an intersectional lens in this chapter is to interrogate the daily rhetoric of power, control, and ownership of a human being. For more information, see Kimberlé Crenshaw, "Demarginalizing the Intersection of Race and Sex: A Black Feminist Critique of Antidiscrimination Doctrine, Feminist Theory and Antiracist Politics," *University of Chicago Legal Forum* (1989): 139; and also Devon W. Carbado, Kimberlé Williams Crenshaw, Vickie M. Mays and Barbara Tomlinson, "INTERSECTIONALITY: Mapping the Movements of a Theory," *Du Bois Review: Social Science Research on Race* 10, no. 2 (2013): 303–12.

26. Glasgow University Media Group (GUMG), *More Bad News*, Bad News 2 (London: Routledge and Kegan Paul, 1980).

27. Ibid., xvii–xviii.

28. Rouba El Helou and Maria Bou Zeid, "Dissonance and Decorousness: Missing Images of Syrian Women Refugees in the Lebanese Media 1," in *In Line with the Divine: the Struggle for Gender Equality in Lebanon*, ed. Rita Stephan, Guita Hourani and Cornelia Horn (Warwick, Rhode Island: Abelian Academic, 2015), 187–207.

29. Cynthia Enloe, *The Curious Feminist: Searching for Women in a New Age of Empire* (Berkeley and Los Angeles, CA: University of California Press, 2004).

30. Ibid., 3.

31. Paolo Freire, "Foreword," in *Nurtured by Knowledge: Learning to Do Participatory Action-Research*, eds. Susan E. Smith, Dennis G. Willms, and Nancy A. Johnson, (Ottawa/New York: International Development Research Centre, 1997), xi–xii.

32. Carolyn Ellis, *The Ethnographic I: A Methodlogical Novel about Autoethnography*, Ethnographic Alternatives (Walnut Creek, CA: AltaMira Press, 2003), xix.

33. Carolyn Ellis and Arthur P. Bochner, "Autoethnography, personal narrative, reflexivity: Researcher as subject," in *The Handbook of Qualitative Research*, eds. Norman K. Denzin and Yvonna Lincoln (Thousand Oaks, CA: Sage Publications Sage, 2nd ed., 2000), 733–768, and also Arthur P. Bochner, "The Functions of Human Communication in Interpersonal Bonding," in *Handbook of Rhetorical and Communication Theory*, eds. Carroll C. Arnold and John W. Bowers (Boston, MA: Allyn and Bacon, 1984), 544–621.

34. David Hayano, "Auto-Ethnography: Paradigms, Problems, and Prospects," *Human Organization* 38, no. 1 (spring 1979): 99–104, doi:10.17730/humo.38.1.u761n5601t4g318v.

35. Stuart Hall, "The Work of Representation," *Representation: Cultural Representations and Signifying Practices* 2 (1997): 13–74.

36. Ellis, *The Ethnographic I*.

37. Andrew Sparkes, "Autoethnography and Narratives of Self: Reflections on Criteria in Action," *Sociology of Sport Journal* 17 (2000): 21–43, doi:10.1123/ssj.17.1.21.

38. Gaye Tuchman, "Introduction: The Symbolic Annihilation of Women by the Mass Media," in *Hearth and Home: Images of Women in the Mass Media*, eds. Gaye Tuchman, Arlene Kaplan Daniels and James Walker Benét. New York: Oxford University Press, (1978), 3–38.

39. Soyini D. Madison, "Performing Ethnography: The Political Economy of Water," *Performance Research* 12, no. 3 (2007): 16–27.

40. "A Milestone National Achievement: Gir Launches a Pioneer COC and Toolkit on GBV With Fe-Male and ABAAD," Notre Dame University *News and Events* web page, accessed September 22, 2019, http://www.ndu.edu.lb/news-and-events/news/a-milestone-national-achievement-gir-launches-a-pioneer-coc-and-toolkit-on-gbv-with-fe-male-and-abaad.

41. Chinua Achebe, "Chinua Achebe, The Art of Fiction No. 139," by Jerome Brooks, *The Paris Review*, no. 133 (Winter 1994), accessed September 8, 2019, https://www.theparisreview.org/interviews/1720/chinua-achebe-the-art-of-fiction-no-139-chinua-achebe.

42. Myra Abdallah, "Al Hawiya Al Jandariya Al Katila Fi Al Iraq," ["Deadly Gender Identity in Iraq"], February 2, 2019, accessed September 10, 2019, https://www.sharikawalaken.media/2019/02/19/الهوية-الجندرية-القاتلة-في-العراق/.

43. Zeinab Mohsen, "Hayat Kayd Al Intizar: Koussass Nissaa Fi Al Mahakem Al Diniya Fi Loubnan," ["Life on Hold: Stories of Women in Lebanese Religious Courts,"] March 20, 2019, accessed September 10, 2019, https://www.sharikawalaken.media/2019/03/20/حياة-قيد-الإنتظار-قصّص-نساء-في-المحاكم/.

BIBLIOGRAPHY

"A Milestone National Achievement: Gir Launches a Pioneer CoC and Toolkit on GBV With Fe-Male and ABAAD." Notre Dame University *News and Events* web page. Accessed September 22, 2019. http://www.ndu.edu.lb/news-and-events/ne ws/a-milestone-national-achievement-gir-launches-a-pioneer-coc-and-toolkit-on -gbv-with-fe-male-and-abaad.

Abdallah, Myra. "Al Hawiya Al Jandariya Al Katila Fi Al Iraq." ["Deadly Gender Identity in Iraq."] February 2, 2019. Accessed September 10, 2019. https://www .sharikawalaken.media/2019/02/19/العراق-في-القاتلة-الجندرية-الهوية/.

Abueish, Tamara. "Palestinian Officials Confirm Israa Ghareeb Died from Physical Assault Wounds." *Al Arabiya English*, September 12, 2019. Accessed September 15, 2019. http://english.alarabiya.net/en/News/middle-east/2019/09/12/Palestinian -officials-confirm-Israa-Ghareeb-died-from-physical-assault-wounds.html#.

Achebe, Chinua. "Chinua Achebe, The Art of Fiction No. 139." Interview by Jerome Brooks. *The Paris Review*, no. 133 (Winter 1994). Accessed September 8, 2019. https://www.theparisreview.org/interviews/1720/chinua-achebe-the-art-of-fiction-no-139-chinua-achebe.

Achebe, Chinua. *Things Fall Apart*. New York: Anchor Books, 1994. First published in 1959.

Avis, William Robert. *Gender Equality and Women's Empowerment in Lebanon*. K4D Helpdesk Report 175. Brighton, UK: Institute of Development Studies, 2017.

BabyFist. "Isra Gharib's Murder Exposes Issues of Power We Can't Ignore." August 31, 2019. Accessed September 5, 2019. https://baby-fist.com/get-inspired/isra-gharibs-murder-exposes-stories-of-power-we-cant-ignore.

Balaa, Aya and Rayane Abou Jaoudel. "Manal Assi's Family Demands Justice." *Daily Star*, February 8, 2014. Accessed September 5, 2019. https://www.dailysta r.com.lb/News/Lebanon-News/2014/Feb-08/246764-manal-assis-family-demands -justice.ashx.

Batliwala, Srilatha. *All about Power: Understanding Social Power & Power Structures*. New Delhi: Creating Resources for Empowerment in Action (CREA), 2019.

Bochner, Arthur P. "The Functions of Human Communication in Interpersonal Bonding." In Handbook of Rhetorical and Communication Theory, edited by Carroll C. Arnold and John W. Bowers, 544–621. Boston: Allyn and Bacon, 1984.

Bowers, Fredson. "Adam, Eve, and the Fall in 'Paradise Lost'." *PMLA* 84, no. 2 (1969): 264–73. Accessed August 28, 2019. doi:10.2307/1261283.

Carbado, Devon W., Kimberlé Williams Crenshaw, Vickie M. Mays and Barbara Tomlinson. "INTERSECTIONALITY: Mapping the Movements of a Theory." *Du Bois Review: Social Science Research on Race* 10, no. 2 (2013): 303–12.

Cherney, Isabelle D. and Brigette Oliver Ryalls. "Gender-Linked Differences in the Incidental Memory of Children and Adults." *Journal of Experimental Child Psychology* 72, no. 4 (1999): 305–28. doi:10.1006/jecp.1999.2492.

Chulov, Martin. "Iran ally Michel Aoun Elected as President of Lebanon." *Guardian*, October 31, 2016. Accessed September 1, 2019. https://www.theguard

ian.com/world/2016/oct/31/michel-aoun-elected-president-lebanon-iran-tehran
-saudi-arabia.

Crenshaw, Kimberle. "Demarginalizing the Intersection of Race and Sex: A Black Feminist Critique of Antidiscrimination Doctrine, Feminist Theory and Antiracist Politics." *University of Chicago Legal Forum* 1989, no. 1 (1989): 139–67.

El Helou, Rouba and Maria Bou Zeid. "Dissonance and Decorousness: Missing Images of Syrian Women Refugees in the Lebanese Media 1." In *In Line with the Divine: the Struggle for Gender Equality in Lebanon*, edited by Rita Stephan, Guita Hourani and Cornelia Horn, 187–207. Warwick, RI: Abelian Academic, 2015.

Ellis, Carolyn. *The Ethnographic I: A Methodlogical Novel about Autoethnography*. Ethnographic Alternatives. Walnut Creek, CA: AltaMira Press, 2003.

Ellis, Carolyn and Arthur Bochner. "Autoethnography, Personal Narrative, Reflexivity." In Handbook of Qualitative Research, edited by Norman K. Denzin and Yvonna S. Lincoln, 733–768. Thousand Oaks, CA: Sage Publications, 2000.

Enloe, Cynthia. *The Curious Feminist: Searching for Women in a New Age of Empire*. Berkeley and Los Angeles, CA: University of California Press. December 15, 2004.

Foster, Johanna E. and Sherizaan Minwalla. "Voices of Yazidi Women: Perceptions of Journalistic Practices in the Reporting on ISIS Sexual Violence." *Women's Studies International Forum* 67 (2018): 53–64.

Freire, Paolo. "Foreword." In *Nurtured by Knowledge: Learning to Do Participatory Action-Research*, edited by Susan E. Smith, Dennis. G. Willms, & Nancy. A. Johnson, xi–xii. Ottawa/New York: International Development Research Centre, 1997.

Glasgow University Media Group (GUMG). *More Bad News*. Bad News 2. London: Routledge and Kegan Paul, 1980.

Hall, Stuart. "The Work of Representation." *Representation: Cultural Representations and Signifying Practices* 2 (1997): 13–74.

Hawari, Yara. "Israa Gharib's Murder Has Nothing to Do with Honour." *AlJazeera Indepth Opinion*, September 5, 2019. Accessed September 8, 2019. https://www.alj azeera.com/indepth/opinion/israa-gharib-murder-honour-190904131045999.html.

Hayano, David. "Auto-Ethnography: Paradigms, Problems, and Prospects." *Human Organization* 38, no. 1 (spring 1979): 99–104. https://doi.org/10.17730/humo.38 .u761n5601t4g318v.

Human Rights Watch. "World Report 2019." *Lebanon Events of 2018*. New York: Seven Stories Press, 2019. Accessed September 9, 2019. https://www.hrw.org/ world-report/2019/country-chapters/lebanon.

Jordan, Matthew. *Milton and Modernity: Politics, Masculinity and Paradise Lost*. Hampshire and New York: Palgrave, 2001.

"Lebanon Let's Talk: Tackling Sexual Violence Requires a Shift in Mentality." *Executive Magazine*, no. 221, February 1, 2018. *Pressreader.com*. Accessed September 7, 2019. https://www.pressreader.com/lebanon/executive-magazine/ 20180201/282050507543827. February 2018, no. 221.

Milton, John. "Paradise Lost." *The John Milton Reading Room*, edited by Thomas H. Luxon. Accessed August 30, 2019. https://www.dartmouth.edu/~milton/readin g_room/pl/book_1/text.shtml.

Peterson, V. Spike. "Feminist Theories Within, Invisible To, and Beyond IR." *The Brown Journal of World Affairs* 10, no. 2 (2004): 35–46.

Peterson, V. Spike. "Transgressing Boundaries: Theories of Knowledge, Gender and International Relations." *Millennium: Journal of International Studies* 21, no. 2 (1992): 183–206. Accessed August 21, 2019. doi:10.1177/03058298920210020401.

Shullenberger, William. "Wrestling with the Angel: 'Paradise Lost' and Feminist Criticism." *Milton Quarterly* 20, no. 3 (1986): 69–85.

Sparkes, Andrew. "Autoethnography and Narratives of Self: Reflections on Criteria in Action." *Sociology of Sport Journal* 17 (2000): 21–43. Doi:10.1123/ssj.17.1.21.

Spradley, James Phillip. *The Ethnographic Interview*. New York: Harcourt Brace Jovanovich College Publishers, 1979.

Soyini Madison, D. "Performing Ethnography: The Political Economy of Water." *Performance Research* 12, no. 3 (2007): 16–27.

Tlaib, Rashida. "Isra's Death Illustrates an Ever-Present Toxic Masculinity and Control Over Women's Bodies and Lives." *Twitter* account @RashidaTlaib, September 2, 2019. Accessed September 5, 2019. https://twitter.com/RashidaTlaib /status/1168310469809119232.

Tuchman, Gaye. "Introduction: The Symbolic Annihilation of Women by the Mass Media." In *Hearth and Home: Images of Women in the Mass Media*, edited by Gaye Tuchman, Arlene Kaplan Daniels and James Walker Benét, 3–38. New York: Oxford University Press, 1978.

Youssef, Samir. "Mohammed Al Nahaily." *Aatel Aan El Horiye*. Season 6. MTV Lebanon. Beirut, November 28, 2018. Accessed September 7, 2019. https://www .mtv.com.lb/vod/en/video/194927.

Zeinab Mohsen. "Hayat Kayd Al Intizar: Koussass Nissaa Fi Al Mahakem Al Diniya Fi Loubnan." ["Life on Hold: Stories of Women in Lebanese Religious Courts."] March 20, 2019. Accessed September 10, 2019. https://www.sharikawalaken.med ia/2019/03/20/المحاكم-في-نساء-قصّص-انتظار-ال-قيد-حياة/.

PART 4

CULTURES AND CONTEXTS
OF SHAME

9

Shame and Social Scripts

Vita Emery

When a person feels shame it indicates that they believe themselves to have done something wrong. In an opposing manner, when we hear that "someone feels no shame," this tends to indicate that the subject being referred to feels as though they have done no wrong, even, and perhaps especially, in a situation in which the said subject may have been judged to have done wrong by others. From such a perspective, heeding the emotion of shame will produce healthy responses to a variety of situations. For example, if some subject exposes himself in public, and then feels ashamed for having done so, perhaps because he believes that someone has seen him, he may think twice about doing so again. And in this case his behavior has been corrected based on his desire to avoid the emotion in the future. Thus, we might think that when a subject experiences shame it always indicates that they have either done actual wrong or believe that they have done wrong. Indeed, Virgil C. Aldrich, in an article published in 1939, claims that shame is a very good indicator of what behaviors are right and wrong. He explains, "It is attendant shame only which gives to actions their peculiar moral character."[1] For this reason we might think that shame would be a helpful tool in shaping moral behavior. Yet, much more has been written about the emotion of shame since Aldrich published his article, which serves to ambiguate the relationship between shame and its cause, and which this chapter seeks to explore.

Even if it is the case that shame always indicates a belief in wrongdoing, it is not clear that it would have a correcting effect even in the most moral of characters. Most, if not all, of us can probably come up with personal examples of moments when shame did not lead to corrective behavior. Michael Lewis claims that many times a subject will respond to shame, not with a change in behavior at all, or at least not with a change that directly affects whatever the subject was originally ashamed of, but instead with some outburst in emotion.

Lewis explains that "responses to shame can be varied: anger, depression, or withdrawal."[2] Lewis also believes that responses to shame are going to be different based on cultural or social context, explaining, "Cultural differences, past and present, can be viewed as differences in the ways in which shame and self-consciousness are experienced and addressed."[3] Thus, it is clear that the emotion itself is not only going to arise in response to different behaviors based on the culture a subject has been raised in, but the way that a subject responds to the emotion itself is going to vary immensely. And here arises another way in which shame isn't always helpful. The emotion may not be tuned correctly to the moral facts.

But what then, if anything, does shame teach us about our behavior? If both the source and the response to the emotion of shame are as inconsistent as indicated in the previous paragraphs, there may in fact be good reasons to work against and even ignore the emotion both in ourselves, and more globally. Yet, shame is not so easily extirpated from our lives. Silvan Solomon Tomkins argues that we are born with multiple innate affective responses, including shame.[4] He contends that shame is then amplified through our experiences. Tomkins describes the way children can learn to tolerate shame, or not, based on the way they see their caretakers handle it.[5] Thus, there is information to be gathered from those moments of shame, but it may well be that a subject's experiences as children both with their own experiences of shame, and those of the adults that surround them, will make it more or less difficult for them to cull such information.

In this chapter, I argue that what shame actually indicates, at least after childhood, is some internalized "should statement," a social norm that has ossified, at least in the consciousness of the individual who experiences the shame, and may also have found a stable and unquestioned place in the broader society.[6] In addition, I claim that many of the norms that will impact our experience of shame have to do with our identity as it relates to the more general community.[7] In other words, a subject's experience of shame is shaped by a sense of who they are in a society, or their social identity and the social scripts they feel compelled to follow.

Given this conclusion, I contend that the best we can do with shame is view it as a therapeutic tool, a way for a subject to understand something of themselves and their relation to society. Shame may also, in some situations, indicate a need to change our political situation, which has a hand in keeping harmful social norms in place.

SOURCES OF SHAME

My central claim is that our experience of shame is inherently tied up in our social identity. But in order to understand how shame might arise from an individual's relation to their social role, it is first important to locate the more general source of the emotion. Paralleling questions that Dan Zahavi asks in *Self and Other: Exploring Subjectivity, Empathy, and Shame*, we might wonder whether shame is indicative of "a (failed) self-concept, and a capacity for critical self-assessment?"[8] Or, instead, does it underscore the socially constructed nature of the self, existing as a human emotion only because of those norms established by a broader society? The answer is a partial yes to both of these questions. Indeed, it seems clear that shame occurs in those moments during which we fail to meet the expectations we have for ourselves. Yet, the expectations that we have for ourselves exist, in an almost dependent fashion, because of the social norms that the society around us embraces.

Martha Nussbaum also argues that shame as an emotion springs from an individual's relation to normalcy. When we try to act "normal" we are attempting to behave in ways that are expected by those in the community surrounding us. When we fail to fit in, or be "normal" we feel shame. In Nussbaum's words, there are moments when our "'abnormal' weaknesses are uncovered anyway, and then we blush, we cover ourselves, we turn away our eyes. Shame is the painful emotion that responds to that uncovering."[9] Michael Lewis holds a similar view on what shame responds to, defining it as "the feeling we have when we evaluate our actions, feelings, or behavior, and conclude that we have done wrong. It encompasses the *whole of ourselves*; it generates a wish to hide, to disappear, or even to die."[10] This definition gets at both the expectation we have of ourselves to "be" a certain way, and the kind of helplessness that can occur when we do not behave this way. But it is important to note how much the expectations of the society around us are going to impact our experience of shame. Individuals will not always be able to gage what their society views as normal. As I will argue, an acknowledgment of our helplessness in relation to social expectations may actually be a first step in creating a different, and helpful relation to the self, using shame. Though we may not be able to affect the exact moment that the emotion arises, we will be able to learn from it.

All of this means that the experience of the emotion itself is premised upon there being some distance between the social world we inhabit and our personal experience. In other words, in order for there to be norms that we are aware of, that we may either accept or reject or less consciously find ourselves internalizing, we must accept the premise that there is a world that we are born or thrown into, and an internal subjective experience of that same world. Another way of distinguishing between these two realms, the thrown and the subjective, can be found in Sartre's analysis of human identity. Sartre, who is borrowing from Hegel, uses the terms "for-itself" (*pour-soi*) and "in-itself" (*en-soi*). In brief, the "in-itself" can be understood as the object of consciousness and the "for-itself" is consciousness itself, which in Sartre's words is "thrown into a world and abandoned in a situation."[11] The "in-itself" exists independently of the "for-itself" as a fully determined and nonrelational object. In contrast, we can think of the "for-itself" as an entity that is self-reflective and can determine itself even within a given situation. The implication is that the "for-itself" has some control over how he or she will respond to a given situation. But within this space of inherent freedom there is a tension that arises, as the "for-itself" of a subject, a subject's consciousness, is unable to fully identify with the "in-itself," or unchosen, objectifiable aspects of personhood.

Within this tension, there is space for a subject to lose control. Indeed, we cannot always grasp how we will perceive or internalize a given situation, nor how we will ourselves be grasped or perceived. We are affected by material, in some cases genetic, in some cases more circumstantial, structures that inevitably shape our perception, and the perception of others. And, in addition to those material conditions which become part of the very shape the "for-itself" takes, we must recognize that from an early age, the gaze of the other will play a part in our self-perception. Sartre is not unaware of the effecting other's gaze. Zahavi, in his own exploration of shame references Sartre, explaining "that there are modes of consciousness which, although they are mine, nevertheless reveal to me a being which is my being without being-for-me."[12] What does this mean? In simple terms, it means that subjects are not always in control of their images.

The narrative which phenomenologist Maurice Merleau-Ponty tells about the mirror stage is a useful illustration of the child's experience when he or she begins to understand the separation between image and subject, and in turn begins to develop a self-image. Merleau-Ponty posits that the child feels very special upon first seeing themselves in a mirror, which is perhaps the reason for the image's hold on the child. But more transformative than this feeling of specialness, the child also experiences a sense of alienation. The image in the mirror indicates to the child that their embodied experience is not simply the feeling of having a body. Merleau-Ponty explains that the child is "captured, caught up" by their spatial image. The child leaves "the reality of my lived *me* in order to refer myself constantly to the ideal, fictitious, or imaginary *me* of which the specular image [mirror image] is the first outline."[13] There is, for the child, a new, "constructed me, a me that is visible at a distance, an imaginary me," built on top of the immediately felt and lived me.[14] Before the mirror stage the child has been in a world of bodies but has not understood their relationship with these bodies. Having discovered that there is a body image that they project, the child begins to grasp how this image relates to others. Returning to Sartre's analysis, shame occurs when we both feel ourselves as object in another's gaze and realize that who we are in their gaze does not match up with the expectations that the society around them has. In other words, Sartre explains that shame is "shame of *self*; it is the *recognition* of the fact that I *am* indeed that object which the Other is looking at and judging."[15]

But what exactly does the other judge? What is the content of the judgment? In the next section, I will discuss what I am calling social scripts. Social scripts are akin to social norms. Yet thinking of our social interactions as scripts makes sense of both the kind of hold that they have over us and the flexibility possible in shaping them. In what follows, I will give some theoretical backing for social scripts and present several illustrative examples, which indicate their dependence on social identity.

SOCIAL SCRIPTS

A script, in basic terms, is a text that when read can give form to a play, movie, or broadcast. A script generally includes different characters with various parts that several individuals must play to create the story or scene. Thus, metaphorically the idea of a script can capture several important features of our existence. These features include the relationship between a given subject and the context or world they find themselves in, the actual tropes that certain characters play, which are akin to roles that subjects end up finding themselves playing, and the dynamism between characters within a given plot or scene. I contend that we follow scripts in our daily lives and that this fact has great significance for the nature and usefulness of shame as an emotion.

Shakespeare puts his own spin on the metaphor between script and life: "All the world's a stage, And all the men and women merely players."[16] Though this often quoted phrase is probably considered by many to be a trite rendering of what human existence actually amounts to, we might consider the rest of the stanza. It continues: "They have their exits and entrances, And one man in his time plays many parts, His act being seven ages."[17] Jacques, the character who gives this speech, goes on to list the seven ages that a man will go through as follows: Infant, school-boy, lover, soldier, justice, lean man with "slipper'd pantaloon" and "spectacles on nose and pouch on side," and, finally, a second childishness.[18] And though individual lives will not follow this exact pattern, we will each go through different phases and play different roles in those phases. Each phase of life will come with certain societal expectations that shape the role we play in our community based on how we conform to these same expectations. Just as in the seven ages, or stages that Jacques describes, when we are young we are allowed to cry and whine. As we grow older we are meant to take on more responsibilities and have certain kinds of relationships. But how do these stages of development connect to behavioral expectations? And how do we learn to "properly" interact with other subjects?

"Proper" interactions with others are learned during our upbringing and tend to be shaped by the larger culture's normative standards. According to Tomkins, who is well known for both his affect and script theory, personality begins to develop almost immediately after we are born. Affective responses to certain situations when we are babies get shaped into more long-term patterns of behavior and become personality traits. Rae Carlson explains that "innately endowed programs for discrete affects are established before birth and remain the well-springs of human motivation."[19] For Tomkins, the fact that we will inhabit social scripts is a given, even as it is also clear that they can shape and be shaped in a multiplicity of ways. Tomkins explains: "Some scripts are innate, but most are innate and learned. The learned scripts originate in innate scripts, but radically transform the simpler, innate scripts."[20] We are both shaped and play a part in shaping ourselves from the first moment. Further, as Tomkins elaborates in his own theorization of social script theory, when a child shows signs of distress the response to this child will indicate to the same child whether the distress was appropriate to the situation. The first script, according to Tomkins, is that of the "birth distress cry and flailing arms and limbs, in response either to excessive stimulation of change of scene or a slap on the behind."[21] The second innate script that can be observed is a baby's "excitement-driven visual tracking of the mother."[22] After the first moments of life the baby will communicate their needs by crying or some similar kind of response. The initial communication of the child is responded to by the other subjects that surround them. This basic level of communication is a script according to Tomkins because already the "stimuli and responses" are being connected. They are both being imprinted "with the same abstract analogic quality, and thus amplify both, as well as amplify, connect, and make similar to each other."[23] In other words, there is an innate response to hunger (or another similar need) that the child produces, which the adult responder will associate with said need. The adult will respond in some appropriate or inappropriate way, and the behaviors of the two individuals will be made more relevant and obvious to each. Tomkins posits that the responses of a young baby impact that same child's understanding of the stimulus and response.

To clarify further how these initial scenes can become important for the child's whole life Tomkins uses the terms amplification and magnification. He tells us: "A single affect is scripted innately to amplify its own activator in a single momentary scene. But when amplified scenes are co-assembled, as repeated, the resulting responses to such a set represent magnification, or amplification, of the already separately amplified scenes."[24] Tomkins again calls on the scene of infant hunger. If that baby is in their mother's arms he or she will express hunger by various movements of their head and will activate a sucking reflex, which will allow milk to be gotten from the breast. Tomkins posits that this situation is, "by any conception of the good life," a "good scene."[25] Yet soon the child seems to indicate a desire to do it themselves. Tomkins explains:

> Psychological magnification begins, then, in earliest infancy when the infant imagines, via co-assembly, a possible improvement in what is already a rewarding scene, attempts to do what may be necessary to bring it about, and so produces and connects a set of scenes which continue to reward him with food, and its excitement and enjoyment, and also the excitement and enjoyment of remaking the world closer to the heart's desire.[26]

In other words, our early experiences build upon those innate affective responses and if similar scenes are repeated, then our affective response will be magnified. As we get older the stimuli will get more complex and the affective responses will co-mingle. This is, in brief, how all social scripts develop for a particular subject.

In adulthood, many scripts are played out every day. We could think of the typical script for a subject who is meeting a person, perhaps a new colleague, for the first time. This subject will probably attempt to make polite small talk, asking general questions about the other person's name, interests, etc. If the other person responds with anger or begins to ask deeply personal questions, the first subject will likely react with surprise or view the person who is going against the assumed script as rude. Yet even such a simple script about how to behave when meeting someone for the first time is dependent on aspects of the social identities of the subjects involved. Indeed, the place that each person is raised may teach different scripts for meeting subjects who are of varying race, class, gender.

Thus, one reason that I use the language of script, instead of, for example, ostensibly normal social behavior, is the way that script as a term can capture both the socially constructed aspect of our social interaction, while also indicating a kind of malleability for these same norms. Additionally, I hold that the term script takes into account the sense that whatever part a person is playing is going to be set within a broader narrative. Thus, scripts not only gesture to the connection between particular social identities and the kinds of norms that are closely tied to said identities, but they also get at the way different experiences with norms, looked at from any given identity perspective, may shift the script. Further, I suggest that certain racial or gendered bodies are going to be expected to play more highly specific parts, or face more moments during which it is not obvious what script is expected. I will argue this point in the following discussion of shame. So, when do we actually feel shame?

SOCIAL SCRIPTS AND SHAME

I suggest that shame occurs when two conditions are met in a particular subject's experience. The first is when some subject feels as though there is a certain script or role that society perceives that individual should be attempting to fulfill and this same subject has internalized said script. Internalization can mean either the active endorsement or the unconscious use of a script. The second condition that must be fulfilled is the script itself being broken or changed in some way. This breaking can happen in one of two ways. The first is a conscious breaking, which a subject engages in because he or she can see something wrong with the script. If the breaking is conscious then shame will only occur if something goes wrong in the attempt, that is, one's efforts to act against a norm are misunderstood or used against one (which may happen most of the time a script is broken). A script can also be broken unconsciously, if a subject does not fully understand the expectations in a given situation. A subject will still feel shame even without active attention to the broken script if he or she receives a lot of negative feedback, that is, is teased or called out in some other way. A subject will "feel no shame" if they are able to live their lives by expected scripts or if they have found a way to entirely disengage with society, such that they have no concern for any kind of script (which seems almost, if not entirely, impossible). In this way, shame stems from a kind of middle ground of recognition of our social scripts.

Though shame often arises when a subject is trying to change or shift some particular part of their identity in relation to a script, the ability more generally to effect and shift scripts may be largely impacted by social identity. Some identities are going to be consistently present, almost impossible to avoid, the very body that one inhabits being the declaration of identity, whereas other identity features will be more subtle. Subtler identity features encompass things like class, level of education, or the town or city that one was raised in, whereas race and gender are going to be much more obvious from the outset. We can, for example, think of a script for a woman who is on a date. Whether that date does something to implicate her gender or not, there are expectations for this woman that are specific to her gender, whether that be how the woman carries her body, or who is expected to make a first move. In contrast, the town that she was raised in may not play any part in the expectations a date could have for her behavior. Karin A. Martin, in her work on the ways that bodies are gendered as early as preschool, claims that "hidden curriculum that controls children's bodily practices serves also to turn kids who are similar in body comportment, movement, and practice into girls and boys, children whose bodily practices are different."[27] Iris Marion Young, in her seminal piece "Throwing Like a Girl," looks at the differences between male and female athletes and the way they use their bodies, claiming that there is no reason that a girl should be throwing, or doing any other number of activities, differently than a boy.[28] Although both of these pieces focus specifically on ways that female physical experience is shaped from a young age, both authors also gesture to the ways that such experiences will affect other areas of behavior and experience for women. We might say that the woman described above, on her first date, is, by being a woman, scripted from the start.[29]

These articles also make it clear that women are not the only subjects to be scripted from the start. Though it may seem that certain bodies are going to be more immediately scripted by the nature of the society they inhabit, every subject is going to experience scripting from a young age, as is also evident in Tomkins's developmental account. For example, there is a different sort of scripting occurring for the boys who went to the same preschools Martin studied, as for the girls. These boys were taught to take up space when they play. Though there is a certain "neutrality" that the white male body still carries in many communities, this neutrality is not born from a lack of scripts, but instead from the fact that the scripts these white male bodies inhabit are often about dominance or power. Additionally, there is less mixed messaging about how a white male body should inhabit space, and so there may be less opportunity for the white male body to face incongruity between place or situation and script. If we look at the prevalence of conversations surrounding "white male toxicity," it is clear that there are many harmful scripts fed to white men. And it may well be the case that these scripts are held in place because of these subject's experiences of and desire to avoid shame. Still, the difficulty remains for those bodies that are more or less complicatedly scripted to figure out when a script has been broken, and by who. Again, as Martin and Young have argued, it is clear that many women have been taught scripts of taking up less space, making themselves discrete, and maintaining modesty. Young explains: "Women in sexist society are physically handicapped. Insofar as we learn to live out our existence in accordance with the definition that patriarchal culture assigns to us, we are physically inhibited, confined, positioned, and objectified."[30] When a sexual assault is perpetrated the response of shame that sometimes occurs may well come from a subject's own belief that she has broken one of these scripts, even though the offending behavior was not hers or in her control.

It is probably the case that social scripts are not the only way that we experience social norms, and may only be one clear, familiar and distinctive way in which conformity to such norms is fulfilled (though it may also be the case that any norm we do enact has an attending script). It certainly is the case that shame, empirically, works very hard to regulate the scripts and the norms by which we operate. In other words, the emotion of shame keeps us as enactors of the conventional. If we were able to follow only those norms that we can critically endorse or approve of after examining them in light of alternatives, it might seem as though we would be able to avoid shame. But of course, this requires an understanding of the social norm that is beyond any agent's capacity (based on the pure number and difference in varying contexts). And even if we were able to critically endorse and act upon the norms of our choosing, we would still have to account for the ways in which norms attach differently to our identities based on both the context in which these identities present themselves and our relationship to that context. Indeed, the term social scripts captures the way that certain roles will be taken up by individuals in a given scenario as it relates to their broader individual lives, in a way that the term norm does not. This is one reason that shame is a less autonomous emotion than guilt or embarrassment. Shame can be imposed on us against our will, and felt despite our thinking that it is mistaken because it is so heavily embedded in the scripts that we actively play in some moments and reject in others. My theory of understanding the relation between self and norms through scripts is probably only one piece of the puzzle (though potentially an empowering piece). In the following section, I consider what we might do with shame, so that it may serve us on an individual level.

RESPONDING TO SHAME, OR SHAME AS THERAPY

So, what do we do with the affect or emotion? How do we respond to those moments in which we feel it? It seems clear that we are not going to be able to eradicate it entirely, unless we were somehow able to eradicate social scripts too. But there are some lessons to be learned from those experiences that bring the emotion to the fore. As argued, shame happens when a script has been broken. I contend that an agent can use the experience of shame to understand their own relationship to norms more clearly.

In exploring what it means to use shame in order to better understand ourselves, I have developed a tripartite axis which explains the different ways scripts may be implicated in our relation to the emotion:

1. When we actively do something and immediately feel as though we shouldn't have. The script that is broken is about the behavior that one expects from oneself all the time, a kind of universal, but subject specific, script. In this case the script broken is not explicitly about a subject's visible or social identity. For example, someone steals something and feels ashamed. If someone feels deeply that they are not the kind of person who steals and then does so, shame will rise to the fore.

2. When we do something that implicates a particular script that is identity dependent, and location or situation specific. For example, a woman might think, "I should not have worn this particular low-cut dress to this particular party." Perhaps the dress would be fine in a different moment, but as a woman in this context showing so much skin gives rise to shame.
3. When something is done to a subject, which draws out a particular aspect of their social identity. The shame arises because the subject being acted upon assumes that they have broken some social script, and yet unless the woman finds some aspect of her own behavior to blame, the shame will be about her whole personhood. In other words, if she hasn't really broken a script at all, but has the general sense that she shouldn't have been "on stage" at all, to use the metaphor to full effect, she may feel a deep sense of shame.

If one can understand their experience of shame as fitting into one of these three categories, then it becomes possible to sift through and find helpful internal responses. Because scripts are internalized over many years, it cannot be said for certain that the cognitive work that I discuss will lead to immediate change, but small shifts may lead to evolving and long-term change, and more informed considerations of the work that shame does. The internal work I describe may also lead to a desire to change certain norms more globally so the same kinds of scripts don't develop, for example, a more general shift in the expectations surrounding what it is to be a woman, so that objectification may become less common.

The first kind of shame can be dealt with by a person either changing their behavior so as to fit into the expected script or internalizing a new script. Indeed, if shame of this first kind arises then it may be that some norms that one would rather not break have been broken, and the subject can learn from that experience and try not to break them again. Or a subject may decide that they held a bad or wrong norm, and through an interrogation of their experience be able to recalibrate what script they will use. The second kind of shame, I argue, is situational. Again, it requires a subject to reflect upon the reasons that some specific script might be required in some situation and the subject can choose whether or not to assent to that reasoning. The third kind of shame indicates a need to break a script, or see that the script is not at all related to the experience of shame. When a subject experiences this kind of shame the best response may very well be to understand why the emotional experience is unfounded. A subject may also use this knowledge to develop a political project, perhaps through an understanding of the power structures that are at work that create the identity category and hold it in place.

As mentioned, it does seem clear that we are often reluctant to break harmful scripts because we want to avoid feeling ashamed. It is easier to accept that one is, for example, an object and let oneself be treated as an object than it is to buck this script in public. Such public bucking will force those who are paying attention to either accept or reject our relationship to the objectification that might be part of the norming that forms our social role. Thus, dramatic social change may come about through a large number of subjects understanding of and decision to reject their social scripts. Indeed, and especially in the above described third category of shame, the emotion might be avoided if the subject who does the social script breaking feels some sense of agency in doing the rupturing, even when it fails. And even if shame itself cannot be avoided, the period during which we experience it may be greatly lessened if we are able to understand how and why we feel the emotion. If breaking the script is part of some larger project that the subject is working on, then a moment of failure may lead to a doubling down on the effort toward change and not invoke as much shame.

CONCLUSION: WHAT'S NEXT?

In addition to the kind of self-work I describe, the understanding of shame and its relationship to social scripts may help make clear what social and political changes are necessary more broadly, particularly which scripts should be broken or dismantled more permanently. Foucault's critical discussion on the notion of power—particularly micro-practices of power—begins to make sense of the complex interactions, which give rise to those very hard to break scripts. For Foucault, power is always present, but is not something that one person or institution possesses over another person or institution. Instead power exists as a relationship between subjects and institutions. Foucault argues that discourse—the institutionalized way of writing or speaking about reality, which literally shapes what people think can be intelligibly said about the world—is created through a relation between power and knowledge. For example, in *The History of Sexuality*, Foucault argues that new discourses surrounding sexuality have dramatically changed the way that subjects relate to pleasure, desire, and even the self. He claims:

> [R]ather referring all the infestimal violences that are exerted on sex, all the anxious gazes that are directed at it, and all the hiding places whose discovery is made into an impossible task, to the unique form of a great Power, we must immerse the expanding production of discourses on sex in the field of multiple and mobile power relations.[31]

These new discourses, despite what many may have thought at the time, are not so progressive, nor do they uncover something more true, or essential about being a subject. Instead the new and disparate discourses produced surrounding sexuality are built through an interaction of power and knowledge.[32] According to Foucault, power and knowledge are wrapped up in each other, knowledge being a kind of exercise of power, and power being a function of knowledge. Again, in *The History of Sexuality*, Foucault explains one particular example of how power and knowledge work together. He describes the way that confession, as originally practiced only within the confines of the church, moved into our secular culture, particularly in the fields of psychology and psychoanalysis.[33] Confession, which can be understood as a form of power, was used to incite people to tell the "truth." In Foucault's words:

> Confession frees, but power reduces one to silence; truth does not belong to the order of power, but shares an original affinity with freedom: traditional themes in philosophy, which a *political history of truth* would have to overturn by showing that truth is not by nature free—nor error servile—but that its production is thoroughly imbued with relations of power. The confession is an example of this.[34]

Thus, whatever "truth" is produced in the confessional realm becomes a kind of knowledge. And according to Foucault, this knowledge, of a subject's desires, pleasures, emotions, creates our notion of sexual identity. Once this notion of sexual identity is created, subjects are pressed to produce more knowledge of themselves. This knowledge translates back to identity, which has to be cultivated and controlled by power. The scripts we follow, though developed from inborn affectual responses, are a kind of identity built, at least largely, through power. And perhaps, in understanding the scripts that we engage in, we may also begin to see what combinations of power and knowledge hold them in place, and work to see them dismantled. Shame if used as a kind of therapeutic tool in the way I have described may productively contribute to this process. Such changes are not going to be enacted by a single individual. It will take time to forge a broader shift in a society's outlook, whatever the perceived social norms of that society are. Still, perhaps it can begin with the shame of one.

NOTES

1. Virgil C. Aldrich, "An Ethics of Shame," *Ethics* 50, no. 1 (1939), 57–77.
2. Michael Lewis, *Shame: The Exposed Self* (New York: First Free Press, 1995), 2.
3. Ibid.

4. Silvan S. Tomkins, *Exploring Affect: The Selected Writings of Silvan S. Tomkins*, ed. E. Virginia Demos (Cambridge: Cambridge University Press, 1995), 217–9.

5. Ibid., 185.

6. Martha Nussbaum argues that we will have "primitive" experiences of shame during childhood, when we feel that physical bonds with our caregivers may be compromised. Later the anxiety which gives rise to shame becomes about losing our social bonds with those in our community. See Martha Nussbaum, *Hiding From Humanity: Shame, Disgust, and the Law* (Princeton, NJ: Princeton University Press, 2004), 185.

7. Erving Goffman, in the now classic *Stigma: Notes on the Management of Spoiled Identity* wrote, "in an important sense there is only one completely unblushing male in America: a young, married, white, urban, northern, heterosexual Protestant father of college education, fully employed, of good complexion, weight, and height, and a recent record in sports" (New York: Simon & Schuster, 1963), 128. In these words, Goffman gets at the idea that shame is often born of difference, and that those bodies which lie outside a very narrow understanding of normal are more likely to experience shame.

8. Dan Zahavi, *Self and Other: Exploring Subjectivity, Empathy, and Shame* (Oxford: Oxford University Press, 2014), xiv.

9. See Nussbaum, *Hiding From Humanity*, 173. In this study of shame, Nussbaum is focused on those cultures or communities that are considered Western and democratic. Yet, the emotional experience of shame, as a response to an abnormality, is itself something that I contend might be traced across cultures. Peter Goldie, in *The Emotions: A Philosophical Exploration* (Oxford: Clarendon Press, 2002) explains the ways that similar emotional experiences can be traced across cultures by viewing them through a narrative model. As an example, the language that is used to locate anger as an emotion in one society might be different than our own. But it is possible to tell a similar story in multiple cultures about the way that some single subject experiences and interacts with said emotion. A similar tracing can occur with the emotion of shame.

10. See Lewis, *Shame*, 2.

11. See Jean-Paul Sartre, *Being and Nothingness*, trans. Hazel E. Barnes (New York: Washington Square Press, 1984), 127.

12. Zahavi, *Self and Other*, 212.

13. See Maurice Merleau-Ponty, "The Child's Relations with Others," in *The Primacy of Perception*, ed. James M. Edie (Evanston, IL: Northwestern Press, 1964), 136.

14. Ibid., 137.

15. Sartre, *Being and Nothingness*, 350.

16. See William Shakespeare and Horace Howard Furness, *As You Like It* (New York: Dover Publications, 1963), Scene vii.

17. Ibid.

18. Ibid.

19. See Tomkins, *Exploring Affect*, 296.

20. Ibid., 313.

21. Ibid.

22. Ibid.

23. Ibid.

24. Ibid., 315.

25. Ibid.

26. Ibid., 317.

27. Karin A. Martin, "Becoming a Gendered Body: Practices of Preschools," *American Sociological Review* 63 (1998): 496.

28. Iris Marion Young, "Throwing Like a Girl," in *"Throwing Like a Girl" and Other Essays* (Oxford: Oxford University Press, 2005).

29. This kind of case has played a major role in the #MeToo movement.

30. Young, "Throwing Like a Girl," 42.

31. Michel Foucault, *The History of Sexuality, Volume 1*, Translated by Robert Hurley (New York: Vintage Books, 1990), 98.

32. Ibid., 6–7, 98.

33. Ibid., 128–9.

34. Ibid., 60.

BIBLIOGRAPHY

Aldrich, Virgil C. "An Ethics of Shame." *Ethics* 50, no. 1 (1939): 57–77.

Foucault, Michel. *The History of Sexuality, Volume 1*. Translated by Robert Hurley. New York: Vintage Books, 1990.

Foucault, Michel. *The History of Sexuality, Volume 3: The Care of the Self*. Translated by Robert Hurley. New York: Vintage Books, 1988.

Goffman, Irving. *Stigma: Notes on the Management of Spoiled Identity*. New York: Simon & Schuster, 1963.

Goldie, Peter. *The Emotions: A Philosophical Exploration*. Oxford: Clarendon Press, 2002.

Keenan, Julian, Gordon G. Gallup and Dean Falk. *The Face in the Mirror: How We Know Who We Are*. New York: Harper Collins, 2003.

Lewis, Michael. *Shame: The Exposed Self*. New York: First Free Press, 1995.

Martin, Karin A. "Becoming a Gendered Body: Practices of Preschools." *American Sociological Review* 63 (1998): 494–511.

Merleau-Ponty, Maurice. "The Child's Relation with Others." In *The Primacy of Perception*, Edited by James M. Edie, 96–155. Evanston, IL: Northwestern Press, 1964.

Nussbaum, Martha. *Hiding From Humanity: Shame, Disgust, and the Law*. Princeton, NJ: Princeton University Press, 2004.

Sartre, Jean-Paul. *Being and Nothingness*. Translated by Hazel E. Barnes. New York: Washington Square Press, 1992.

Shakespeare, William, and Horace Howard Furness. *As* You *Like It.* New York: Dover Publications, 1963.

Tomkins, Silvan. *Exploring Affect: The Selected Writings of Silvan S. Tomkins.* Edited by E. Virginia Demos. Cambridge: Cambridge University Press, 1995.

Young, Iris Marion. "Throwing Like a Girl." In *"Throwing Like a Girl" and Other Essays.* Oxford: Oxford University Press, 2005.

Zahavi, Dan. *Self and Other: Exploring Subjectivity, Empathy, and Shame.* Oxford: Oxford University Press, 2014.

10

An Ecological Feminist Perspective on Violence

Cecilia Herles

Although ecological feminist theorists tend to focus on issues of environmental degradation, in this chapter I will reflect on the possibilities of extending an ecological feminist framework to examine issues of violence experienced by humans and nonhumans. Through an extension of the ecological feminist framework, I hope to widen the scope of understanding violence and to emphasize strategies for interconnectedness and empathy toward others.

Ecological feminism is a social and political framework that aims to expose the interlocking forms of oppression as they connect to the environment and nonhuman beings. Drawing from the work of ecological feminist philosopher Val Plumwood, I examine how her framework can offer the necessary tools for critiquing the logic behind systems of violence.[1] Her insight can also be useful for resisting against violence by developing sustainable relationships and promoting human and ecological flourishing. By providing a nuanced critical examination of power relations and dualisms, this nonhierarchical framework can be implemented to create strategies for resisting against a mindset of violence. I see possibilities for this ecological feminist framework to connect to broader social movements in sustainable peace making.

AN ECOLOGICAL FEMINIST CRITIQUE OF DUALISMS

Val Plumwood's examination of the role of dualistic thinking in Western philosophy sheds light on a logic of colonization and legacy of oppression that impacts humans and nonhumans. Dualisms are deeply embedded in notions of power and they form a "system, an interlocking structure."[2] Plumwood explains that a dualistic way of thinking is rooted in domination and accumulation. This mindset subordinates the Other and denies dependency on the Other. She notes, "the colonised are appropriated, incorporated, into the selfhood and culture of the master, which forms their identity."[3] Examples of dualistic elements in Western thought dating back to ancient Greek philosophy include culture/nature, reason/nature, male/female, mind/body, master/slave, reason/matter (physicality), human/nature.[4] As Simone de Beauvoir argued in 1949 in *The Second Sex*, "it is understandable that the duality of the sexes, like all duality, be expressed in conflict."[5] In her reference to the Hegelian notion of Master and Slave, Beauvoir asserts that if one of the two in the dualistic relationship imposes its superiority, it establishes itself as absolute.[6] In Plumwood's ecological feminist view, it is important to note how these dualisms are dynamic and subject to change, but they are used as tools of power. Plumwood argues, power constructs difference in these dualisms to set up a subordinate and alien realm. This construction of difference is a mechanism to power over the other.

DUALISTIC THINKING AND VIOLENCE

Although these dualisms are not entirely fixed, they are often used repeatedly to reinforce power structures. Plumwood notes, "culture thus accumulates a store of such conceptual weapons, which can be mined, refined and redeployed for new uses. So old oppressions stored as dualisms facilitate and break the path for new ones."[7] Dualistic thought is found in the use of violence against the other such as gang rape and sexual assault as a war tactic as well as environmental degradation and trophy hunting. Plumwood's framework includes specific features of dualistic thinking, including the following:

Backgrounding (other as inessential)
Radical Exclusion (hyperseparation) (maximize distance between the two)
Incorporation (relational definition)
Instrumentalism (objectification)
Homogenization or stereotyping (disregard for diversity and difference)

Descriptions of these features can be used to examine how power is operating in patterns of violence.

Backgrounding is evident in how nonhumans and the environment are often unseen, and considered inessential. In addition to nonhumans and the environment, humans are often also rendered as inessential, made invisible, and subjected to violence. This denial of the Other sets up the Self as universal and not dependent upon the Other. An example of this backgrounding can be seen in the power dynamics in gang rape. Sociologist, Michael Kimmel argues, in the case of gang rape there is a bonding taking place among the perpetrators (self) that brings the men together and in which the women function as a means through which the male bond is enacted through an act of violence.[8] An ecological feminist perspective suggests that this act of exploitation is rendering the Other as inessential. Judith Butler recently noted in an interview with George Yancy that "one reason men feel free to dispose of women's life as they see fit is because they are bound to see one another through a silent (or not-so-silent) pact of brotherhood. They look the other way; they give each other permission and grant each other impunity."[9] This does not suggest that men alone are capable of violence, or that they are somehow predisposed to violent actions. Rather, this illustrates that violence can be more easily enacted through both a sense of togetherness and a backgrounding of the Other. Despite the Self often requiring the Other, this dependency on the Other is often not only ignored and rejected, but even feared. An ecological feminist approach could help shed light on ways in which backgrounding occurs in patterns of violence and could shift focus to facilitate an understanding and appreciation of those living on the margins. This perspective could also raise critical questions about the very process of how studies of violence are conducted. For example, in studies of violence, are the voices of the survivors of violence being fully considered and heard? If not, why are their voices being overlooked or even erased?

In addition to backgrounding, Plumwood explains another feature of dualist thinking she calls radical exclusion. Radical exclusion involves a hyperseparation that maximizes distance between the Self and Other. Those who are Other are deemed not only radically different, but inferior. This can be set up with denying any overlapping qualities and suggesting the Other is incapable of having similar qualities as the Self. This hyperseparation is enacted through setting up rigid barriers to focus solely on differences between the categories in order to cover up any commonalities. This radical exclusion is a feature usually embedded in violence. One illustration of radical exclusion can be found in environmental degradation and pollution in which the environment and nature is constructed as radically separated from culture. For example, the transportation and dumping of toxic waste assumes this radical exclusion. This radical exclusion is evident in the practices of environmental racism both within and beyond the borders of the United States of America in which marginalized groups are subject to concentrations of toxic "time bombs" as environmental justice scholars, Robert D. Bullard and Beverly Wright note.[10] Bullard and Wright cite the prevalence of toxic polluting industries along Cancer Alley, the 85 mile stretch from Baton Rouge to New Orleans as one example of environmental racism.[11] They also note how environmental racism can be found in how many safety regulations were waived and much of the unregulated waste from Hurricane Katrina was dumped in landfills such as the Chef

Highway Landfill, built near a mostly African American and Vietnamese community.[12]

Radical exclusion is also featured in the rhetoric of "us" versus "them" in anti-immigration policies, and it is particularly evident in the building of walls and buildings to separate from the other. These structures are constructed out of a sense of fear in order to physically enforce and maintain these strict barriers. These are attempts to obscure any commonalities shared with these humans who are often forcibly separated from their families. Yet, those in favor of such anti-immigration measures of radical exclusion are often proponents of missionary trips to other regions to "save them," so the location and proximity of the Other to the Self is relevant. Radical exclusion can also be viewed in the prison system and the higher rates of incarceration of men of color in the prison industrial complex in the United States. There is a disturbing widely held view of prison rape as a supposed deserved punishment for the radically excluded inmates, and 60 percent of all sexual violence against inmates is perpetuated by institutional staff.[13] Radical exclusion is also connected to the growing number of acts of domestic terrorism in which anti-immigrant and white nationalist ideology is held by those committing acts of mass violence in El Paso, Texas, and many other recent attacks.[14]

Violence is closely connected to these first two features of dualist thinking, and these features of backgrounding and radical exclusion are often utilized and referenced in unison. These attributes deny dependency of Self to Other and emphasize a hierarchical boundary between the Self and Other by making the Other no longer visible or connected. Plumwood explains several other features of dualistic thought which involve a denial of the Other's independence from the Self.

One of these features is incorporation which is defining and recognizing the Other only in relation to the assimilation of the Self. Through incorporation, the Other is only recognized as relational to the Self. Nature is often portrayed in this relational definition and becomes subsumed into culture and humanity, despite the fact that humanity is largely dependent upon nature. This tendency comes from a place of assumed superiority over the Other. Incorporation fails to recognize and appreciate difference, but instead masks the Other as the Self and aims to collapse the Other into the Self. This is evident in how pollution, violence to the environment, and overall environmental degradation are not factored into calculations of the Gross National Product, as Vandana Shiva and other ecofeminists have noted.[15] Indeed, Plumwood explains, "In this model, nature is seen as only accidentally related to human identity."[16] Incorporation is often a pattern in acts of domestic violence in which risk factors for domestic violence include the victims of domestic violence being subject to separation from anyone else, as well as possessiveness and control over activities.[17] A United Nations

Office on Drugs and Crime report indicates that more than eight out of ten victims of homicides committed by intimate partners are females and that "intimate partner violence continues to take a disproportionately heavy toll on women."[18]

Instrumentalism is another feature of dualistic thought in which no intrinsic value is recognized for the Other. This mindset deems the Other as only useful to the Self as a means to an end, and this can often be found in ways nature/environment are conceived. Plumwood argues, "The master model of egoism and instrumentalism, in which the systems of class, gender and colonial oppression have a heavy and connected investment, have been immensely influential in shaping the way the human relation to nature has been conceived in the west."[19] An example that illustrates this instrumentalism is found in the spectacle of trophy hunting and the images displaying the dead bodies of nonhumans as spectacles. These violent images depict dead nonhumans, such as lions or elephants, as mere objects and trophies. These graphic images are similar to images of the lynchings of people of color. In both sets of these images, the celebration and glorification of this violence ties into the ideals of conquering over the Other as an object without any intrinsic value.

Another example of instrumentalism is found in the dangerous conditions for those working in food production and the prevalence of sexual assault of workers in the fields. When there is an instrumentalist treatment of the Other, such as workers being sexually assaulted in the fields, they are shamed about their bodies. This often reflects a historical legacy of how their bodies are constructed by race and class as well as gender. One central characteristic of the objectification is to shape her into a thing, but this is also molded by race, class, citizenship, and sexuality. This is an act of reduction that constrains the realm of possibilities for the Other to navigate the world.

The last feature of dualist thinking of homogenization or stereotyping is when multiplicity is ignored. It often relies upon appeals to the "nature" of the Other as being "all the same" and having fixed and static qualities. Consider the racial stereotyping and homogenization of those subject to the violence of being sex trafficked. For example, Asians, and younger Asian girls in particular, are depicted as inherently hypersexual and submissive. As North American Asian feminist scholar and activist, Jo-Anne Lee notes, "the fevered yearnings of White heterosexual masculinity have long represented Asian women as 'naturally' hypersexual beings; as China Dolls, Suzie Wongs, Miss Saigons, Dragon Ladies, Madame Butterflies."[20] This stereotype helps to perpetuate the trafficking of Asian bodies in a global system of sexual violence linked to a historic legacy of occupation and colonization.

Through this analysis of the five features of dualistic thinking, Plumwood presents an ethical framework with tools to make sense of the world. I will now examine how dualistic thinking is linked to the prevalence of victim blaming and shame.

VIOLENCE AND VICTIM BLAMING

An ecological feminist framework can be used to examine how violence can be normalized. Violence is connected to the dualistic way of thinking that solidifies and glorifies hierarchies, at times celebrating domination and coercion in times of tragedy and suffering. Victim blaming can be a tool of power used to maintain these patterns of violence. Sonya Renee Taylor describes the concept of body terrorism that closely relates to dualistic thinking.[21] Taylor states, "Body terrorism is made of both systems and structures, hearts and minds. It is the constant stratification of bodies, placing us into hierarchies where we are valued and denigrated often at the same time, in the same body."[22] Further, Taylor discusses how binary thinking is a mindset that is both limiting and narrowing our possibilities and how we are allowed to navigate the world.[23] This mindset is closely linked to the violence directed toward some bodies more than others. As Sara Ahmed points out, "feminist consciousness can be thought of as consciousness of the violence and power concealed under the languages of civility, happiness, and love, rather than simply or only consciousness of gender as a site of restriction of possibility."[24] Particularly in acts of sexual violence, victim blaming and the glorification of sexual violence are rampant, and these features contribute to the shaping of rape culture.

From an ecological feminist perspective, victim blaming is closely connected to notions of the "wild," "feminine," and "body" as inherently seductive and dangerous, thereby women who are victims must be "asking for it." Historically, constructions of nature have often been linked to ideas of femininity too, so it's also helpful to consider how the legacies of violence can be understood in relation to these ideas. Hélène Cixous argues that in violence wielded by the master over the passive slave, "the *body* of what is strange must not disappear, but its force must be conquered and returned to the master."[25] Both nature and the feminine other are often viewed as natural prey in the form of the Other, reinforcing a "naturalness" to a supposed prey-predator relationship evident in the myth that men cannot control their natural impulses and that's why rape occurs.[26] Ecofeminist Susan Griffin argues in her work on rape, "according to the male mythology, which defines and perpetuates rape, it is an animal instinct inherent in the male."[27] As Sara Ahmed puts it, it's gender fatalism, "boys will be boys"[28] and Ahmed argues, "gender fatalism has already explained the violence against you as forgivable and inevitable."[29] However, cis women, whose gender identities match the sex they were assigned at birth, are not the only survivors of violence.[30] Consider the alarming rates of violence against trans women in the United States, particularly trans women of color.[31] Greta Gaard's work on queer ecofeminism illustrates the ways in which ecofeminism and queer theories connect, and Gaard argues how "liberating women requires liberating nature, the erotic, and queers."[32] These connections are evident in the ways sexism operates against transgender women, and Julie Serano argues that the media hyperfeminizes trans women, hypersexualizes trans women, and objectifies trans women's bodies.[33] These constructions of gender, sexuality, and nature are linked to the myths operating as explanations of these acts of violence.

Victim blaming is related to gendered constructions of vulnerability, and the tool of shaming can enforce a continued state of vulnerability. When survivors of violence are shamed, it may limit their process of healing. Sara Ahmed describes this emotional turmoil, "The world is experienced as a sensory intrusion. It is too much. . . . Perhaps you try to forget what happened. You might be ashamed. You might stay silent. You might not tell anyone, say anything, and burn with the sensation of a secret. It becomes another burden: that which is not revealed."[34]

Notions of victimhood are closely related to the notions of white womanhood as purity and the expectations of chastity to maintain this purity, as noted by Susan Griffin and Greta Gaard.[35] These ideas of victimhood for white women in particular can also negatively impact engagements with the natural world as a space not meant to be occupied by women. In contrast, Val Plumwood's response to surviving a crocodile attack illustrates her deeper understanding of what it means to be prey.[36]

In order to address violence against humans and nonhumans, I acknowledge that perpetration of male violence is not the only form of violence in operation and of concern. Only addressing male violence overlooks the ways in which coercive power operates through violent means. It is important to note how women often participate in violence too, and they exert power in doing so, as in the case of child abuse, for example. As feminist scholar, bell hooks notes, "We must see *both* men and women in this society as groups who support the use of violence if we are to eliminate it."[37] hooks emphasizes the importance of seeing women as political beings who are not inherently passive or necessarily caring toward others. She argues, "feminist efforts to end male violence against women must be expanded into a movement to end all forms of violence."[38] This challenge to end violence requires dismantling interconnecting systems of oppression that rely on a cultural acceptance of violence.

EMPOWERMENT

Despite the prevalence of shame and victim blaming, it is important to learn from the many ways in which survivors empower themselves in times of violence. I do not intend to paint a picture of survivors, particularly women, as a somehow monolithic, singular, and homogenous group that lacks agency. These damaging representations often evoke a distorted picture of these women's realities. I am reminded of Chandra Mohanty's critique of the Western assumptions of third world women as powerless.[39] In developing strategies to resist against systems of violence, I turn to the potential of an ecological feminist ethics to guide agency and empowerment to enact a promising ethics of peace. This ecological feminist approach asserts that change is possible. Decision-making based on dualistic thinking can be disrupted and rejected. This critique of dualist thinking provides strategies for moving beyond these binaries and resisting against violence as an endless cycle. As Chris Cuomo notes in her work on *Feminism and Ecological Communities*, it is possible to "articulate and develop feminist, ecological ethics that aim toward human and ecological flourishing without representing humans, women or nature in ways that are static and bounded."[40]

Victim blaming is situating the Other as background, not as relevant. Instead of backgrounding, Plumwood emphasizes the need to "recognize the contribution of what has been backgrounded, and which acknowledge dependency."[41] Feminist scholars ought to recognize how difference and dependency can not only be accepted, but indeed can be a source of meaningful connections. Lori Gruen states, "Only from a place of privilege might one even formulate the illusion that dependency is something that can be completely overcome."[42] Audre Lorde and many other women of color have drawn attention to the ways in which difference is systematically misused in order to separate from the other. As Lorde emphasizes, "it is not our differences which separate us . . . but our reluctance of recognizing those differences and to deal effectively with the distortions which have resulted in the ignoring and misnaming of those differences."[43] Lorde advocates for "ways to use each others' differences to enrich our visions and our joint struggles."[44] Embracing differences and their potential can be coupled with Elsa Barkley Brown's idea of pivoting the center, as described by Patricia Hill Collins.[45] In such an epistemic approach, Hill Collins notes, "each group becomes better able to consider other groups' standpoints without relinquishing the uniqueness of its own standpoint or suppressing other groups' partial perspectives."[46]

In order to shift toward an appreciation of difference, the patterns of backgrounding and other features of dualistic thought need to be questioned. Recognizing interconnections to break down rigid polarization is a necessary response to radical exclusion. One model for this affirmation of difference and recognition of continuity can be found in a program in The Coalition of Immokalee Workers which started in Florida and has spread beyond the Southeast of the United States.[47] They have been addressing issues of workers' rights and pushing for accountability in cases of sexual violence in the fields. The workers themselves have developed the project, and the workshops and trainings about sexual assault and harassment are happening during company time. As Bernice Yeung points out, The Coalition of Immokalee Workers has been able to convince growers to sign onto the program, and this means "they must abide by a strict code of conduct that includes better pay and zero tolerance for sexual harassment. In exchange, these growers are given an opportunity to sell to retailers such as Whole Foods or Taco Bell, which have also promised to only buy tomatoes from Fair Food farms."[48] In the past seven years, Yeung reports that "35 supervisors have been disciplined for sexual harassment, and 10 have been fired"[49] and now the numbers are dropping. This program has the potential for redefining the workspace and calling sexual harassment and violence as a workplace issue that everyone has a responsibility to actively prevent. This can be more effective as a preventative measure, as it emphasizes collectivity.

Another illustration of collective movement is the Ni Una Menos ("Not One Less").[50] This movement is addressing violence against women, trans people, and the indigenous in Latin America. This movement recognizes and appreciates difference, and it's mobilizing across differences. Judith Butler calls attention to this movement because it "has distinguished itself from individualist modes of feminism that are based on personal liberty and the rights of the individual subject"[51] and these collectives are created with a recognition that "what is happening to one life, whether it is violence, debt or subjection to patriarchal authority, is also happening to others."[52]

To avoid incorporation, focusing on strategies to encourage resistance through the Other's voices is preferable. Such resistance could involve drawing attention to ways in which the Other is not merely an extension of the Self. Instead of incorporation, Plumwood aims to "rediscover a language and story for the underside."[53] This reminds me of the Coalition of Immokalee Workers in terms of their development of a language and story for the underside that translates their stories for discussion. Instead of incorporating and asserting a denial of independence of Other, this endorses an opportunity for these voices to be heard.

In her ethical framework, Plumwood emphasizes relationality and noninstrumentality. Instead of instrumentalism, she advocates for shifting to view the other as having needs and value on its own account. Plumwood suggests "A view of self as self-in-relationships can not only explain how instrumentalism can be avoided but also an appropriate foundation for an account of the ecological self, the self in noninstrumental relationship to nature."[54]

Relationality and reciprocity are needed to resist objectification of the other and to recognize interdependency between humans and with the environment. In Sunaura Taylor's ethic-of care, she emphasizes the importance of "recognizing that we are all vulnerable beings, who during our lives go in and out of dependency, who will be giving and receiving care (and more often than not, doing both), and that contribution cannot be understood as a simple calculation of mutual advantage."[55] Taylor raises important points about how vulnerability and dependence are both unsettling, but also holds the potential for "new ways of being, supporting, and communicating."[56]

Responses to dualistic thinking cannot simply eliminate distinction and distort differences or merely fall into a cavern of reversal either.[57] Instead of homogenization/stereotyping with a mindset that x are all the same, Plumwood is urging for a deeper understanding of multiplicity. She promotes "a non-hierarchical concept of difference" (that) involves recognising the complexity and diversity of the "other nations" which have been homogenized and marginalized in their constitution as excluded other, as the "rest."[58] This is not a reversal or denial of difference. Rather, this understanding of multiplicity illustrates valuing and appreciating difference. In order to resist against the notion that we are doomed in this dualistic thinking and the inevitability of violence, there needs to be a transformation in approaching difference without fear, as this chapter has argued.

The work and the life led by Plumwood continues to inspire feminist scholarship and activism and serves as a template for both living in connection with the environment and for resisting against violence. The complex pattern of continuity and difference, particularly human continuity with nature, needs more affirmation. Plumwood promotes "a dialectical movement to recognize both the relationship and continuity denied by backgrounding and radical exclusion, and also to affirm the difference and independence of the other denied by incorporation and the definition of the other in relation to the self as lack and as instrument."[59] She further notes that "an ecological identity which aims to resolve the legacy of alienation from the earth must seek a ground of continuity not in separation from nature but in connection with it."[60] This ecological feminist framework could be a path away from violence, destruction, and coercion; hopefully it can lead us toward a more sustainable ethics of peace, creating the space for all of humanity to fully appreciate our interconnections including the intrinsically valuable connection to our environment.

NOTES

1. Val Plumwood, *Feminism and the Mastery of Nature* (London: Routledge, 1993).

2. Plumwood, *Feminism and the Mastery of Nature*, 41.

3. Ibid., 40.

4. Ibid., 43.

5. Simone de Beauvoir, *The Independent Woman: Extracts from The Second Sex*, trans. Constance Borde and Sheila Malovany-Chevallier (New York: Vintage, 2008), 16.

6. Ibid., 16.

7. Plumwood, *Feminism and the Mastery of Nature*, 43.

8. Michael Kimmel, *Guyland: The Perilous World Where Boys Become Men* (New York: Harper Collins, 2008).

9. George Yancey, "Judith Butler: When Killing Women Isn't a Crime," *New York Times*, accessed July 10, 2019.

10. Robert D. Bullard and Beverly Wright, *Race, Place, and Environmental Justice After Hurricane Katrina: Struggles to Reclaim, Rebuild, and Revitalize New Orleans and the Gulf Coast* (Boulder, CO: Westview, 2009), 23.

11. Ibid., 23.

12. Ibid., 26–7.

13. See RAINN in https://www.rainn.org/statistics/victims-sexual-violence, quoting statistics from the United States Department of Justice, Office of Justice Programs, Bureau of Justice Statistics, Sexual Victimization in Prisons and Jails Reported by Inmates, 2011–2012 (2013).

14. Dan Frosh, Zusha Elinson and Sadie Gurman, "White Nationalists Pose Challenge to Investigators," *Wall Street Journal*, Aug. 4, 2019.

15. Vandana Shiva, "Development, Ecology and Women" in *Staying Alive* (London: Zed Books, 1989).

16. Plumwood, *Feminism and the Mastery of Nature*, 53.

17. See Georgia Fatality report for 2018, accessed at http://georgiafatalityreview.com/reports/report/2018-report/.

18. See BBC, "The Women Killed in One Day in the World," *BBCnews.com*, November 25, 2018.

19. Ibid., 147.

20. Jo-Anne Lee, "Issues in Constituting Asian-Canadian Feminisms" in *Asian Women: Interconnections*, ed. Tineke Hellwig and Sunera Thobani (Toronto: Women's Press, 2006), 25.

21. Sonya Renee Taylor, *The Body is Not an Apology* (Oakland, CA: Berrett-Koehler, 2018), 86.

22. Ibid., 86.

23. Ibid., 104.

24. Ahmed, Sara, *Living a Feminist Life* (Durham, NC: Duke, 2017), 62.

25. Hélène Cixous, "Sorties: Out and Out: Attacks/Ways Out/Forays" in *The Newly Born Woman*, trans. Betsy Wing (Minneapolis: University of Minnesota, 1986), 6.

26. Susan Griffin, *Rape: The Politics of Consciousness* (New York: Harper & Row, 1979), 16.

27. Ahmed, *Living a Feminist Life*, 16.

28. Ibid., 26.

29. Ibid., 26.

30. Jen Christensen, "Killings of Transgender People in the US saw Another High Year," *CNN*, January 17, 2019.

31. Christensen, "Killings of Transgender People."

32. Greta Gaard, "Toward a Queer Ecofeminism" in *New Perspectives on Environmental Justice: Gender, Sexuality, and Activism*, ed. Rachel Stein (New Brunswick: Rutgers Press, 2004), 29.

33. Julie Serano, "Trans Woman Manifesto."

34. Ahmed, *Living a Feminist Life*, 24.

35. Griffin, *Rape: The Politics of Consciousness*.

36. See Freya Matthews' tribute to Val Plumwood in Freya Matthews, "Val Plumwood," *The Guardian*, March 26, 2008.

37. bell Hooks, *Feminist Theory from Margin to Center* (Cambridge, MA: South End, 2000).

38. Ibid., 132.

39. Chandra Mohanty, "Under Western Eyes: Feminist Scholarship and Colonial Discourses." In *Third World Women and the Politics of Feminism*, ed. Chandra Talpade Mohanty, Ann Russo, and Lourdes Torres (Bloomington: Indiana University Press, 1991).

40. Chris J. Cuomo, *Feminism and Ecological Communities: An Ethic of Flourishing* (New York: Routledge, 1998), 34.

41. Plumwood, *Feminism and the Mastery of Nature*, 60.

42. Lori Gruen, "Facing Death and Practicing Grief," in *Ecofeminism: Feminist Intersections with Other Animals & the Earth*, ed. Carol J. Adams and Lori Gruen (New York: Bloomsbury, 2014), 131.

43. Audre Lorde, "Age, Race, Class, and Sex: Women Redefining Difference," in *Feminist Theory: A Reader*, 4th edition, ed. Wendy K. Kolmar and Frances Bartkowski (New York: McGraw Hill, 2013), 292.

44. Ibid.

45. Elsa Barkley Brown, quoted in Patricia Hill Collins, *Black Feminist Thought* (New York: Routledge, 1990).

46. Hill Collins, *Black Feminist Thought*.

47. http://ciw-online.org, accessed July 10, 2019.

48. Bernice Yeung, "What Hollywood Can Learn From Farmworkers," *Slate*, September 19, 2018.

49. Ibid.

50. https://www.lanacion.com.ar/tema/niunamenos-tid53941, accessed September 19, 2019.

51. Judith Butler, quoted in George Yancey, "Judith Butler."

52. Butler quoted in Yancey, George, "Judith Butler."

53. Plumwood, *Feminism and the Mastery of Nature*, 60.

54. Ibid., 154.

55. Sunaura Taylor, "Interdependent Animals: A Feminist Disability Ethic-of-Care," in *Ecofeminism: Feminist Intersections with Other Animals & the Earth*, ed. Carol J. Adams and Lori Gruen (New York: Bloomsbury, 2014), 124.

56. Ibid.
57. Lorde, "Age, Race, Class, and Sex: Women Redefining Difference," 292.
58. Ibid., 60.
59. Ibid., 66–7.
60. Plumwood, *Feminism and the Mastery of Nature*, 102.

BIBLIOGRAPHY

Ahmed, Sara. *Living a Feminist Life*. Durham, NC: Duke University Press, 2017.
BBC.com. "The Women Killed in One Day in the World," *BBC.com*, November 25, 2018. Accessed July 10, 2019. https://www.bbc.com/news/world-46292919.
Beauvoir, Simone de. *The Independent Woman: Extracts from The Second Sex*. Translated by Constance Borde and Sheila Malovany-Chevallier. New York: Vintage, 2008.
Bullard, Robert D. and Beverly Wright. *Race, Place, and Environmental Justice After Hurricane Katrina: Struggles to Reclaim, Rebuild, and Revitalize New Orleans and the Gulf Coast*. Boulder, CO: Westview, 2009.
Christensen, Jen. 2019. "Killings of Transgender People in the US Saw Another High Year." *CNN*, January 17, 2019.
Cixous, Hélène. "Sorties: Out and Out: Attacks/Ways Out/Forays," *The Newly Born Woman*. Translation by Betsy Wing. Minneapolis: University of Minnesota, 1986.
Collins, Patricia Hill. *Black Feminist Thought: Knowledge, Consciousness, and the Politics of Empowerment*. New York: Routledge, 1990.
Cuomo, Chris. *Feminism and Ecological Communities: An Ethic of Flourishing*. New York: Routledge, 1998.
Frosh, Dan, Zusha Elinson, and Sadie Gurman. "White Nationalists Pose Challenge to Investigators." *Wall Street Journal*, Aug. 4, 2019.
Gaard, Greta. "Toward a Queer Ecofeminism." In *New Perspectives on Environmental Justice: Gender, Sexuality, and Activism*, edited by Rachel Stein, 21–44. New Brunswick, NJ: Rutgers Press, 2004.
Georgia Fatality Review, *Reports 2018*. Accessed July 20, 2019. http://georgiafatalityreview.com/reports/.
Griffin, Susan. *Rape: The Politics of Consciousness*. New York: Harper & Row, 1979.
Gruen, Lori. "Facing Death and Practicing Grief." In *Ecofeminism: Feminist Intersections with Other Animals & the Earth*, edited by Carol J. Adams and Lori Gruen, 127–141. New York: Bloomsbury, 2014.
Hooks, bell. *Feminist Theory: From Margin to Center*, 2nd edition. Cambridge, MA: South End Press, 2000.
Kimmel, Michael. *Guyland: The Perilous World Where Boys Become Men*. New York: Harper Collins, 2008.
Lee, Jo-Anne. "Issues in Constituting Asian-Canadian Feminisms." In *Asian Women: Interconnections*, edited by Tineke Hellwig and Sunera Thobani, 21–46. Toronto: Women's Press, 2006.

Lorde, Audre. "Age, Race, Class, and Sex: Women Redefining Difference." In *Feminist Theory: A Reader*, 4th edition, edited by Wendy K. Kolmar and Frances Bartkowski, 289–293. New York: McGraw Hill, 2013.

Matthews, Freya. "Val Plumwood," *The Guardian*, March 26, 2008.

Mohanty, Chandra. "Under Western Eyes: Feminist Scholarship and Colonial Discourses." In *Third World Women and the Politics of Feminism*, edited by Chandra Talpade Mohanty, Ann Russo, and Lourdes Torres. Bloomington: Indiana University Press, 1991.

Plumwood, Val. *Feminism and the Mastery of Nature*. London: Routledge, 1993.

RAINN. United States Department of Justice, Office of Justice Programs, Bureau of Justice Statistics, Sexual Victimization in Prisons and Jails Reported by Inmates, 2011–2012 (2013). Accessed July 10, 2019. https://www.rainn.org/statistics/victims-sexual-violence.

Serano, Julie. "Trans Woman Manifesto," in *Feminist Theory: A Reader*, edited by Wendy K. Kolmar and Frances Bartkowski, 4th edition, 547–550. New York: McGraw Hill. 2013.

Shiva, Vandana. *Staying Alive*. London: Zed Books, 1989.

Taylor, Sonya Renee. *The Body Is Not an Apology: The Power of Radical Self-Love*. Oakland, CA: Berrett-Koehler, 2018.

Taylor, Sunaura. "Interdependent Animals: A Feminist Disability Ethic-of-Care." In *Ecofeminism: Feminist Intersections with Other Animals & the Earth*, edited by Carol J. Adams and Lori Gruen, 109–126. New York: Bloomsbury, 2014.

Yancey, George. "Judith Butler: When Killing Women Isn't a Crime," *New York Times*, July 10, 2019. https://www.nytimes.com/2019/07/10/opinion/judith-butler-gender.html.

Yeung, Bernice. "What Hollywood Can Learn from Farmworkers," *Slate Magazine*, Sept 19, 2018. Accessed July 20, 2019. https://slate.com/human-interest/2018/09/farmworkers-janitors-sexual-harassment-training.html.

11

Embodying Freedom and Truth within the Compass Rose

Spiritual Leadership within the Revolution of Love

Eleanor Sanderson

PERCEIVING PATHWAYS OF PEACE

It is painstaking work to articulate the denigration of the feminine within our societies. Spiritual and religious postures are critically interwoven in this task. A commitment to this work is vital if the repressive, and shame-inducing, power of such cultures for individuals, communities, and the flow of the divine itself is to be abated. Articulating these connections and generating alternative cultures is a compassionate gift.[1] It can bring peace to individuals who have embodied the hooks of shame that are not of their making, or of divine desire, but belong more broadly to cultivated human society. As broader awareness grows of these connections, so too does the capacity to correct deeply embedded unconscious bias and therefore to enable more personal and collective freedom from shame and denigration.

This work is particularly important in religious institutions and spiritual movements. Religious and spiritual ways of being often implicitly express an intentional relationality which is focused on human relationships, humanity's relationship with other parts of our world, and the relationship between humanity and the divine. The increasing awareness of the complexity of human intersubjectivity requires religious and spiritual leaders to embody a greater attentiveness to, and corresponding humility within, human interrelationality. Specifically, this human interrelationality requires the identification of prevailing cultural challenges which limit the fullness of life in the context of dominant and enduring philosophical, political, religious discourse, and practice. Religious and spiritual leaders are also called to embody the culture of the divine whom they, in many ways, represent. As such, a priority for spiritual and religious leadership should be to speak in relation to past perpetuations of shame-inducing oppressive cultural bias. Yet it is important to do so in such a way as to embody hope and creativity in generating new cultures of compassion and peace.

My desire, in the context of this edited volume, is to speak personally and passionately as someone who embodies this possibility and priority in my own identity and vocation. I am one of the first[2] women bishops in the Anglican Communion. Alongside my vocation within the church, I have invested much of my life in hearing and sharing the stories of women from around our Anglican Communion[3] from a grassroots community development practitioner perspective as an academic geographer and as a public theologian. From these various positionalities, I have perceived and experienced profound human and divine pain, as well as the possibilities of transformational sacred pathways of peace. A persistent motivation throughout my work has been that the rich variety of spiritual women's voices and experiences are frequently absent from dominant discourse. Their wisdom, and the pathways into other ways of knowing that such wisdom may open, risk being lost.

Stepping into an episcopal office has meant that this passionate motivation has also been brought into sharp relief in relation to the intersubjective formation of my own identity and ability to speak or not. The liberating speech acts that I have sought to discern and facilitate in various communities particularly, explicitly engage "with spiritual bodies and as a spiritual body."[4] They now have a fresh poignancy as I seek to live purposefully within the continued cocreativity of the Christian Church. Reflecting upon the ongoing challenge of agency and vocality expressed by feminist public theologians and spiritual women in public discourse,[5] here I want to offer intimate reflections on the challenge of facilitating and embodying liberating speech acts between men and women facilitated in community with the Christian Triune God. I do so within the framing of the symbol used to depict the Worldwide Anglican Communion: the compass rose.

Canterbury Cathedral, the home cathedral of the Anglican Communion located in the United Kingdom and a sacred site marked by both peace and violence, has upon its stone floor an imprint of the compass rose accompanied by the words, "the truth will set you free."[6] The points of the compass purposefully extend beyond the confines of the image, symbolizing the global spread of the Anglican Church. At the center of the compass is the crest of St George, the Patron Saint of England, a military saint who was martyred for refusing to renounce his faith. On the top point of the compass is a miter, the symbol of the episcopal ministry that marks the nature of the Anglican Church around the world. Each aspect of this imagery could be critiqued as evocative of different vehicles of oppression.[7] I therefore intentionally use this symbol re-creatively. I engage with the compass rose as an invitation to cultivate the "manifold wisdom of God"[8] by calling forth an enlivened global community to expose oppressive forces and liberate humanity from violence, denigration, and shame through the gift of grace in Christ.[9] I seek to articulate and celebrate the call to spiritual leadership as an embodied and nonviolent revolution of love shaped by the way of the cross.

Being a bishop within an Anglican Episcopal office means that I function as an embodiment of covenantal unity. One aspect of that function is the role of liturgical authority—to hold together the spoken words of collective worship in a way which reflects both the local contextual wisdom from within our global fellowship and our inherited historical tradition. In this piece of writing I want to highlight these functions of covenantal partnership and liberating speech acts as means of embodying this revolution of love and exploring the gifts from the Christian tradition that can be used in broader society. I want to highlight and celebrate spiritual resistance to enduring cultures of shame for women, but also the compassionate creativity of intentional partnerships between women and men that transforms rather than transfers such shame.

This writing will include personal stories and poetry, interwoven with historic and contemporary Anglican liturgy, as a means of destabilizing normative writing processes. I desire to add to the poetics as well as the politics of public theology, which is desired by feminist theologians to generate alternative spaces of speech. I also seek to embody both the mystical and political endeavors of liberation theology, as articulated by Mary Grey:

> Our dreams of peace and reconciliation are nurtured and grounded by God's generosity. For it has always been a straight choice: choose life, or death. Acquiesce in the dominating culture of violence or keep alive the torch of the political and mystical spirituality of resistance.[10]

These personal, and, in most cases, previously hidden, expressions of my feminine voice, and therefore agency and wisdom, articulate an intentional partnership with divine creativity contained within the Christian tradition. Importantly, such an articulation pushes into the complex possibility of embodying peace in sites marked by violence, particularly sites juxtaposed by their resonance as simultaneously most intimate and highly public.

FINDING A PATHWAY BETWEEN THE VIOLENCE OF SILENCE OR THE VIOLENCE OF SPEECH

Critiquing the limited access and resources belonging to women in order to cultivate a language and culture according to their own genesis is a long-standing refrain among feminist philosophers and theologians.[11] *Ecriture Feminine*, for example, has been used to describe the rupture of feminist approaches to vocality and subjectivity (particularly using psychoanalytic tools) within mainstream philosophy from continental Europe. In the words of Luce Irigaray:

> [T]he real exists as at least three: a real corresponding to the masculine subject, a real corresponding to the feminine subject, and a real corresponding to their relation. These three reals thus correspond to a world but these three worlds are in interaction. They never appear as proper in the sense of independent of each other. And when they claim to do this, they neglect one of the three reals, which distorts the whole.[12]

Destabilizing masculine normative assumptions of knowledge and speech both highlights and invites intersubjective relationality. Feminist scholarship, as it grows in its diversity and depth, generates fresh insights into the worlds that exist and are created by us. For example, voices of divine wisdom have gained increasing recognition through Womanist Theology, and from indigenous and majority world women[13] in both theology and community development. These voices often strongly illustrate the interconnection between the cultivation of society, tangible indices of deprivation with a gendered reality, and the available pathways and perception of divine participation.[14]

This intermingling variety and tenacity powerfully resonate with the eco-theology of theologians such as Mary Grey[15] and the relatively recent resurgence of new Celtic theologies. Within this writing is a critical analysis of dominant theological streams and a search for, and rediscovery of, more ancient wisdoms within the Christian tradition. Mary Grey passionately asks, "who has paid much attention to the consequences of centuries of powerlessness, inequality, misogyny, marginalisation and violence on the female psyche?"[16] and urges, "how profound must be the understanding of the strategies of healing needed."[17] J. Philip Newell, speaking from within Celtic renewal, identifies the Latin root of the word religion (*religare*), which means "to bind back together" and mourns the reality that religious history "has been used to tear apart, to divorce heaven from earth, spirit from matter, one people from another."[18] He reconnects this passion for binding together with the Anglo Saxon origin of the words whole and holy with *hale*, which means health, and writes:

> We live in the midst of a new consciousness of life's interrelatedness. And this awareness relates both to life's essential oneness and to life's shared brokenness. Like never before in the history of humanity, we are becoming aware that what we do to a part we do to the whole, that the parts will not be well as long

as the whole is neglected, and that the whole will not be well if the parts are neglected.[19]

Despite this invitation into a new harmony, the challenge of its possibility remains for women in terms of how to navigate the violence of silence and the violence of speech. In relation to feminist voices within public theology, Heather Walton[20] asserts "you have to say you cannot speak," while Marcella Althaus-Reid, in a dialogue with Duncan Forrester about progressive possibilities within public theology, insists that "in the centre there are no fragments."[21] Elsewhere, Newell asserts that "Wellness is found (. . .) not in isolation but in relationship."[22] Sadly, the personal testimony of women (seen particularly in the #MeToo Movement) and in ongoing sexism and gender inequality within institutional, cultural, and philosophical realms indicate that dominant masculine discourses have yet to perceive and cultivate healthy relational culture involving women.[23] More hopefully perhaps, Newell also argues that we are experiencing a "unique moment" of "grace (. . .) in which we are being offered a new-ancient way of seeing with which to transform the fragmentation of our lives and world back into relationship."[24]

That way of seeing, I believe, is an explicitly relational theology, philosophy, and pedagogy of practice. Relational consciousness is central to the Christian tradition: relationships between humanity and God; relationships between humanity and creation; relationships within humanity; God revealed as a loving community in continual trinitarian relationship. The liturgical life of a church intentionally shapes participation and consciousness of these relationships.

Further a crucial component of this expressly relational awareness is the concept of grace. Grace (which can be understood as an unmerited gift extended by the giver) *is* a way of relational transformation and is both a revelation and a wisdom at the center of the Christian tradition as illustrated by the common exchange within the liturgy:

Leader: Grace and Peace to you from God
Congregation: God fill you with truth and joy[25]

This liturgical greeting is founded on one of the most ancient invitations into the presence of God from within the Anglican liturgical tradition. It expresses the divine relational posture toward humanity (grace and peace): a posture anchored in the words of forgiveness spoken by Jesus upon the cross, "forgive them, for they do not know what they are doing."[26] I believe that the corresponding invitation into truth and joy is particularly pertinent to our contemporary consciousness of embodied truths and the deep griefs and hidden shame[27] that steals joy-filled living. Grace, particularly grace toward self and other, is a pathway of compassion and peace that opens the possibility of fresh truth and joy being spoken aloud.

In an effort to provide a more grounded and embodied experience of the mystical poetics deemed necessary in broader public discourse, I now wish to turn from speaking about things beyond myself, but which inevitably constitute my cultural and religious self, to speak from my own auto-ethnography in a way that connects to the themes introduced so far:

I wasn't really aware of the beginning of the #Me Too movement. I had given up all social media and news apps as part of my discernment season with God leaning into an episcopal calling. Jesus was extending a hand of intimate friendship again in a new way. "Withdraw, for now," He said, "I want you to concentrate on our friendship. I want us to be very, very close." And so, I withdrew a little from the world and drew myself more deeply into the companionship of Christ and the mystery of God.

It was a message from a long faithful friend and prayer partner that prompted me to find out what #me too was all about. "I am thinking about you," she said, "with #me too and praying about how, or when, or if, you speak." So I crept out of my self-imposed media solitude and found out what #Me Too referred to.

A long familiar physiology of the body awoke. The shallowness of breath. The numbness. The heartbeat. The clammy feeling of constriction.

Here is a door.

A door that it seems utterly impossible to walk through.

And every time I stand at this door it looks different, it opens into a slightly different way. Each time I find myself at this door again I peer through its crack to a different dimly lit possibility, varying each time. The same door. Always different. But, the same door. Each time I walk away from that door I feel its oppression in my life and the grief. Each time I walk away from that door I feel my wisdom and freedom in doing so and yet I also feel the pain and the grief that I have walked away. Each time I stand at that door, standing with my forehead pressed against it, feeling the weight of myself and the metal, the cold unknown, the force of repression and yet utter impossibility of freedom overwhelms me in its alien, foreign materiality against my skin. And in some odd way another lash of the 40 minus 1 whips across my back and the skin is torn afresh; the public and private interplay of abuse, violation and shame.

Since being called so emphatically into an episcopal ministry, by both God and the church, that door has been put before me with a frequency I could never have anticipated.

The door often looks the same: an invitation to speak about sexual violence or gender-based abuse. Each time I have that invitation I have to go to another door within myself and ask if that inner door of personal experience is opened or do I speak, as I have for many years, with an insight and perspective that comes from a deeper place than people realise and with a voice that remains silent on the depths from which it is drawn.

I have also found my new female episcopal presence to be a door to others. Again and again the flow of conversation erupts from an initial greeting into a story-telling, a sharing of experiences, either personal or of a friend or family members whose female identity, call in Christ and experience of the church drips with grace, forgiveness and pain and I am immediately perceived as a safe and reassuring place where those stories can be told. Sometimes other stories begin to flow. Stories of the pain, violence and shame visited on women and the male leaders who share these stories from around our globe with me ask if I will come and minister to their women in places where female priestly or episcopal ministry is not present. These stories add to an already full cup of my own priestly ministry which has included supporting men and women who have experienced or perpetrated abuse. I experience myself as a doorway; a door of healing, a door of reconciliation, a door of possibility for peace. An episcopal ministry also necessarily requires a door of safety in which those communities within our oversight have appropriate safeguarding. I inherit shared oversight of a church deeply and sincerely wrestling with fresh awareness and concern for this part of our community life from its past, its presence and looking to its future.

And whilst these different doors have come into my new life with an unexpected frequency, I actually stand at a different doorway with Jesus distinct and yet implicit with all these.

I stand with Jesus, our hands together over the handle of another door: a very ancient one. "Be lifted up you ancient doors" (Psalm 24:7). A very old call to recognise the divine tenure of all creation and to respond to that knowledge with an invitation into relationship with God. As we stand together at this door, Jesus presses his head against the wood alongside me and speaks in embodied transference. I am taken to his earthly life and through his eyes and heart see his humanity, his very real humanity, his very real masculinity. I see through his eyes the ministry of women to him and he leans into my heart and says, "I could not have done what I did without the ministry of women to me and you will not be able to do what you will do without the ministry of men to you." Our heads feel the wood, feel the long cut grain of wood and I hear afresh the invitation to partner with God.

The social scientist within me has noticed with poignancy the pathways and prompts that necessitate and invite my ongoing journey transforming complex post-traumatic stress disorder into post-traumatic growth: "out of loss there is gain (. . .) at a time when one is vulnerable as never before, there is a sense of strength."[28] I have experienced this noticing in similar ways to noticing the once hidden aspects of humanity that, when articulated, transgress established epistemologies and disciplinary norms and consequently expand the boundaries of knowledge and analytical tools.[29] Now, in the context of leadership within a religious and spiritual community, I recognize the foundational posture of grace and peace as a particular gift within my Christian tradition that is able to cultivate both the possibility and pathway of personal and communal growth in relation to a present and a past shaped by trauma and shame. I particularly notice the need for this posture of grace alongside the need for more intentional partnerships between men and women intersubjectively and spiritually. A posture and pathway of grace is needed in order to create cultures of transformation and liberation, so that there truly is freedom from the shame that women have been particularly subjected to, rather than such cultures of shame being perpetuated in their transference onto men.

Grace is therefore needed in and for the relationships that constitute human community because of the violence and brokenness of human community. Grace is also a revelation and wisdom for human and *divine* community; a gift from a generous God (to speak in relation to Mary Grey) inviting humanity into a covenant of life and peace:

> *Differentiation* is the gift and grace offered by God (. . .) diversity between peoples is also part of the brilliance of creation, if liberated from a culture of violence (. . .) the grace of differentiation emanates from the trinitarian economy, offering itself as the very ground of communion, a communion that respects the boundaries of difference, and as the enhancement of an identity grounded in creation in the image of God.[30]

An essential part of the continued creativity of this Christian community is therefore intentionally enlivening grace-filled partnerships across human difference, particularly partnerships between men and women.

PATHWAYS OF SACRED PARTNERSHIP

In articulating *a New Harmony*, Newell speaks of "a comprehensive change of consciousness" perceivable in "countless realms of reality (. . .) including the Christian household."[31] If this consciousness is pivoting, as I perceive it to be, on an intentional and conscious relationality, there is much within both the ancient roots and the voices of female consciousness finding new spaces of expression within Christian spirituality. Christianity, at its core, is an expression of human and divine intentional partnership. In a world scared by interrelational violence, of which women have been the most subjected, it is important that interrelational spiritual wisdom is explicitly cultivated.

The Christian tradition is filled with remarkable partnerships across difference as covenantal relationships are formed and reformed. A function of the episcopal role is to act as a covenantal anchor post to communion and community. Whatever canonical law and institutional forms of power, authority, and transformation are created, the bishop's role remains to maintain an enduring covenantal community of people who intentionally choose to be subject to one another out of reverence to the divine self-emptying example.

In my ordination and installation service in the Diocese of Wellington, we created a new section of liturgy which spoke of intentional partnership between, Justin Duckworth, the Bishop of Wellington, and myself. This new liturgy acted as a leadership covenant that we undertook together. The language is intentionally evocative, combining fragments of ancient liturgical phrase and Biblical reference with contemporary intersubjective awareness and the explicit articulation of power, boundaries, and the necessary pathway of choosing a posture of humility, grace, and blessing:

> With God's will, we commit to this journey together. Humbly we come before God in partnership; not weighing our merits but committing to seek, receive and give pardon for our offenses. We enslave ourselves afresh to the Gospel of Christ, confident in the goodness of God's Kingdom coming. We beg God's passion to be ours, so that we may listen, speak and act with, and through, the unconditional love of God. In so doing, we relinquish our egos and self-protection into the hands of the crucified Christ, inviting God's Spirit to humble us and make us a merciful and whole people. We commit to walking the way of Jesus together: in places of power and powerlessness, inside and outside the boundaries of the church. We therefore give permission to God to build us and the people we lead and serve into the living temple, Christ's body and bride, symbol and reality of true partnership with God. We therefore commit to love and trust each other in this partnership, because we recognise that we each respond in obedience to God's call and because we joyfully entrust each other into the grace, anointing and blessing of Almighty God.[32]

In the following year, the words of this new liturgy began to be integrated in different ways in other new covenantal partnerships which began within our diocese—chosen and adapted by our priests and people. It was also then used in our annual Chrism service, which traditionally takes places during Holy Week, and in which the oils for baptism and healing are blessed by the bishops and the community rededicate their covenantal promises to God and to each other. Explicitly articulating relationality, power and partnership is an important way of fostering a new culture of compassion and peace, particularly when men and women intentionally lead religious communities together. By finding grace-filled language to both acknowledge our *fragmentation* as Marsella Althaus-Reid[33] has suggested, and that expressly, and with intersubjective consciousness, *binds together*,[34] can be a potential liberating speech act. Such awareness and agency has relevance beyond religious communities and can contribute to the ongoing development of grassroots participatory partnerships within community development, social science, and contextual theologies—sites of partnership in which power difference and past traumatic history resides. Such intentional liberating speech acts also have a role in cultivating broader public culture and are resonant with the feminist public theology critique of consensus-driven rationality and a desire for a greater poetics in both public theology and the public discourse it coconstructs. Within such a poetics, the "irruption of an unmanageable transcendence"[35] is an important liberation.

PATHWAYS OF SACRED RELATIONALITY: SUBJECTION, SURRENDER, SUBVERSION, AND SUBMISSION

In the day-to-day life of ministry with women, and men, I often talk of a matrix of subjection, surrender, subversion, and submission, as a way of navigating pathways of peace in the messy reality of relational life. I point to these pathways in the divine life expressed in the stories and songs of Christian spirituality and in the person of Christ. Things to which we are subject, such as the power and freedom that another's will can exercise over us and to which we ourselves can be powerless. Things to which we ourselves surrender, such as maintaining our agency, power, and selfhood, but letting go of certain control. Things to which we, with divine energy, inspiration, and power subvert, such as unconscious bias, inequality, arrogance, and violence. Things to which we consciously submit, specifically to relational partnerships and community, "submit to one another out of reverence for Christ"[36] as a basis of common life.

In order to perceive and navigate this matrix in the Christian context, I argue that we need vulnerability to one another and persistent openness to the presence of God. This perception takes compassion and care. The cultivation of this perception can often correspond to the cultivation of grace—a human grace and a divine grace and the weaving together of the two. This is because to cultivate this perception means to grow in our intersubjective competency and our own self-awareness. The limitations of our competency, with which we then become more coherently aware, also solicit the necessity of grace. Noticing the juxtaposition of imperfect human community and unconditional divine love generates an embodied humility and an intentionality of care.

One of the greatest potential injustices of physical and psychological violence against women is that it has the potential to further steal life-giving, joyful, and truthful relationship across and between the genders. This stealing occurs threefold (to speak in relation to the three worlds articulated by Irigaray earlier). Firstly, in the perpetuation of a masculine unconscious bias for men. According to Jean Byrne, "Irigaray (. . .) thinks that, from Plato onward, virtually all philosophers are complicit in the forgetting inherent in [the] universalisation of man's subjectivity."[37] This is a challenge that could also be applicable to traditional theology. This is a stealing which then robs men from perceiving and participating in, secondly, the worlds of women *and*, thirdly, the worlds of relationality with women. This stealing also occurs for women in both the unopened space of intentional relationality with them by men, but also in the withdrawing from such relational space that trauma and violence by men can create. Walking the way of love, which is a commitment to nonviolence, is an invitation into this mutual vulnerability and care for self and other as well as increasingly competent consciousness of self and other.

There is an immutable influence in the interconnected transcendent and immanent relationality of humanity and divinity. The fluidity and potential fecundity of this relationality is critical, and to this the wisdom of Irigaray, again, can speak: "Poetic language sometimes keeps available a part of the energy of the coming into relation, and that of thinking when it exists."[38]

I wish to share the following poetry as a means of bearing witness to that interconnection and energy. I wrote the following three poems during a forty-day period of spiritual discipline. The discipline of writing a poem a day was a divine invitation to which I responded, that served to create a space of my own voice, self-awareness and self-care. Each of these poems relates to interactions with men that occurred during those days. In sharing them in this context, I seek to again give a more grounded and embodied articulation of love and grace and, again, increase the poetic and mystical interruption within normative written discourse.

I am visited today
by Godly men
who speak to me
words of heartfelt
apology and ask
permission to journey
with me, to walk
with me, to stand
with me and pray
with me:

my heart is full
of love

We talk of forgiveness
narcissism and the
projection of ego
and pain
as a sermon for
the wounded healer
sits in a corner
part of my brain,
in view and waiting,
whilst I speak to a
church full of people about
the Word becoming flesh
in us
I sense we have always
enjoyed each other's
gentleness and wisdom;
I know you are a balm
to my current wounds.
It is very windy today
and I couldn't find
the way into the church.
I am glad I found you
I am glad God found
a path for us to share
in which we can
be weathervanes
for the blowing of God's
Spirit through each other's
lives

My heart is so
satisfied with love;
to think you have
prayed for me
for years
and as I put
the kettle on
I feel Christ
lean into my
consciousness and

drop the truth
that he has
prayed for me
without ceasing
since before I
was born and
such knowledge is
too wonderful for
me to hold in
my heart:
how hard it is
for us to know
the love of God
which I proclaim
in blessing over others
and receive from
your hands afresh
today myself

During the forty days in which these poems were written, I met with an academic colleague and friend involved in monastic Christian community and at the forefront of international refugee work. We had both been involved in hard public and private conversations and as we met together we shared poetry spontaneously between us, reflecting that in the cultural context of Aotearoa New Zealand the role of women is often to bring songs to balance the more masculine space of speech making. She gifted me a poem to mark the new pathway of relationality between myself and the church in my ordination as a bishop. The poem spoke of the way women found different paths of agency and physicality as the countering actions of love in relation to Jesus's challenge to bind the "strong man."[39] I affirmed my understanding that blessing is a form of binding—choosing relational connection but also choosing relational postures of nonviolent love.

The strength of personhood required to bless in the face of terror and violence must never be underestimated, nor hurried, nor forced on anyone, if we take our cues from the ministry of Jesus. But, from my own embodied revolution of love, I take ownership of the invitation from God to own the act of blessing. Once experienced in such an extreme demonstration of grace, choosing to bless and not curse then becomes a more readily accessible posture within the smaller everyday interactions of humanity. I believe the action of choosing to pray blessing in the face of oppression is an action that retains, or regains, agency and overcomes and eradicates shame, because it requires and embodies dignity and power.

Painstaking resilience is required to live with the triggers of post-traumatic stress. To pray blessing again and again on the shadowy past and the stark present, to proclaim blessing from a generous posture of grace, unmerited, undeserved gift, given again and again, carves fresh pathways of grace and peace in a world upon which fresh truth and joy will then have chance to walk. Blessing is a pathway of compassion and peace that can be found in every facet of the matrix of subjection, surrender, submission, and subversion and it is a power of God given to humanity that cannot be taken away. Blessing is also a pathway of fresh relational subjectivity between the self and the other—a gift relinquished to us by a God choosing intersubjectivity with humanity. Grace and blessing remain the agency of the giver. When we receive grace and blessing, we have to choose to receive it, but choosing *not* to receive it does not remove the agency of the giver who has given it freely. When we either choose to give grace and blessing or to receive grace and blessing, we create new relational possibilities and new pathways of peace by embodying or enabling liberating speech acts.

The analysis of post-traumatic growth identifies a number of areas of positive change where it is possible to thrive at a new level of higher functionality for people exposed to trauma. The traumatic events themselves "are not viewed as desirable—only the good that has come out of having to face them."[40] These areas of higher functioning include appreciation of life, more meaningful personal relationships, increased personal strength, a richer existential and spiritual life, and the ability to perceive and prioritize new possibilities.[41] These growth areas closely align with the areas of calling for the cultivation of transformative Christian community and which the Christian community is called to contribute, in turn, with the surrounding world.[42] The lens of post-traumatic growth is therefore a very powerful lens to reframe leadership for a religious community, particularly a community founded on following the divine self-revealed as a human who experienced violent and shameful death, resurrection, and commissioning of humanity into fresh spiritual strength and release. Given the statistical prevalence of GBV (one in three women in New Zealand),[43] as more women come to operate in spaces of such leadership, the likelihood that they will be able to do so drawing on the potential gifts cultivated through post-traumatic growth is a hopeful possibility. I therefore bear witness here to my own embodied revolution of love which has been shaped by the way of the cross.

RETURNING TO THE COMPASS ROSE

Sites marked by violence (uncovered and unhidden) and yet the persistent determination of peace are powerful sacred sites of holiness and wholeness, particularly when embodied and intimate, they (we) testify to grace-filled human and divine partnerships in and through trauma and pain. Here, perhaps, is the red cross on a white shield (the center of the compass rose image), evoking the words of Jesus, "blessed are the peacemakers, for they shall be called children of God."[44] These are words which simultaneously acknowledge violence and invite the transformation of trauma into a movement of nonviolent love and post-traumatic growth. The compass, perhaps reseen as an orientation of that pathway, a road of freedom and truth that extends continually outwards, leading the fabric of institutional church into constant re-creative transformation. Within the Anglican Communion this is an intentionally global transformation, in which the manifold wisdom of God, the many colored wisdom from global cultures, and from women, men, and children increasingly language the tradition of the church and form grace-filled covenants of intentional partnership.

A new era of awareness regarding interrelational subjectivity has emerged. And with this era comes new possibilities and new demands for spiritual and religious leadership to be both attentive to the perpetuation of shame-inducing unconscious bias and in finding pathways beyond. Such leadership, when it intentionally cultivates awareness of the multiple worlds of and between men and women, can, in turn, contribute new possibilities and pathways of peace within broader culture and society. I particularly offer the proactive posture of grace (culminating in the liberating speech act of blessing) and the explicit intersubjective work required for intentional partnership across humanity and across humanity and divinity as possibilities from the Christian tradition to contribute to the cultivation of new cultures of compassion and peace. I therefore publicly offer the immanent and transcendent poetics in these very personal reflections as a contribution to the ongoing transformation of our inherited cultures, recognizing the public significance of freshly articulating possible, and powerful, nonviolent pathways of love.

I end this contribution with words of liturgy from one of the new monastic communities covenanted into our Anglican Diocese and which I, along with the men, women, and children of our own residential Christian community, pray every morning together:

Leader: You call us together as your body
All: Help us to share the day well with others
Leader: Yours is a revolution of love[45]

NOTES

1. See, for example, the work of Ramona Boodoosingh, Melanie Beres and David Tombs, "Research Briefing: Violence against women in Samoa," in *Women's Studies Journal* 32, no. 1 (2018): 33–56, which illustrates and explores how the Christian church in Samoa can be complicit in perpetuating gender inequalities yet also has undeniable potential as a source for transformation.

2. The first female Anglican Diocesan Bishop, Rt Rev Dr Penelope Jamieson, was ordained in 1990 in the Anglican Church of Aotearoa New Zealand and Polynesia (see Jenny Chambers and Erice Fairbrother, *Vashti's Banquet: Voices from her Feast. Essays to mark the 25th Anniversary of the First Woman Bishop in the Anglican Communion* (Auckland: General Synod Office, 2016)). I am only the fourth woman since then to serve as bishop in this same Province and the first female bishop serving within the Diocese of Wellington. The first female bishop in my home country of England was ordained in 2015.

3. See, for example, Eleanor Sanderson, "The Sacred Thread: Weaving our Bonds of Affection," *Anglican Theological Review* 98, no. 2 (2016): 255–69.

4. Eleanor Sanderson, "Emotional Engagement in the Context of Development and Spirituality Research," *Emotion Space and* Society 5, no. 2 (2012): 123. This concern to honor positional knowledge and experience is central within feminist methodologies and within the growing body of participatory methodology within both Development Studies theory and practice and within qualitative research methodologies (see Eleanor Sanderson, "Participatory Cartographies: Reflections from Research Performances in Fiji and Tanzania," in *Participatory Action Research Approaches and Methods: Connecting People, Participation and Place*, eds. Sara Kindon, Rachel Pain and Mike Kesby (New York: Routledge, 2006), 122–31; and Sara Kindon and Eleanor Sanderson, "Progress in Participatory Development: Opening up the Possibility of Knowledge Through Progressive Participation," *Progress in Development Studies* 4, no. 2 (2003): 114–26.

5. In the context of feminist public theology, see Heather Walton, "You Have to Say You Cannot Speak: Feminist Reflections Upon Public Theology," *International Journal of Public Theology* 4 (2010): 21–36. For a powerful illustration of the depth of challenges facing the cultivation of both breath and voice in the context of womanist theology, see Teresa Fry Brown, "Avoiding Asphyxiation: A Womanist Perspective on Intrapersonal and Interpersonal Transformation," in *Embracing the Spirit: Womanist Perspectives on Hope, Salvation and Transformation*, ed. Emile Townes (New York: Orbis Books, 1997), 72–94.

6. For an explanation of the origin of this symbol, see the Canterbury Historical and Archaeological Society http://www.canterbury-archaeology.org.uk/compass/4 590809642.

7. The compass, for example, is a navigation tool connected to the European colonization of the world. The constellation of the Southern Cross would be an alternative imagery of navigation and movement from the Southern Hemisphere and the cultural legacy of Polynesian navigation. The military imagery can be particularly confronting, particularly recognizing the gender-based violent atrocities carried out against women in the context of war. The miter represents an office of ecclesiastic authority to which only one gender, one part of the image of God, has been allowed to occupy for many centuries.

8. To speak in relation to Ephesians 3:10 "through the church, the manifold wisdom of God should be made known" (New International Version [NIV] (London: Hodder & Stoughton, 2011). The language of "manifold" depicts many colored wisdom and could therefore indicate a celebration of both the multicultural reality of the

church coming into its fulfillment and the full expression of male and female ways of knowing, which reflect the likeness of God.

9. Such a call is anchored in the Anglican Communion by the fivefold definition of mission adopted by the Anglican Consultative Council which includes the transformation of unjust structures of society. The Anglican Communion Office includes a dedicated Women and Society office which specifically undertakes this work of education and transformation in relation to the global Anglican Communion.

10. Mary Grey, *To Rwanda and Back: Liberation Spirituality and Reconciliation* (London: Darton, Longman and Todd, 2007), 192.

11. This detailed exposition is particularly expressed in the work of Luce Irigaray. See, for example, Luce Irigaray, *This Sex Which Is Not One* (New York: Cornell University Press, 1985); Luce Irigaray, *Speculum of the Other Woman* (New York: Cornell University Press, 1985); Luce Irigaray, *To be Two* (London: The Athlone Press, 2000).

12. Luce Irigaray, *The Way of Love* (London and New York: Continuum, 2002), 111.

13. In relation to early and yet enduring critiques of community development, see Sinith Sittirak, *Daughters of Development: The Stories of Women and the Changing Environment in Thailand* (Bangkok: WENIT, 1996). In relation to indigenous theological critique, see Jenny Plane Te Paa, "Listening to the Spirit: Preparing the Way . . . ," *First Peoples Theology Journal* 4, no. 1 (2006): 64–73.

14. Eleanor Sanderson, "The Challenge of Placing Spirituality within Geographies of Development," *Geography Compass* 1, no. 3 (2007): 389–404.

15. Mary Grey, *Sacred Longings: The Ecological Spirit and Global Culture* (Minneapolis, MN: Fortress Press, 2004).

16. Grey, *To Rwanda and Back*, 172.

17. Ibid., 173.

18. J. Philip Newell, *A New Harmony: The Spirit, the Earth, and the Human Soul* (Edinburgh: Saint Andrews Press, 2012), xxiii.

19. Ibid., xvii.

20. Walton, "You Have to Say You Cannot Speak."

21. Marcella Althaus-Reid, "In the Centre There Are No Fragments: Teologias Descejadas (Reflections from Unfitting Theologies)," in *Public Theology for the 21st Century*, eds. William Storrar, Andrew Morton and Duncan Forrestor (London and New York: T&T Clarke a Continuum Imprint, 2004), 365–83. It is also significant to recognize the impact of colonization on the systematic suppression of indigenous language, which further compounds challenges for indigenous women.

22. Newell, *A New Harmony*, xvii.

23. Again, the progressive scope in the work of Luce Irigaray powerfully critiques and illustrates this challenge. This is particularly expressed in her assertion that without a cultivation of a culture of the two (between men and women) then a progression to a culture of the many is not possible. See, for example, Luce Irigaray, *Elemental Passions* (New York: Routledge, 1992) and Irigaray, *The Way of Love*.

24. Newell, *A New Harmony*, xxx

25. *A New Zealand Prayer Book/He Karakia Mihinare O Aotearoa* (Christchurch, New Zealand: Genesis, 2002), 404.

26. Luke 23:34 (New International Version [NIV])

27. See Curt Thompson, *The Soul of Shame: Retelling the Stories We Believe About Ourselves* (Downers Grove: InterVarsity Press, 2015).

28. Post-traumatic growth refers to the now recognized possibility of developing higher than usual functioning in a range of cognitive and personality traits as a consequence of experiencing and processing the reality of post-traumatic stress disorder and complex post-traumatic stress disorder. See Richard Tedeschi and Lawrence Calhoun, "Posttraumatic Growth: Conceptual Foundations and Empirical Evidence," *Psychological Inquiry* 15, no. 1 (2004), 6.

29. Sanderson, "Emotional Engagement in the Context of Development and Spirituality Research." This work particularly identifies the similar experience of transgression that emotional awareness and spiritual awareness have in intercultural qualitative research.

30. Grey, *To Rwanda and Back*, 197.

31. Newel, *A New Harmony*, xxi.

32. Eleanor Sanderson and Justin Duckworth, "The Bishops' Commitment to Partnership" in Episcopal Ordination of the Reverend Canon Dr Eleanor Ruth Sanderson and Licensing as the Assistant Bishop of the Diocese of Wellington, 2017, The Anglican Church in Aotearoa New Zealand and Polynesia, p 17.

33. Althaus-Reid, "In the Centre There Are No Fragments."

34. Newel, *A New Harmony*.

35. Walton, "You Have to Say you Cannot Speak," 36.

36. Ephesians 5:1 (New International Version [NIV])

37. Jean Marie Byrne, "Breath of Awakening: Nonduality, Breathing and Sexual Difference," in *Breathing with Luce Irigaray*, edited by Emily Holmes and Lenart Škof (London and New York: Bloomsbury, 2013), 68.

38. Irigaray, *The Way of Love*, 136. It is important to note that in this section of Irigaray's writing she refers to human (s) and divinity (ies).

39. Mark 3:27 (New International Version [NIV]).

40. Tedeschi and Calhoun, "Posttraumatic Growth," 7.

41. Ibid.

42. The increased nuance in appreciating the link between religion and spirituality and post-traumatic growth can be seen in Annick Shaw, Stephen Joseph and Alex Linley, "Religion, Spirituality, and Posttraumatic Growth: A Systematic Review," *Mental Health, Religion and Culture* 8, no. 1 (2005): 1–11.

43. A confronting statistic highlighted and supported by New Zealand Women's Refuge (www.womensrefuge.org.nz) and part of the motivation behind the commissioning of a Perspex statue of Kate Shepherd (one of the founders of the Women's Christian Temperance Movement and who was instrumental in the suffrage movement that resulted in New Zealand becoming the first country in the world to give women the vote) which is a literal embodiment of letters of petition from women's refuge members. This statue stands in the National Library of New Zealand, based in Wellington and opposite our Anglican Cathedral.

44. Matthew 5:9 (New International Version [NIV]).
45. Ngatiawa River Monastery, *Daily Devotions* (Reikorangi: Ngatiawa River Monastry, 2017), 9.

BIBLIOGRAPHY

A New Zealand Prayer Book/He Karakia Mihinare O Aotearoa. Christchurch, New Zealand: Genesis, 2002.

Althaus-Reid, Marcella. "In the Centre There Are No Fragments: Teologias Descejadas (Reflections from Unfitting Theologies)." In *Public Theology for the 21st Century*, edited by William Storrar, Andrew Morton and Duncan Forrester, 365–83. London and New York: T&T Clarke a Continuum Imprint, 2004.

Boodoosingh, Ramona, Melanie Bres and David Tombs. "Research Briefing: Violence against women in Samoa." *Women's Studies Journal* 32, no. 1 (2018): 33–56.

Byrne, Jean Marie. "Breath of Awakening: Nonduality, Breathing and Sexual Difference." In *Breathing with Luce Irigaray*, edited by Emily Holmes and Lenart Škof, 67–82. London and New York: Bloomsbury, 2013.

Canterbury Historical and Archaeological Society. http://www.canterbury-archaeol ogy.org.uk/compass/4590809642.

Chambers, Jenny, and Erice Fairbrother, eds. *Vashti's Banquet: Voices from her feast. Essays to mark the 25th Anniversary of the first woman Bishop in the Anglican Communion*. Auckland, New Zealand: General Synod Office, 2016.

Fry Brown, Teresa. "Avoiding Asphyxiation: A Womanist Perspective on Intrapersonal and Interpersonal Transformation." In *Embracing the Spirit: Womanist Perspectives on Hope, Salvation and Transformation*, edited by Emilie Townes, 72–94. New York: Orbis Books, 1997.

Grey, Mary. *Sacred Longings: The Ecological Spirit and Global Culture*. Minneapolis: Fortress Press, 2004.

Grey, Mary. *To Rwanda and Back: Liberation Spirituality and Reconciliation*. London: Darton, Longman and Todd, 2007.

Irigaray, Luce. *Elemental Passions*. Translated by Joanne Collie and Judith Still. New York: Routledge, 1992.

———. *Speculum of the Other Woman*. New York: Cornell University Press, 1985.

———. *The Way of Love*. London and New York: Continuum, 2002.

———. *This Sex Which Is Not One*. New York: Cornell University Press, 1985.

———. *To be Two*. London: The Athlone Press, 2000.

Kindon, Sara and Eleanor Sanderson. "Progress in Participatory Development: Opening up the Possibility of Knowledge through Progressive Participation." *Progress in Development Studies* 4, no. 2 (2003): 114–26.

New International Version (NIV) International Bible Society, London: Hodder and Stoughton, 2011.

Newell, J. Philip. *A New Harmony: The Spirit, the Earth, and the Human Soul*. Edinburgh: Saint Andrews Press, 2012.

Ngatiawa River Monastry. *Daily Devotions*. Reikorangi: Ngatiawa River Monastry, 2017.

Plane Te Paa, Jenny. "Listening to the Spirit: Preparing the Way. . ." *First Peoples Theology Journa* 4, no. 1 (2006): 64–73.

Sanderson, Eleanor. "Participatory Cartographies: Reflections from Research Performances in Fiji and Tanzania." In *Participatory Action Research Approaches and Methods: Connecting People, Participation and Place*, edited by Sara Kindon, Rachel Pain and Mike Kesby, 122–31. London and New York: Routledge, 2006.

———. "The Challenge of Placing Spirituality within Geographies of Development." *Geography Compass* 1, no. 3 (2007): 389–404.

———. "Emotional Engagement in the Context of Development and Spirituality Research." *Emotion Space and Society* 5, no. 2 (2012): 122–30.

———. "The Sacred Thread: Weaving our Bonds of Affection." *Anglican Theological Review* 98, no. 2 (2016): 255–69.

Sanderson, Eleanor and Justin Duckworth, "The Bishops' Commitment to Partnership." In *Episcopal Ordination of the Reverend Canon Dr Eleanor Ruth Sanderson and Licensing as the Assistant Bishop of the Diocese of Wellington*. The Anglican Church in Aotearoa New Zealand and Polynesia, 2017.

Shaw, Annick, Stephen Joseph and Alex Linley. "Religion, Spirituality, and Posttraumatic Growth: A Systematic Review." *Mental Health, Religion and Culture* 8, no. 1 (2005): 1–11.

Sittirak, Sinith. *Daughters of Development: The Stories of Women and the Changing Environment in Thailand*. Bangkok: WENIT, 1996.

Tedeschi, Richard and Lawrence Calhoun. "Posttraumatic Growth: Conceptual Foundations and Empirical Evidence." *Psychological Inquiry* 15, no. 1 (2004): 1–18.

Thompson, Curt. *The Soul of Shame: Retelling the Stories We Believe About Ourselves*. Downers Grove: InterVarsity Press, 2015.

Walton, Heather. "You Have to Say You Cannot Speak: Feminist Reflections Upon Public Theology." *International Journal of Public Theology* 4 (2010): 21–36.

Index

About the Contributors

Janet H. Anderson is an independent journalist and trainer, working with multidisciplinary teams of civil society activists, media professionals, and academics to improve their storytelling skills, create persuasive human rights campaigns, and navigate social media. The founder of Justice Connection, she also manages on and offline spaces for engagement on peace and justice. She is vice president of the Journalists Association at the International Criminal Court, and supports fellow journalists through training and visits to courts and tribunals. She has been published in the *Guardian*, the *Economist*, BBC World Service, IWPR, Justice-Info, Justice Hub, *RNW Media*. She has also authored several books on monitoring atrocity crime trials, including *Reporting Justice: A Handbook on Covering War Crimes Courts* (2006), *Reporting Transitional Justice: A Handbook for Journalists* (2007), *and Assignment Justice: A Practical Guide for Sudanese Journalists* (2009).

Jane Barter is professor of Religion and Culture at The University of Winnipeg, Canada, on Treaty One, the traditional land of the Anishinaabe, Cree, Dene, Oji-Cree, and Dakota peoples, and the homeland of the Métis Nation. She is author of several books on theology, and currently writes at the intersection of religion, philosophy, and feminist theory.

Benjamin Duerr is an international lawyer and foreign policy expert. He is also an award-winning journalist who has reported from ten African countries about conflicts, peace, and humanitarian affairs. He works as a strategist for governments and organizations. Most recently, he worked as a lawyer and policy maker in the Department for International Affairs of the Ministry of Justice and Security of the Netherlands, and as advocacy specialist with the foundation of the Congolese Nobel Peace Prize laureate Dr. Denis Mukwege.

He studied political science and diplomacy at the LSE and holds an LLM in international law from the United Nations Interregional Crime and Justice Research Institute in Turin, Italy.

Rouba El Helou-Sensenig is a university lecturer in the Faculty of Law and Political Science at NDU in Lebanon. She is gender and political communication coordinator at the GCGM studies unit at NDU. As a PhD candidate at the University of Erfurt she is working on Arab-on-Arab Othering in the digital sphere. She is an experienced UNESCO trainer for the field of journalism and information disorder. Her areas of inquiry include political communication, GBV, intersectional gender studies, digital rights, and rule of law in media. She also has a background in social justice activism and journalism in Lebanon and Syria.

Vita Emery is a PhD candidate at Fordham University. She is currently finishing a dissertation that seeks to revitalize existential ethics through an analysis of freedom, subjectivity, and social scripts. In particular, the project explores the ways in which subjects are able to interact with and have control over the roles they take up and put down throughout a lifetime. Her other research interests include social and political philosophy and philosophy of literature and very recently she has been exploring the intersection of contemplative practice and existential ethics. Currently, Emery is a teaching associate at Fordham University, and regularly teaches Philosophical Ethics and Philosophy of Human Nature to undergraduate students.

Shé M. Hawke is an interdisciplinary scholar, social justice advocate, and poet, originally from Australia. She is head of the Mediterranean Institute of Environmental Studies at the Science and Research Centre, Koper, Slovenia, where she now lives. She is also an honorary associate in the Department of Gender and Cultural Studies at the University of Sydney, where she gained her PhD in 2008 and taught from 2005 to 2013. Her research orbits around water and the elemental worlds as it intersects with biosocial cultural studies, philosophy, theology, psychoanalysis, and geopolitics. Her last book *Aquamorphia: Falling for Water* (Interactive Publications, Brisbane) appeared in 2014 as a tribute to water in all its forms.

Cecilia Herles is assistant director of the Institute for Women's Studies at the University of Georgia. She has developed service-learning courses on *The Gendered Politics of Food* and *Environment, Gender, Race, Class*, and a course on *North American Asian Feminisms*. She is the recipient of the 2019 Service-Learning Teaching Excellence Award and the 2016 Creative Teaching Award at the University of Georgia. Herles's research examines feminist philosophies, environmental ethics, and philosophies of race. Her current focus is global climate change, local and global food systems, and activism. She currently serves as faculty advisor for WSSO, Campus Kitchen Project at UGA, and Triota Honorary Society.

Farida Khalaf (Farida Global Organization) is one of more than 6,500 Yazidi survivors of ISIS enslavement and genocide. She was born in Kocho village near Sinjar in northern Iraq. She was a high school student when ISIS attacked her village, killing men and taking women and children hostages. She lost her father and her older brother, and was taken then into captivity with her mother and her other brothers. Her mother escaped after nine months in captivity. Farida was held in captivity for four months where she was subjected to unimaginable suffering including physical and mental abuse. Since her escape, Farida has been an effective part of Yazda organization global advocacy campaign to bring ISIS militants to justice, raise awareness, and bring international attention to the genocide. So far, Farida has spoken in UK, France, Germany, Spain, Sweden, Portugal, Lebanon, Italy, Netherlands, Poland, Brazil, and Belgium. Farida published her book, *The Girls Who Beat ISIS*, which has been published in more than fourteen languages. Farida is the winner of Polish Foreign Minister's Pro Dignitate Humana Prize 2017 and the 2017 Marsh Award for Peacemaking and Peacekeeping, by Wilton Park, an executive agency of Foreign and Commonwealth Office-UK government, and has also received the LiberPress Award for 2017. She also has a documentary film: *With Words Against the IS—a Yazidi Raises the Voice*, and she has spoken with numerous international media outlet including BBC, SWR, Reuters, DW, RT, CBC.

Aaron Looney is assistant professor of Philosophy at Eberhard Karls University in Tubingen, Germany. His research interests focus on anthropology, ethics, and the philosophy of religion, especially in contemporary continental philosophy. He is the author of the first English-language monograph on the French Jewish philosopher Vladimir Jankélévitch, *Vladimir Jankélévitch: The Time of Forgiveness* (Fordham University Press, 2015) in which he investigates the relations between trauma and memory and the tensions between crimes against humanity and reconciliation processes. He is currently working on a book project on shame and confessions in Augustine.

Danny Marrero is course director and instructor of Critical Thinking at Verto Education (USA). He also teaches legal research and methodology in the doctoral program of Juridical Sciences at Pontificia Universidad Javeriana (Bogotá, Colombia). The fascinating issues that arise at the intersection between Law and Philosophy have been the inspiration for his academic growth, leading him to earn two bachelor's degrees: one in philosophy, one in law, plus an LLM, and an MA and a PhD in Philosophy. His research interests include critical thinking, epistemology, philosophy of law, criminal law, and applied ethics.

Melissa McKay is an international criminal lawyer who focuses on the integration of feminist legal theory, international criminal law, and strategic litigation to better address the structural inequalities that facilitate sexual violence in conflict and transitioning societies. She currently works at the Office of the Co-Prosecutors at the Extraordinary Chambers in the Courts of Cambodia, and has previously worked at the International Criminal Tribunal for the former Yugoslavia and appeared before the African Commission on Human and People's Rights. She has additional experience as a consultant on gender rights in Nepal, the Philippines, and Rwanda. Melissa holds a BA (Hons) from St. Francis Xavier University, a JD from Queen's University, and an LLM in International Legal Studies from New York University.

Eleanor Sanderson is assistant bishop, and first female bishop, in the Diocese of Wellington in the Anglican Church of Aotearoa New Zealand and Polynesia. She is also a research associate in the School of Religious Studies, Victoria University of Wellington, and former Fellow for Public Theology at the Centre for Anglican Communion Studies at Virginia Theological Seminary. She has an enduring commitment to social justice and advocacy, and has had a long involvement in international community development. Sanderson has a range of academic publications in the fields of international development, feminist geography, spirituality, and public theology. She and her family currently live in an intentional residential community, which they cofounded, which resources young adult students in Wellington, New Zealand.

Sashinungla is professor of Philosophy at Jadavpur University, Kolkata, India. She is the author of *Environment Preservation: A Philosophical Critique* (Decent Books, 2005), and coeditor of *Tradition and Modernity: Essays on Women of India* (Suryodaya Books, 2015), *Ethics and Culture: Some Indian Reflections* (Decent Books, 2010), and *Patient-Physician Relationship* (Decent Books, 2007). She has published widely on feminist philosophy, insurgency, ethnic conflict, foreign policy, and tribal philosophy and culture with a particular focus on the Indian context, and is associate editor of *Jadavpur Journal of Philosophy*. Her current research projects focus on philosophy of dialogue, cosmocentric environmental thinking, and tribal epistemology and metaphysics.

Lenart Škof is professor of Philosophy and head of the Institute for Philosophical Studies at Science and Research Centre of Koper (Slovenia) and professor of humanities at Alma Mater Europaea (Maribor, Slovenia) where he is also a dean of Institutum Studiorum Humanitatis faculty. He received a Fulbright grant (Stanford University) and Humboldt fellowship for experienced researchers (Max Weber Institute for Advanced Studies, Universität Erfurt). His main research interests lie in new cosmology and new materialism, philosophical theology, the philosophy of American pragmatism, and feminist philosophy. His most recent books include *Atmospheres of Breathing*, ed. by L. Škof and P. Berndtson (SUNY Press, 2018), *Ethik des Atems* (Herder/Karl Alber, 2017), *Poesis of Peace*, ed. by K-G. Giesen, C. Kersten and L. Škof (Routledge, 2017), and *Breath of Proximity* (Springer, 2015). Homepage: https://zrs-kp.academia.edu/LenartŠkof

Vojko Strahovnik is associate professor at the Department of Philosophy and senior research fellow at the Faculty of Theology (University of Ljubljana, Slovenia). He was a Fulbright research scholar in 2016 at the University of Arizona. His main research interest is the structure and phenomenology of normativity, cutting across the philosophical fields of ethics, epistemology, philosophy of science, and aesthetics. The impact of his work ranges from new and important theoretical insights into the nature of normativity (the role of moral principles in the formation of moral judgments, epistemic agency, and epistemic virtuousness) to considerations related to practical dimensions of our lives, such as the role of guilt and moral shame in reconciliation processes, the importance of intellectual and ethical virtues in dialogue and education, and animal ethics. He has published several scientific papers and chapters, as well as five monographs: *Practical Contexts* (Frankfurt, 2004), *Challenging Moral Particularism* (New York, 2008), *Moral Judgment, Intuition and Moral Principles* (Velenje, 2009; trans. Zagreb, 2019), *Moral Theory: The Nature of Morality* (Maribor, 2016; trans. Zagreb, 2018), and *Global Ethics: Perspectives on Global Justice* (Berlin, 2019).

www.ingramcontent.com/pod-product-compliance
Lightning Source LLC
Chambersburg PA
CBHW022313280326
41932CB00010B/1081